IMAGES
of America

NEW HAMPSHIRE OLD HOME CELEBRATIONS

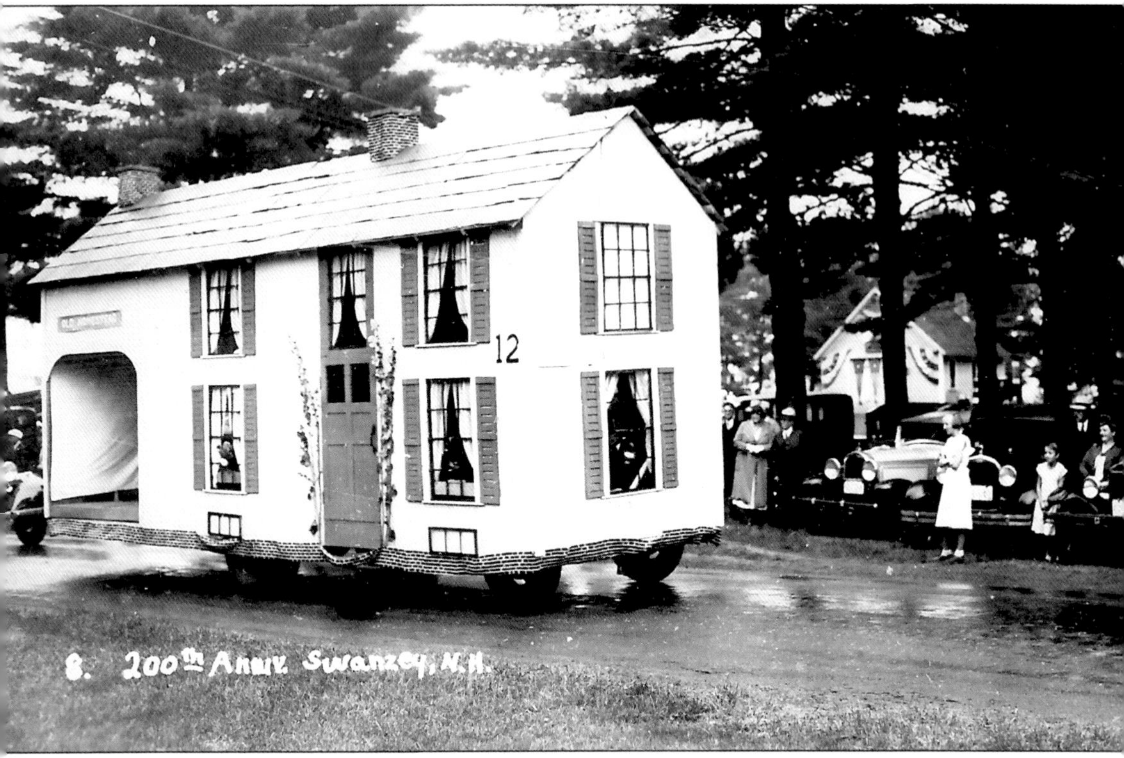

In 1933, Swanzey went all out celebrating the town's bicentennial, old home days, and the 100th anniversary of the birthday of Denman Thompson, author of *The Old Homestead.* A Swanzey native, Thomson's play is produced every year in the Potash Bowl, the town's natural outdoor theater. This float in the 1933 parade took third place in the old homestead competition. (Author's collection.)

On the cover: New Hampshire old home observances have always been used to honor local citizens, and this Wilton float from 1959 honored the town's schoolteachers. Seated at the instructor's desk is Florence Rideout after whom the community's elementary school was named in 1992. Seated students from left to right are Kenneth Sargent, Nancy Fox, Carlene Boutwell, George Fox, and Carl Boutwell. (Courtesy of Dick Putnam.)

IMAGES
of America

NEW HAMPSHIRE OLD HOME CELEBRATIONS

Gary Crooker

ARCADIA
PUBLISHING

ISBN 978-0-7385-6529-3

Published by Arcadia Publishing
Charleston SC, Chicago IL, Portsmouth NH, San Francisco CA

Printed in the United States of America

Library of Congress Catalog Control Number: 2008940187

For all general information contact Arcadia Publishing at:
Telephone 843-853-2070
Fax 843-853-0044
E-mail sales@arcadiapublishing.com
For customer service and orders:
Toll-Free 1-888-313-2665

Visit us on the Internet at www.arcadiapublishing.com

To old home day committees and workers throughout the state who have kept New Hampshire's local holiday alive for over 100 years.

Contents

Acknowledgments 6

Introduction 7

1. Monadnock Region 9

2. Seacoast Region 35

3. White Mountains and Great North Woods 47

4. Dartmouth–Lake Sunapee Region 59

5. Lakes Region 71

6. Merrimack Valley 83

Acknowledgments

America's very first historical societies were local affairs formed in New England to record the region's beginnings. I wish to thank the dozens of town historians and historical societies that have aided me in the research that made this book possible. Theirs is truly a labor of love, and New Hampshire's local historical societies deserve not just my thanks but also the gratitude of everyone who values the heritage of the region. That goes also for the New Hampshire State Historical Society Library and the local library in Wilton where I was able to spend many hours researching New Hampshire old home celebrations from their beginnings.

In addition to these organized groups that serve to preserve their local history, there are individuals who do the same. One of those preservers of New Hampshire's history, in particular the old home movement, is Sam Allen of St. Anselm College. Allen's Granite State Collection of New Hampshire town and city anniversary and old home memorabilia is saving the legacy of this New Hampshire holiday, and I am most grateful for the help he has so unselfishly given me in the making of this book.

Technical support can be a great aid in a project like this even for one who has an aptitude for the technical. I do not. For that reason, my thanks are particularly heartfelt to Brian Broderick, Kelby Erdody, Casey Carpentiere, Lori Jensen, and Michael Dell'Orto for the help they gave along the way.

To Erin Rocha of Arcadia, I offer thanks for being an editor who has a knack for knowing exactly when a gentle nudge in the right direction is needed.

Thanks to my father for riding shotgun. A lot of travel was involved in the project, and I thank him for being with me in body and my mother for being with me in spirit.

I thank my entire family for their patience, particularly my wife, Melissa. Her support, both technical and emotional, was a constant throughout the project. It could not have been completed without her. Like everyone else, she can now look forward to sentences that do not begin or end with the phrase, "as soon as the book is finished."

INTRODUCTION

If anyone were sailing around the area of Monterey Bay, California, in the late summer of 1899, they might have witnessed a sight that would have left them understandably baffled. In full view of those August mariners was a group of revelers celebrating the virtues of the Granite State of New Hampshire, some 3,000 miles to the west. Described in a letter back to New Hampshire from Pacific Grove, California, the transplanted celebration consisted of a group of expatriate New Hampshire natives answering a call to honor their erstwhile home. There were picnic lunches, poems, speeches, and a banner inscribed, "the Granite State's Old Home Week from Atlantic to Pacific."

The scenes that seemed so strange to seagoing passersby were simply faraway reflections of dozens of similar celebrations that were taking place in New Hampshire at the same time. They were the brainchild of one-term New Hampshire governor Frank Rollins. Over 100 years later, Rollins's idea is still going strong, as communities in all sections of the Granite State turn out to welcome home wayward sons and daughters. The sincere flattery of the old cliché comes from imitation of all of the other New England states as well as much of the East Coast and northern tier of United States, as the tradition has spread, and old home celebrations welcome home wandering natives.

Rollins came from a prominent New Hampshire political family. He first proposed his idea for a statewide homecoming celebration while speaking before a Sons of New Hampshire gathering. From the start, it was Rollins's plan to rejuvenate both the spirit and the economy of his home state by building upon the already long-established idea of town and family picnics that were in vogue throughout the Victorian era. Towns such as Hancock and Cornish along with many others had traditions of gatherings that were long established.

At the end of the 19th century, New Hampshire appeared, at least outwardly, to be in economic decline from years of emigration by native residents. While urban manufacturing was keeping the mills of Manchester humming, much of rural New Hampshire was acquiring a shabby look from the increasing number of abandoned farms and homesteads. Rollins saw an opportunity to capitalize on his idea for a statewide homecoming celebration while at the same time encouraging visitors and natives alike to rehabilitate aging farms and communities by way of investment. Many rundown farms became summer homes and main streets received face-lifts in the way of municipal additions such as monuments and public buildings.

The governor's plan was a success in stimulating the economy as well as revitalizing the spirit of his home state. New Hampshire old home celebrations gave residents a chance to spruce up the old community and show it off to visitors and returning natives. The idea of reunions and picnics on a large scale was already a fixture in history-conscious New Hampshire. Family reunions in a small town almost took on the nature of a town-wide event. The same was true of town picnics in villages where everyone knew their neighbors. Much of that same spirit is what Granite State towns try to preserve or recapture today in their old home festivities.

In 1899, when the governor sent out his first call for old home week, the response was what might be expected from a state already in tune with the idea of getting together for fairs and celebrations during particular times of the year. Although more towns may have formed committees, 44 actually responded to the call by preparing reports and sending them in to the state to record their activities during that initial celebration.

On board with reports in 1899 were Andover, Antrim, Bethlehem, Boscawen, Bristol, Carroll, Chesterfield, Concord, Dunbarton, Epsom, Freedom, Gilsum, Greenland, Hancock, Hanover, Henniker, Hopkinton, Kensington, Lempster, Litchfield, Londonderry, Marlborough, Marlow, Merrimack, Milan, Mont Vernon, New Hampton, Newington, Newport, Pembroke, Penacook, Plainfield, Rochester, Rollinsford, Salem, Sandwich, South Hampton, Springfield, Stoddard, Surry, Temple, Walpole, Webster, and Westmoreland.

Several of those towns still celebrate today. In 1899, they celebrated with bands and bonfires, parades and poetry, dances and dinners, and statesmen and speeches. Today the bonfires have given way to fireworks in many communities, and the speeches have mercifully grown markedly shorter. The spirit of camaraderie and community, however, has remained a constant.

In the early years of the old home movement in New Hampshire, operations were run from the top down. The state decreed the date for each year's festivities, and a report was issued annually with towns giving their version of events that took place. In time and in typical New Hampshire fashion, old home celebrations took on individual, local flavor, reflecting the plans laid out in Concord less and less. Originally New Hampshire Old Home Week was held during the final week of August. Today communities can be found celebrating anywhere on the calendar from June through October. Originally old home week was indeed one week in duration. Today it is more likely to be an old home day or weekend. Initially observances were held every year, but some towns now celebrate sporadically or every two, three, or even five years. The inclination of New Hampshire folks to do it their own way has held sway over time.

Of course, the important thing is that whenever or however they do it, New Hampshire residents still celebrate their beginnings and their future through old home days. It has been over 100 years since Rollins first issued his call for the New Hampshire born to return to the scenes of their youth. This book includes a representative sampling of how communities throughout the state have laid out the welcome mat. Each town has done it a little differently through the years, but the message has remained the same: welcome home.

One

Monadnock Region

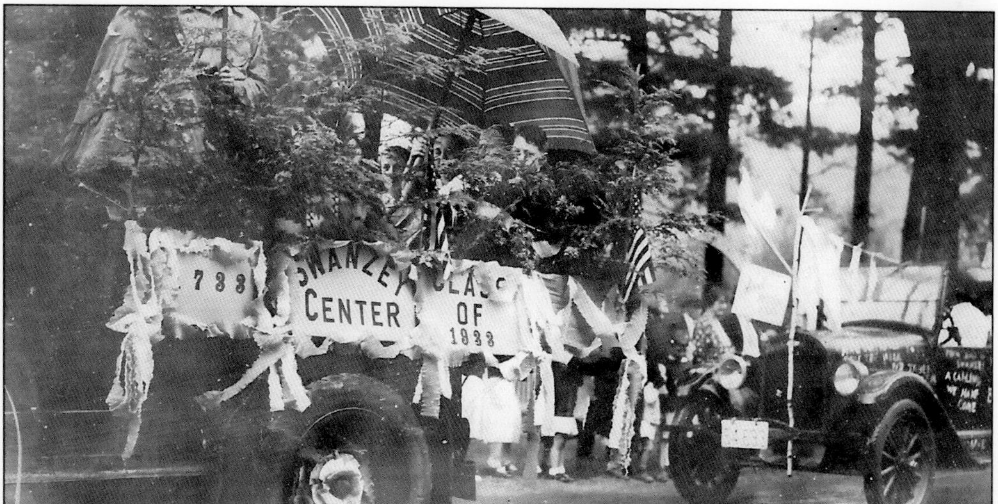

Swanzey Center is represented by this float in the 1933 parade. All the activities took place on August 17 of the town's bicentennial year, including the mile-long parade that had 49 float entrees. Today Swanzey continues to celebrate the tradition with a full day of activities every year in July. (Author's collection.)

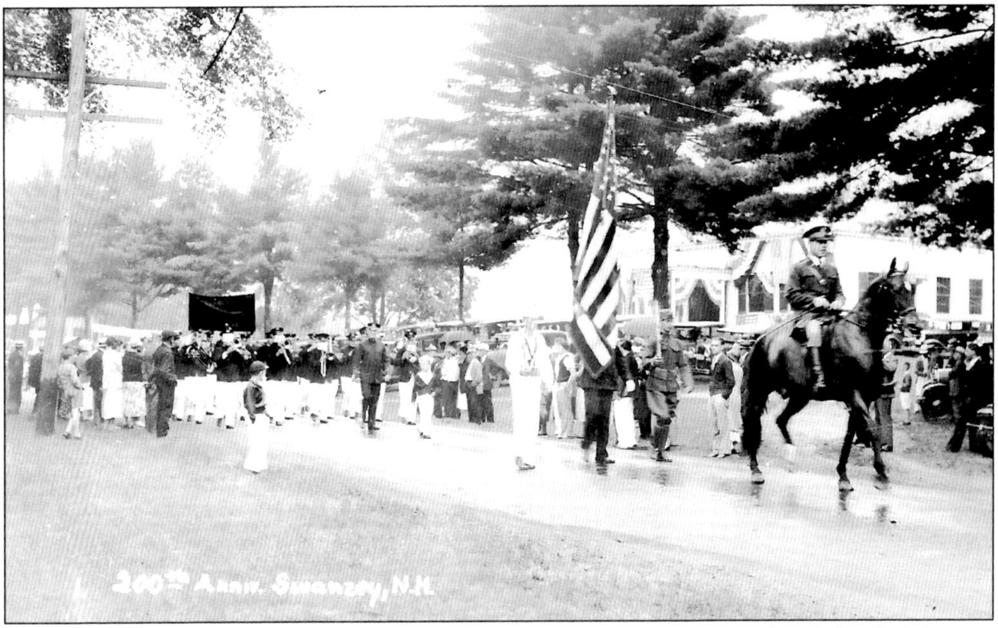

Everyone loves a parade, and in Swanzey in 1933, it was the visiting Keene band that led the way for the old home/bicentennial festivities. On horseback in front of the band is Sumner E. Brown of West Swanzey, who was designated chief marshall of the parade. Even during World War II, Swanzey held its old home day. In 1944, ceremonies were held on the lawn of the Mount Caesar Library. (Author's collection.)

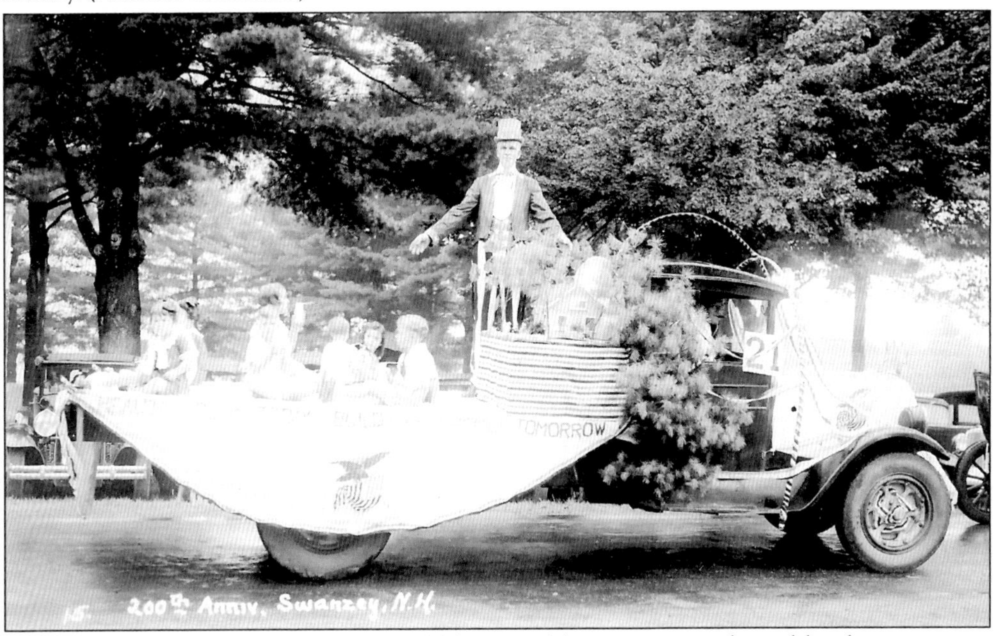

One does not have to be old to enjoy old home celebrations, as evidenced by the youngsters crowded on board this 1933 Swanzey parade float. The group in this entry represented the local 4-H club, while the role of Uncle Sam was portrayed by Leland Bogue. In 1946, Swanzey Old Home Day welcomed home local World War II veterans with performances by the Keene American Legion Band. (Author's collection.)

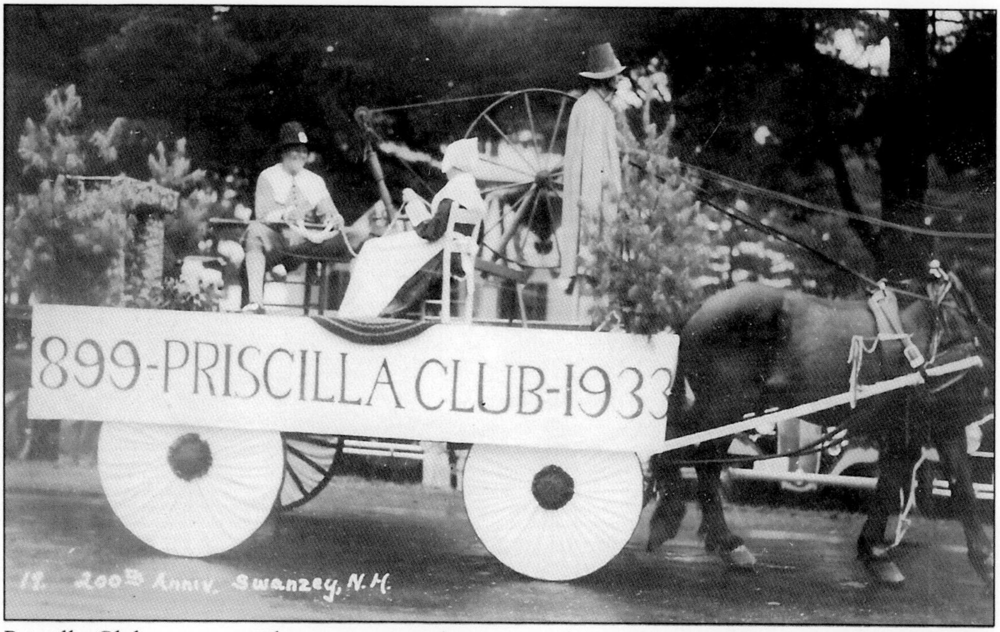

Priscilla Clubs were social organizations for women that were originally formed in 1902. The clubs' purpose was to honor the toil and perseverance of America's early female settlers. That was the theme of this 1933 Swanzey Old Home Day float. Years earlier in 1919, Swanzey Old Home Day welcomed home World War I soldiers with music supplied by the Winchester Cornet Band. (Author's collection.)

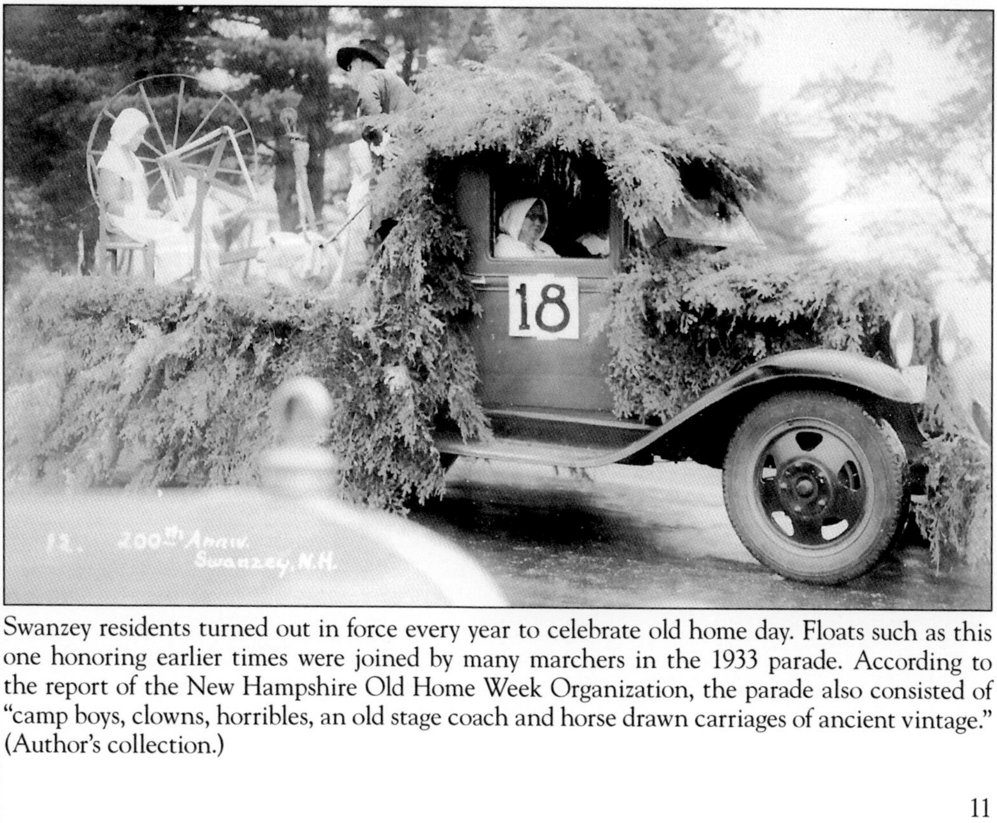

Swanzey residents turned out in force every year to celebrate old home day. Floats such as this one honoring earlier times were joined by many marchers in the 1933 parade. According to the report of the New Hampshire Old Home Week Organization, the parade also consisted of "camp boys, clowns, horribles, an old stage coach and horse drawn carriages of ancient vintage." (Author's collection.)

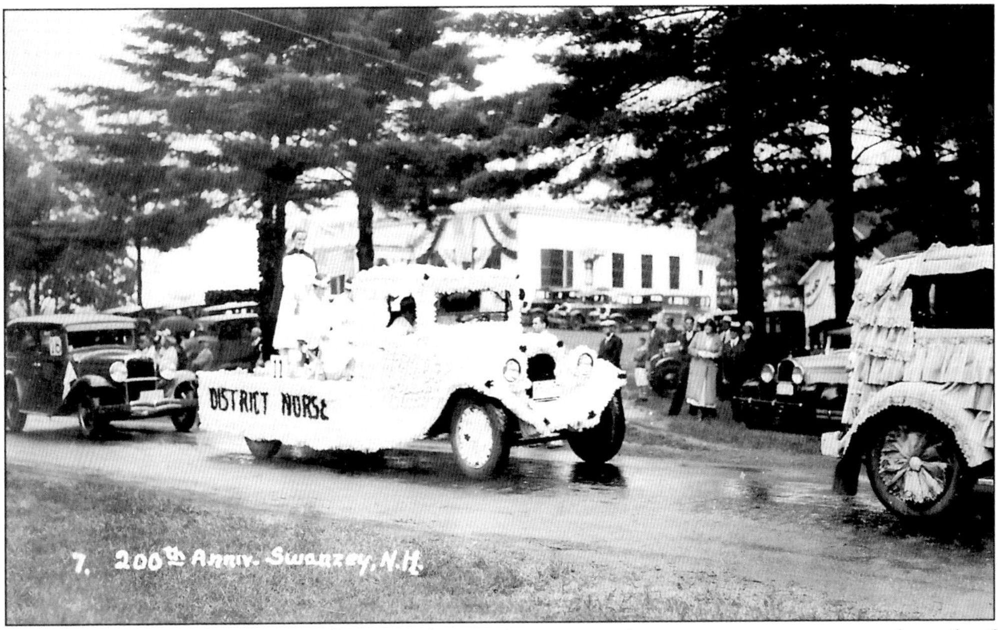

Recognition of citizens who make special contributions to their communities is a trademark of old home day holidays, and in 1933, Swanzey honored its District Nurse Association. Riding on the float that was awarded first place in the parade was nurse Helen Rogers of Swanzey. In 1919, residents got together at Richardson's Park and honored soldiers returning from World War I. (Author's collection.)

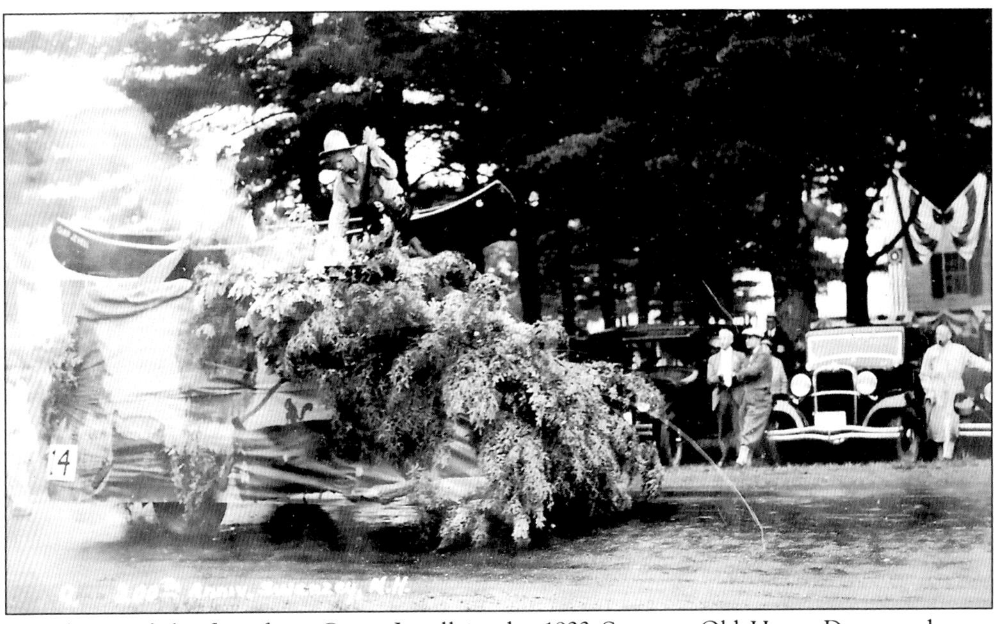

The theme of the float from Camp Jewell in the 1933 Swanzey Old Home Day parade was youthful activities. Established in 1901, Camp Jewell was a YMCA camp located on Swanzey Lake. The camp operated there until the 1950s when it moved to Colebrook, Connecticut, where it is still in existence today. (Author's collection.)

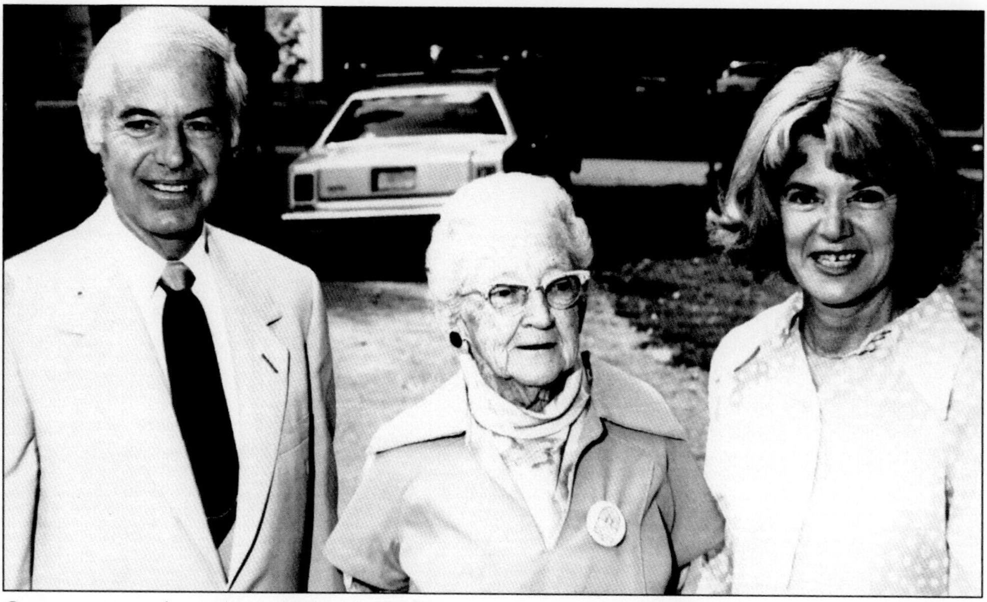

Communities throughout New Hampshire continue to use their old home celebrations to recognize and honor native residents. Seen here at Wilton's 1981 old home days celebration, longtime community leader and schoolteacher Florence Rideout is flanked by one of her former pupils and his wife. William French Smith was born in Wilton in 1917 and went on to become the nation's 74th attorney general under Pres. Ronald Regan. He took time out from his duties to come home for a weekend to meet many old friends and neighbors. (Author's collection.)

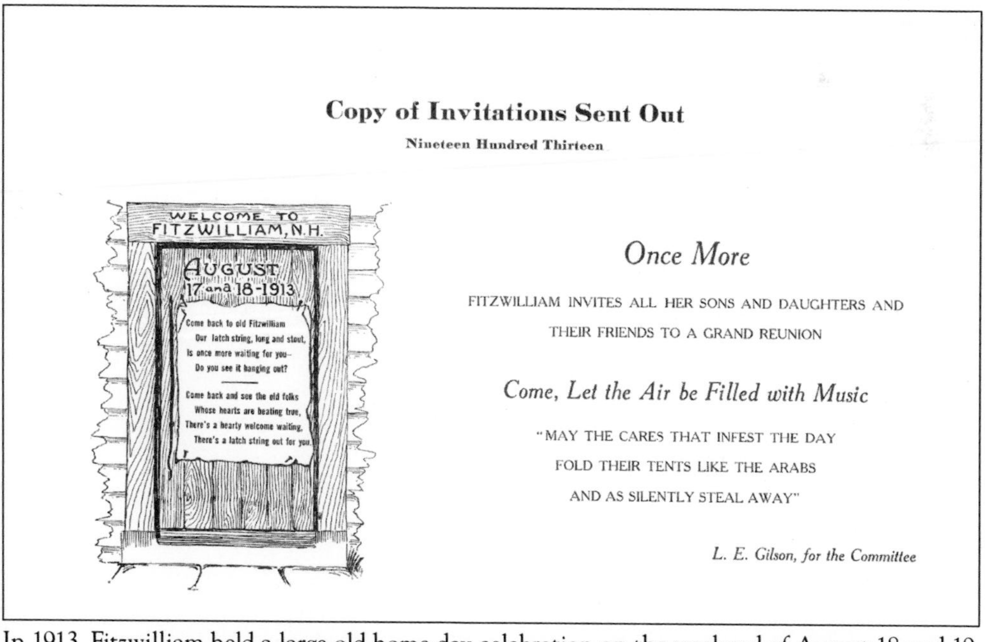

Copy of Invitations Sent Out

Nineteen Hundred Thirteen

WELCOME TO
FITZWILLIAM, N.H.

AUGUST
17 and 18-1913

Come back to old Fitzwilliam
Our latch string, long and stout,
Is once more waiting for you—
Do you see it hanging out?

Come back and see the old folks
Whose hearts are beating true,
There's a hearty welcome waiting,
There's a latch string out for you.

Once More

FITZWILLIAM INVITES ALL HER SONS AND DAUGHTERS AND THEIR FRIENDS TO A GRAND REUNION

Come, Let the Air be Filled with Music

"MAY THE CARES THAT INFEST THE DAY
FOLD THEIR TENTS LIKE THE ARABS
AND AS SILENTLY STEAL AWAY"

L. E. Gilson, for the Committee

In 1913, Fitzwilliam held a large old home day celebration on the weekend of August 18 and 19. This copy of the town wide invitation includes a poem referring to the "latch string," which was a term used often when speaking about old home celebrations. To find the latch string out meant to meet with welcome and hospitality for returning sons and daughters. (Courtesy of Fitzwilliam Historical Society.)

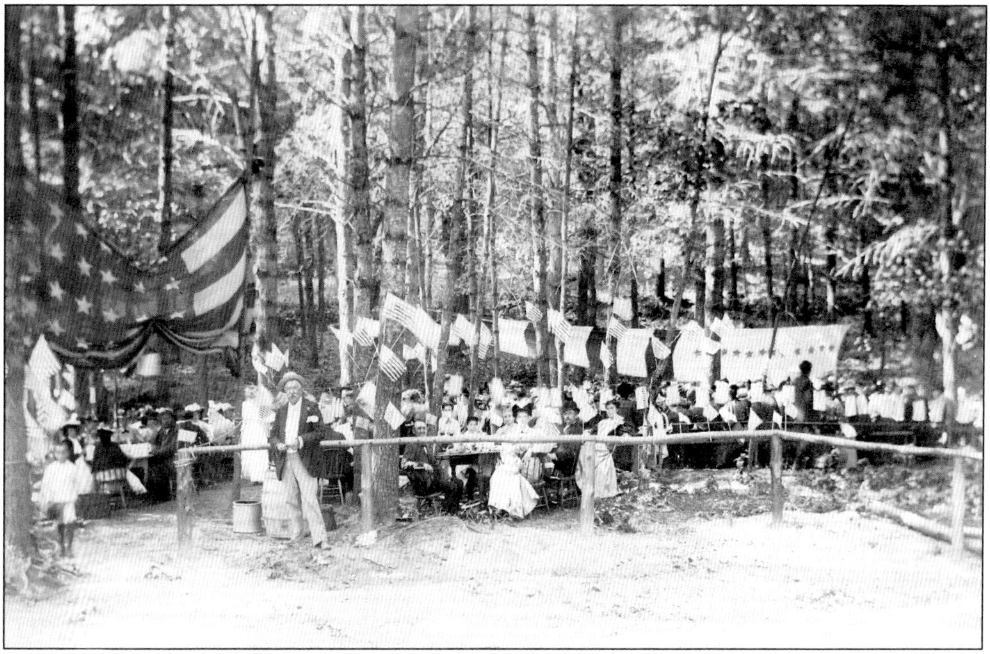

In the days of the grand resorts, there were few that were more majestic than Chesterfield's Silverdale Hotel, located on the shore of Lake Spofford. Here a large gathering enjoys a Chesterfield Old Home Day picnic on the hotel's grounds. (Photograph by Austin O. Foster, courtesy of Chesterfield Historical Society.)

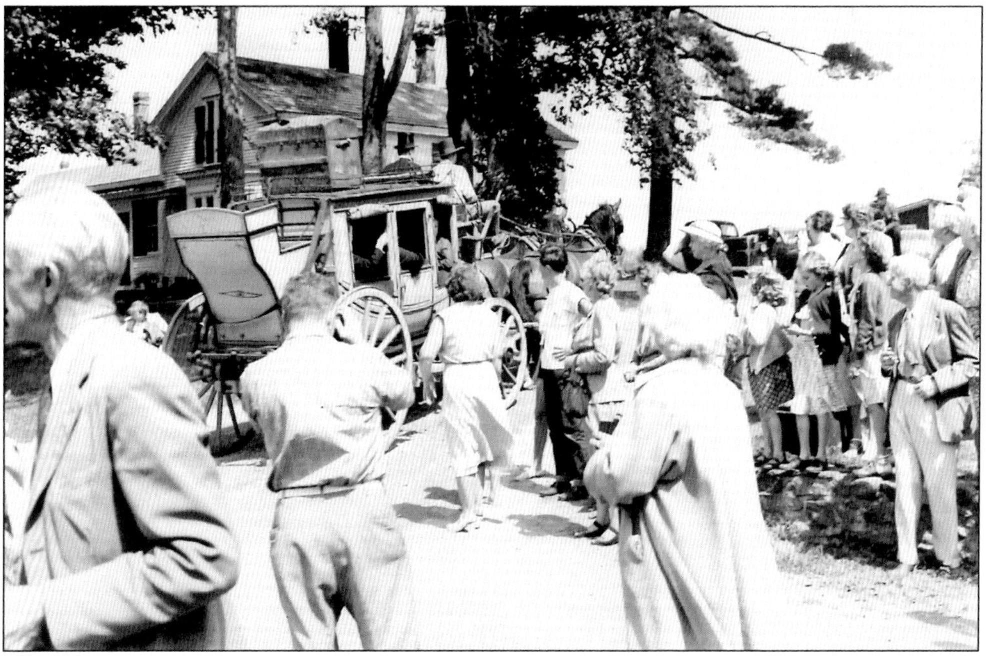

In 1951, Chesterfield residents celebrated old home day along with the 100th anniversary of their town hall. One of the most popular attractions of the day was the old stagecoach that was driven around the town common and on display for all to see. (Photograph by Paul Penning, courtesy of Chesterfield Historical Society.)

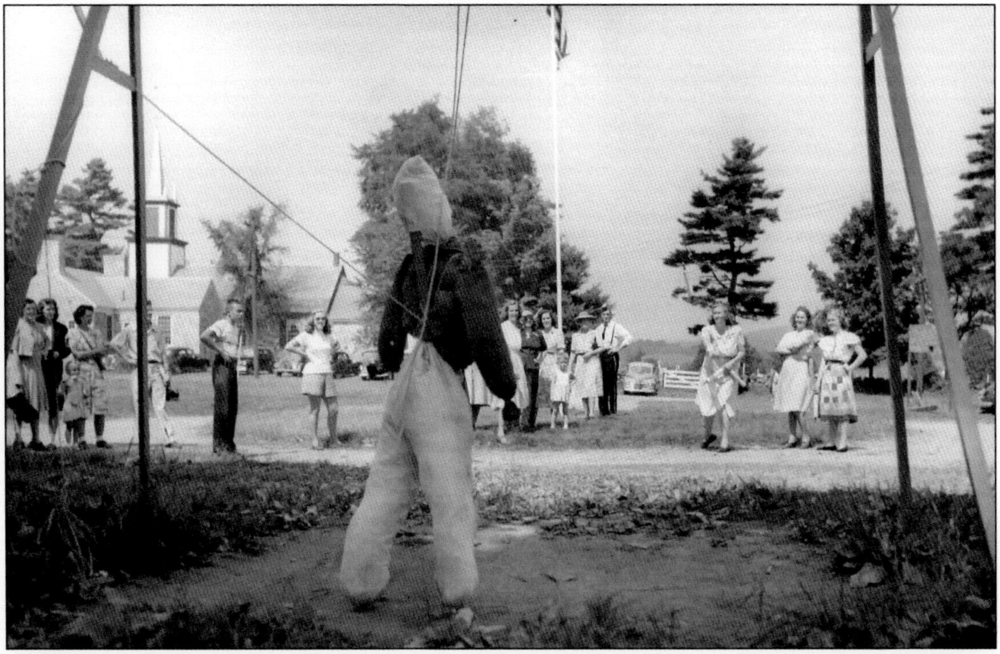

While he might not seem appropriate for today's list of activities, "Oscar the Dummy" was a huge hit at the 1948 Chesterfield Old Home Day festivities. Ladies in town took turns hurling rolling pins at poor, defenseless Oscar and scored points for striking various parts of his anatomy. (Photograph by Bernice Perry, courtesy of Chesterfield Historical Society.)

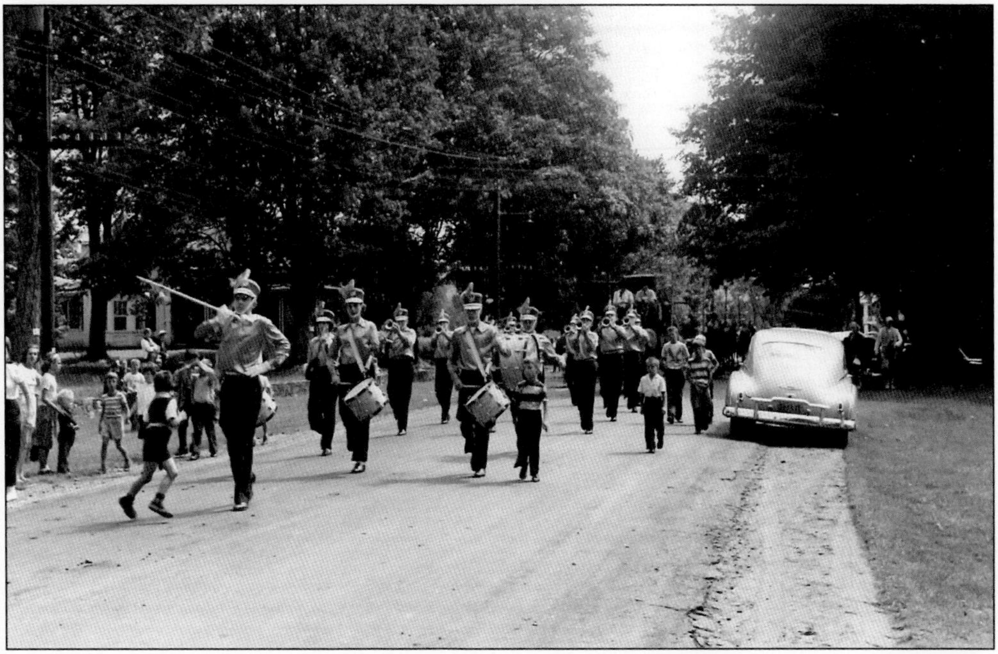

The Kurn Hattin Band from the school of the same name in Westminster, Vermont, was a highlight of Chesterfield's 1951 old home day parade. Here the band is pictured marching down Route 63 much to the delight of several local youngsters who have fallen right in step. (Photograph by Paul Penning, courtesy of Chesterfield Historical Society.)

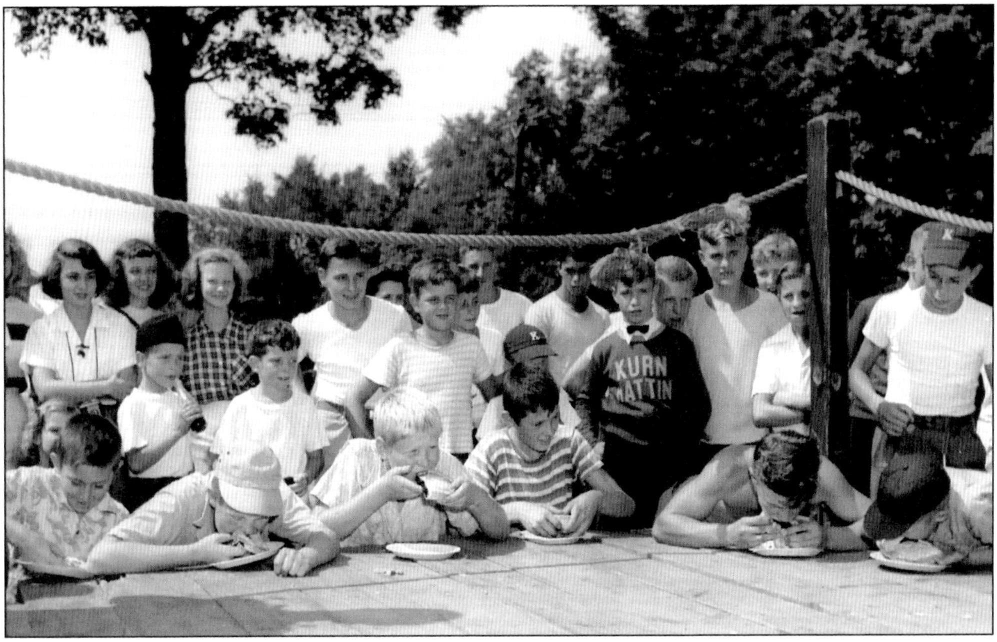

In 1948, Chesterfield had one of its largest and best-attended old home celebrations. Among the attendees were New Hampshire governor Sherman Adams and several members of the U.S. Supreme Court. The dignitaries were on hand for the dedication of the stone plaque in honor of former chief justice Harlan Fiske Stone, who was born in Chesterfield. For these local boys and campers, however, the biggest event of the day was the pie-eating contest pictured here. (Photograph by Bernice Perry, courtesy of Chesterfield Historical Society.)

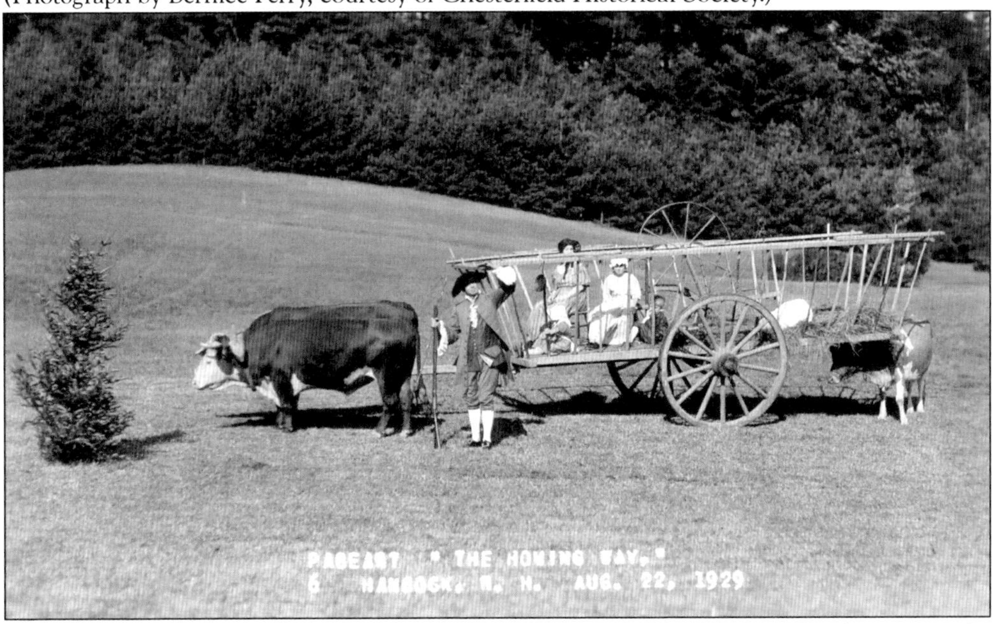

Citizens of Hancock combined old home week with the town's sesquicentennial in 1929. The biggest event of the week was a pageant called the *Homing Way*. Seen here are a few of the characters in the play. About one third of the town's population of 600 took part in the event. (Courtesy of the Granite State Collection, Sam Allen.)

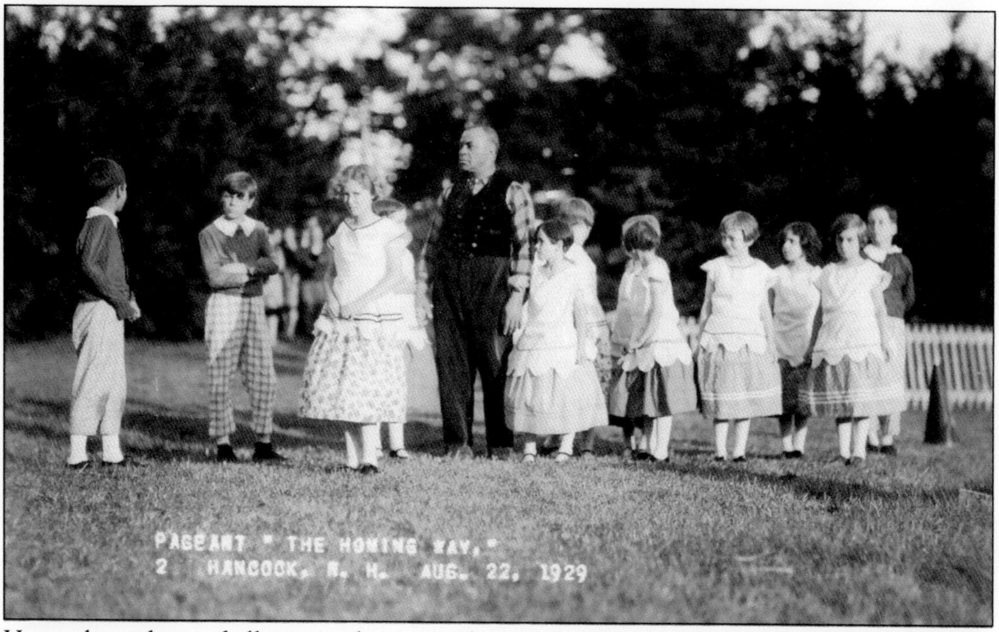

Hancock residents of all ages took part in the town's 1929 old home week pageant. The play covered the time from the arrival of settler John Grimes right up until 1929. Leila Church directed the play, which was in rehearsal for an entire week prior to the celebration. (Courtesy of the Granite State Collection, Sam Allen.)

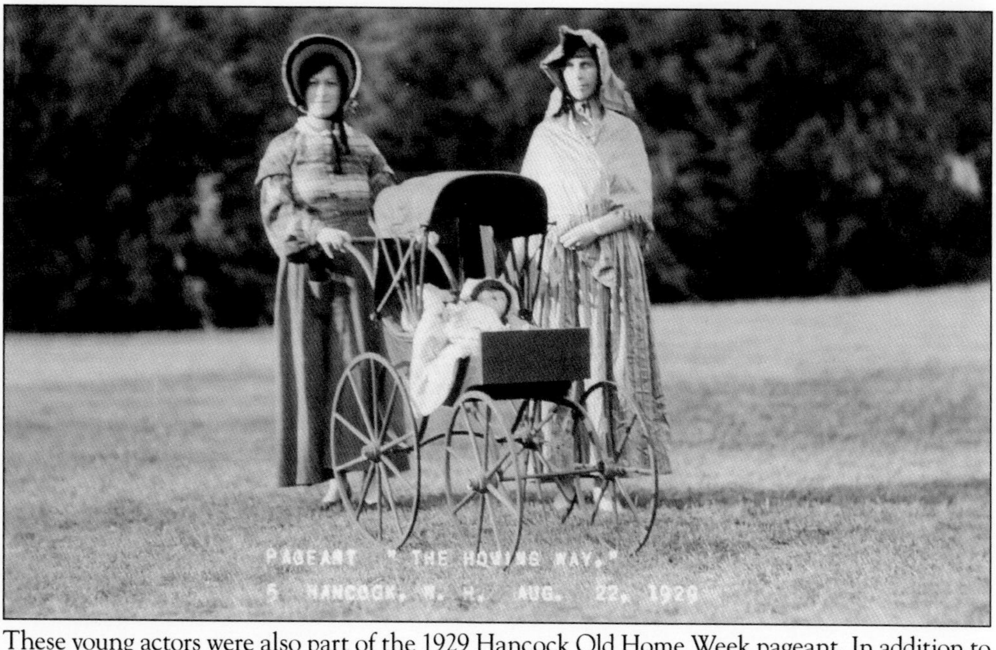

These young actors were also part of the 1929 Hancock Old Home Week pageant. In addition to being one of the communities that responded to Gov. Frank Rollins's call for the first old home celebration in 1899, Hancock had a long tradition of town reunions and picnics stretching back 20 years before it became official. (Courtesy of the Granite State Collection, Sam Allen.)

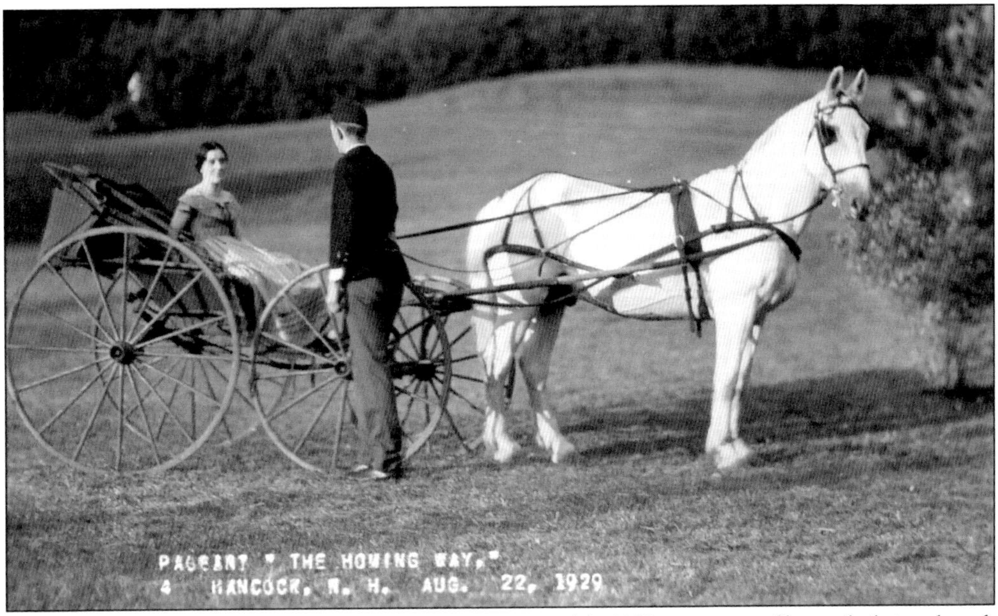

Dressed as a Civil War soldier, this actor in Hancock's 1929 pageant offers a helping hand. According to the Hancock history *The Second Hundred Years*, many in similar Union uniforms were pressed into service of a different kind. During a dress rehearsal, many of the actors, who were also volunteer firemen, answered the alarm to fight a house fire while still dressed in military costume. (Courtesy of the Granite State Collection, Sam Allen.)

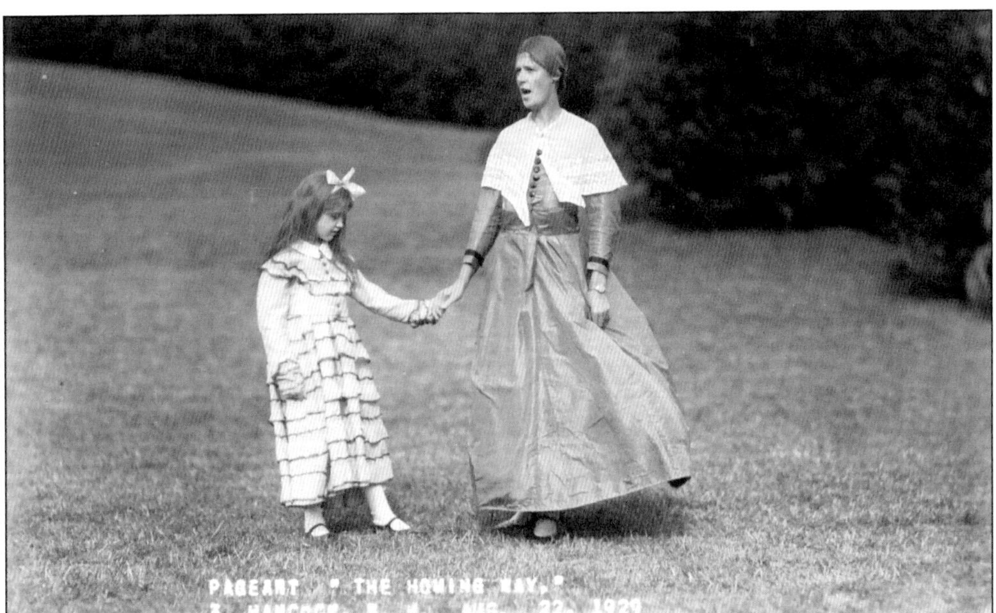

Hancock's history, including Colonial times, was depicted in the "Homing Way," a pageant staged for the 1929 bicentennial/old home week celebration. Only an outdoor stage was deemed large enough to house such a story. The entertainment was staged in a local valley with spectators seated on a neighboring hillside. (Courtesy of the Granite State Collection, Sam Allen.)

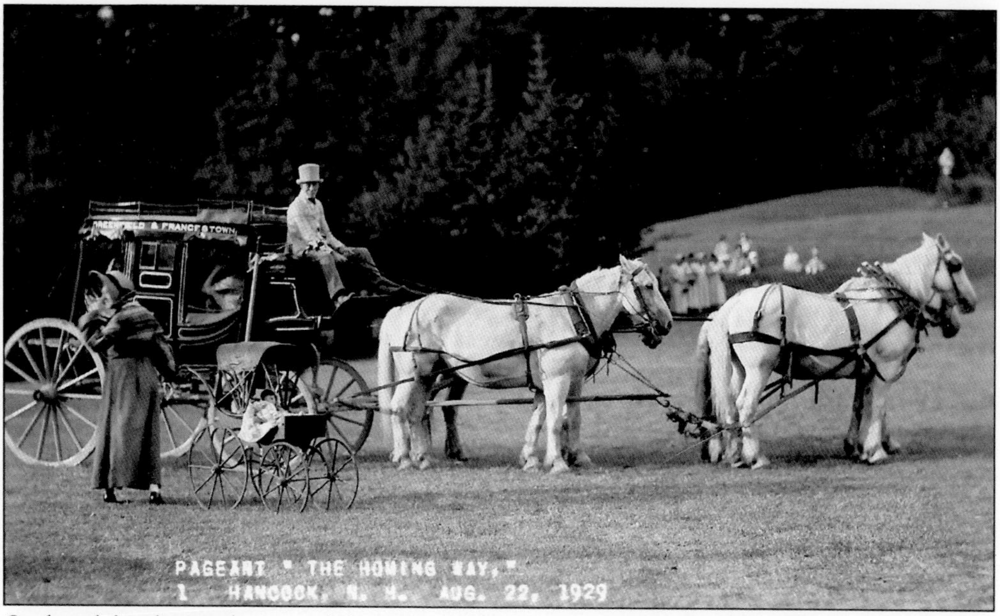

On hand for the production of the 1929 old home day pageant in Hancock was the Concord coach, which for many years ran passengers between Greenfield and Francestown and other lines in New Hampshire. Notice the hillside in the background where crowds were able to enjoy the show. (Author's collection.)

MARLOW

WELCOMES YOU TO ITS

180th Anniversary and Old Home Day

August 21, 1941

All-Day Program of Sports, Speaking, Music.
Play and Dance in the Evening.
Auspices Golden Rule Rebeckah Lodge.

PRESIDENT: W. M. DAVIS
VICE-PRESIDENTS:
MRS. MARIAN PERKINS
A. W. PHELPS
A. M. DAVIS

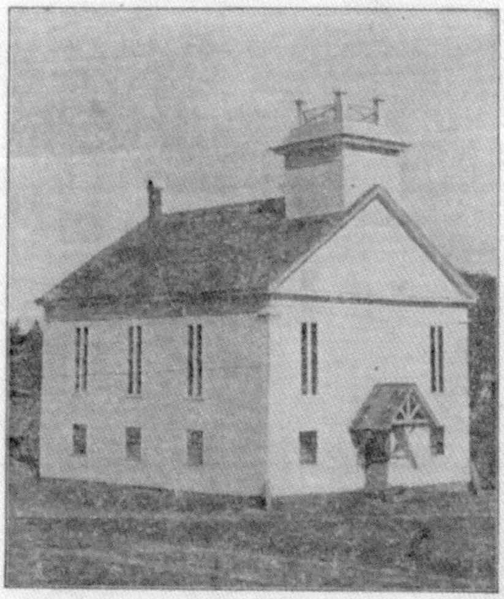

JONES HALL

Even mid-week was a good time to return home for old home day, as Marlow planned its celebration for a Thursday in 1942. In addition to directing all of the activities listed above, the very busy Golden Rule Rebekah Lodge members also found time to provide dinners for everyone following the grand parade. (Courtesy of the Granite State Collection, Sam Allen.)

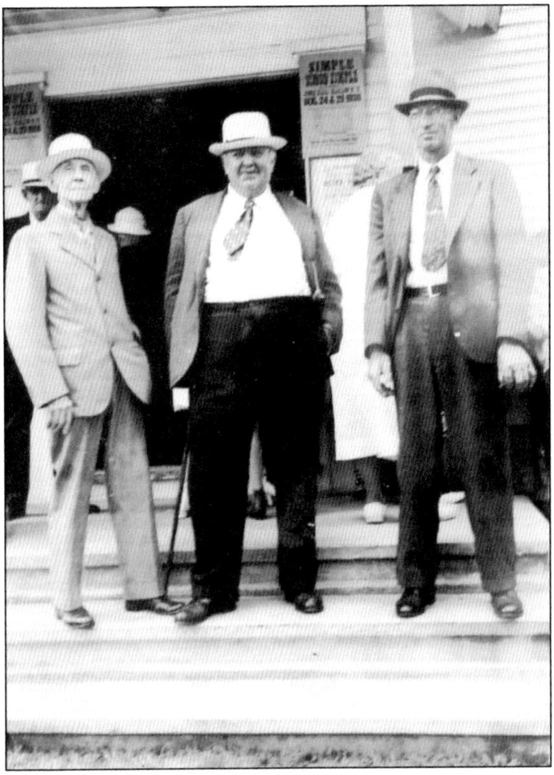

These three gentlemen stopped to pose for the camera during the 1938 Marlow Old Home Day. Behind them is a poster for the play that was performed at that year's festivities, *Simple Simon Simple*. Marlow was one of the town's that celebrated during the first New Hampshire Old Home Week in 1899. (Courtesy of Marlow Historical Society.)

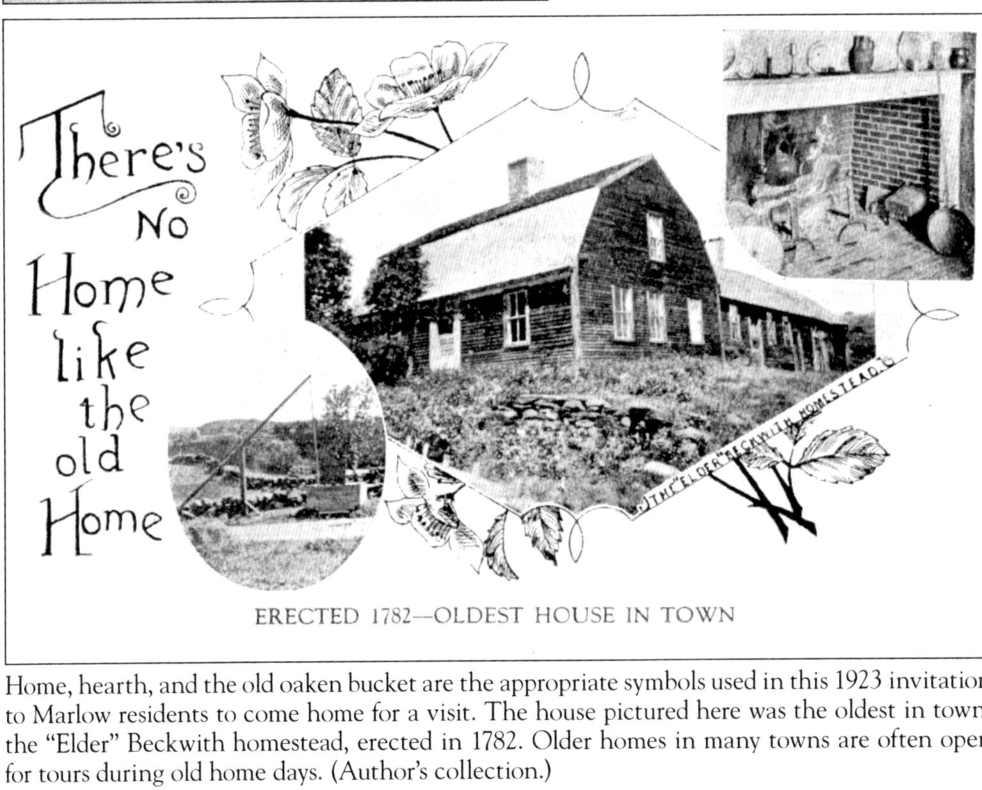

Home, hearth, and the old oaken bucket are the appropriate symbols used in this 1923 invitation to Marlow residents to come home for a visit. The house pictured here was the oldest in town, the "Elder" Beckwith homestead, erected in 1782. Older homes in many towns are often open for tours during old home days. (Author's collection.)

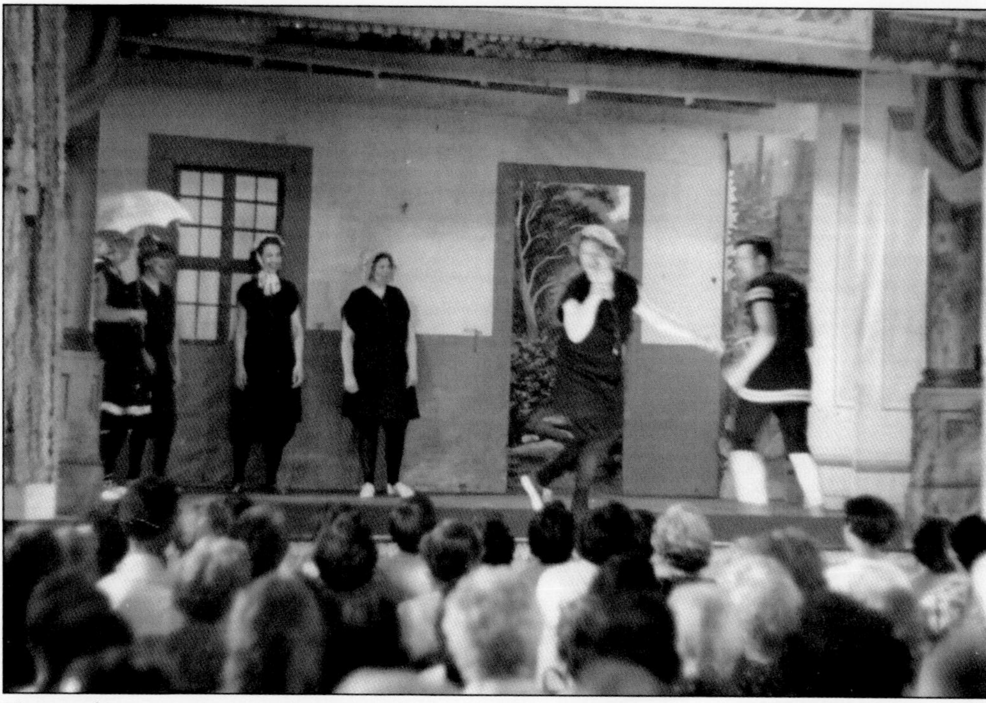

Having fun on stage was always a key part of the day at Marlow Old Home Day. Hopefully the audience was enjoying themselves as much as the performers appear to be in this 1955 performance of *Bathing Beauties*. Identified here are Mrs. Peterson, Mrs. Larsen, Mrs. Cushing, Ralph Winhan, and Johnnie Monte. (Courtesy of Marlow Historical Society.)

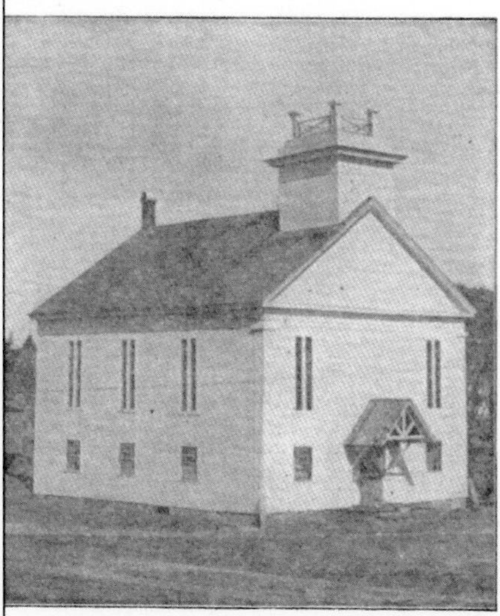

Marlow Old Home Day

Thursday, August 19, 1937

Parade 9:30, Sports, Dinner, Afternoon Program

Home Talent Play, "Ready-Made Family"
Two Nights, August 18th and 19th

OFFICERS

President, Warren M. Davis

Vice-Presidents
A. W. Phelps, M. J. Huntley
Sec. Martha L. Strickland
Treas. Sara E. Phelps

EXECUTIVE COM.

Mr. and Mrs. Harry Newton
Mr. and Mrs. Frank Whippie
Mr. and Mrs. Fred G. Huntley

ENTERTAINMENT COM.

Walter Dorr
Mrs. M. Watson
Mr. and Mrs. Halsted Compton
Gerald Morrill

RECEPTION COM.

Rev. and Mrs. N. J. Langmaid
Mrs. Marion Perkins
Mrs. Addie Tinker
Henry Dodge
Henry Spaulding

Sports, food, and homegrown talent were on tap for old home day 1937 in Marlow. Those are still high on the lists of entertainment today, as towns gather to celebrate. In 1937, Marlow, like many towns in their early old home celebrations, included a play such as *Ready Made Family* noted here. Pictured on the card is the Marlow Town Hall. (Author's collection.)

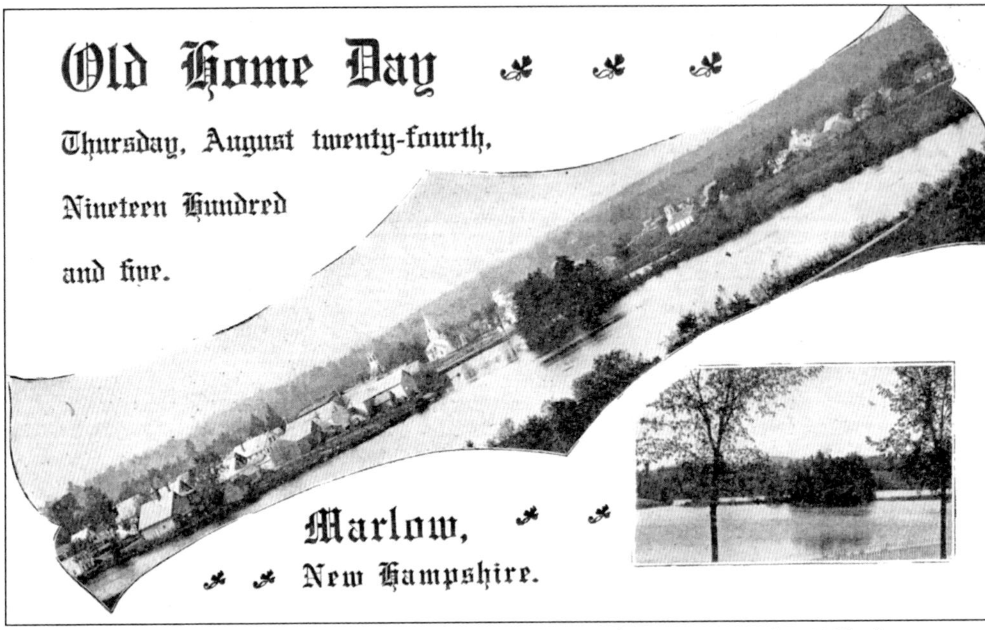

Nearly the entire village of Marlow is pictured on this card announcing the 1905 observances. Marlow celebrated the very first New Hampshire Old Home Week in 1899. After celebrating its 150th anniversary in 1911, interest waned in the activities of old home week. For several years following, residents made it a movable feast, as several Marlow residents who had moved to Keene got together yearly in Wheelock Park to observe the holiday. (Author's collection.)

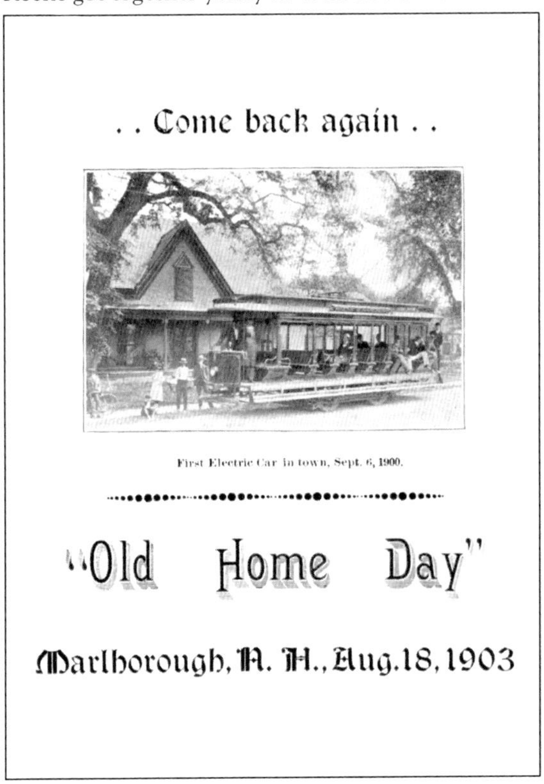

Today old home day is thought of as mostly a time to look back with former residents. However, since its beginnings, it has also been a time when communities take pride in the advancements that have been made. This 1903 call to Marlborough residents to come home features the town's first electric car put into service just three years earlier. (Courtesy of Marlborough Historical Society.)

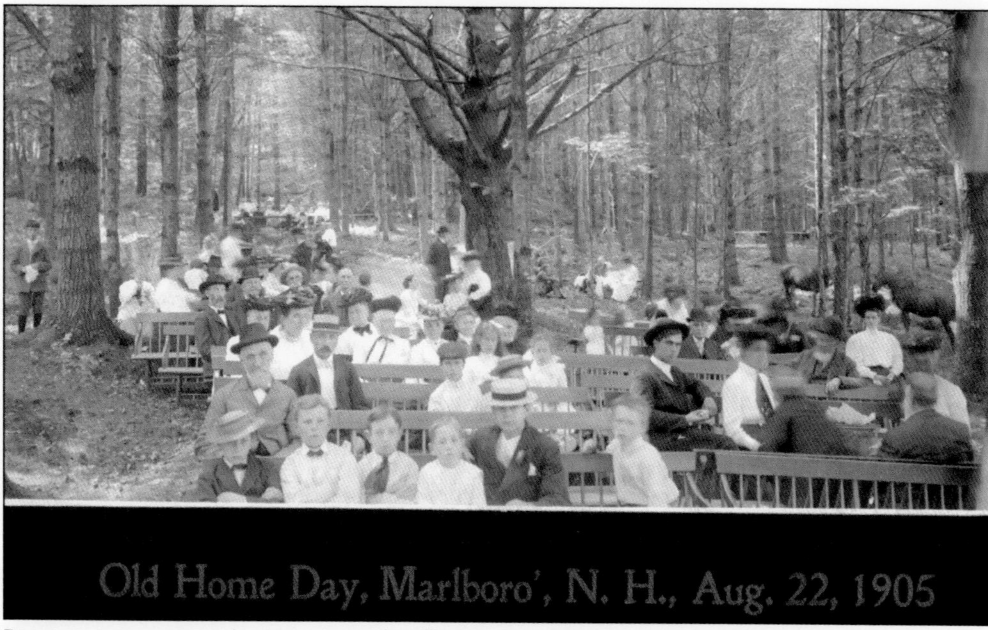

Picnic groves were a feature in nearly all New Hampshire towns around 1900 and were often the site of old home day gatherings and picnics. This 1905 Marlborough old home photograph shows residents enjoying the town picnic at Richardson Grove at Cummings Pond. (Courtesy of Marlborough Historical Society.)

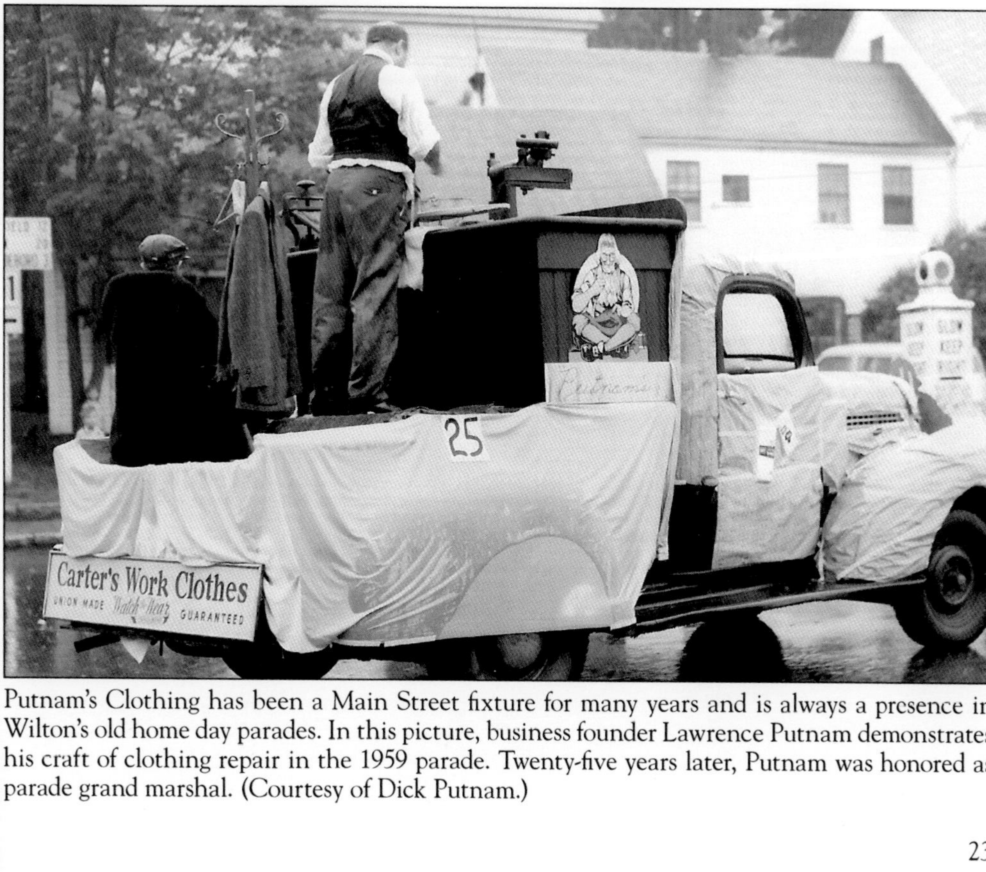

Putnam's Clothing has been a Main Street fixture for many years and is always a presence in Wilton's old home day parades. In this picture, business founder Lawrence Putnam demonstrates his craft of clothing repair in the 1959 parade. Twenty-five years later, Putnam was honored as parade grand marshal. (Courtesy of Dick Putnam.)

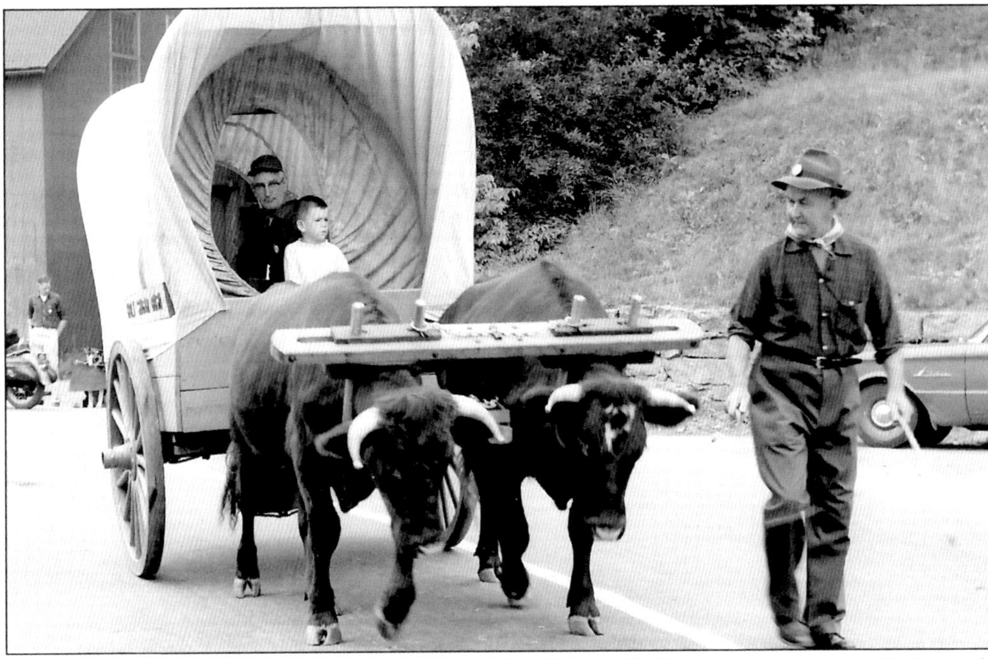

For many years, Jason Holt's oxen were on hand for Wilton Old Home Days. In this 1964 parade photograph, he is seen with his oxen. Riding inside the wagon are Guy Holt (left) and Chris Gregoire. Mildred Gibbons successfully chaired the weekend celebrations for many years. (Courtesy of Dick Putnam.)

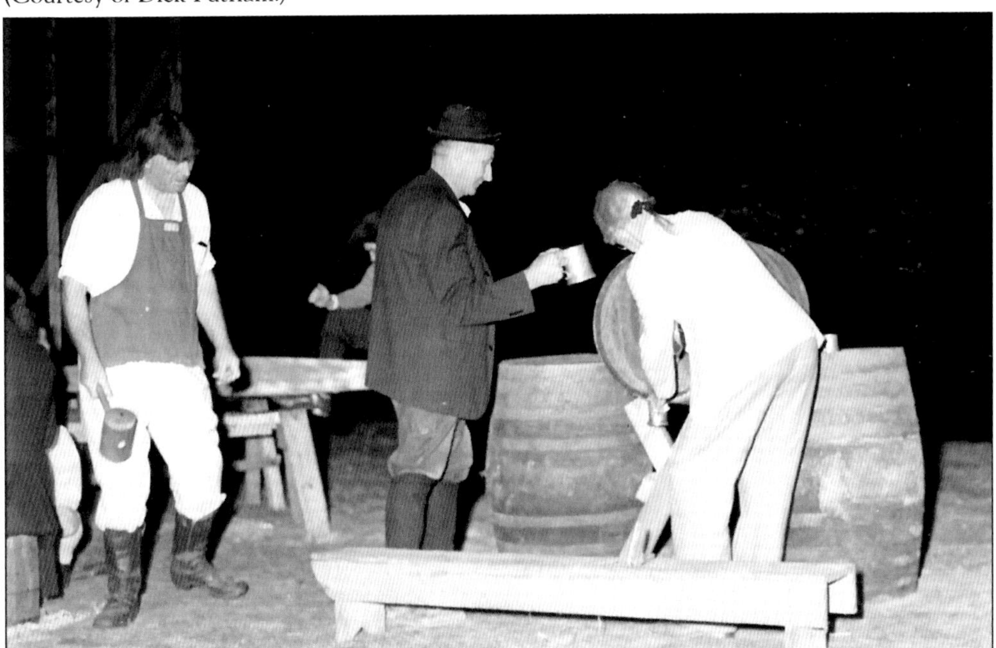

Wilton first celebrated old home day in 1939 in conjunction with the town's 200th anniversary. Like many other communities, one of the ways it acknowledged the holiday was by acting out scenes from earlier times. Heading for refreshments here are Luther Langdell, Eugene Rideout, and Judge Harold Cheever. (Courtesy of Dick Putnam.)

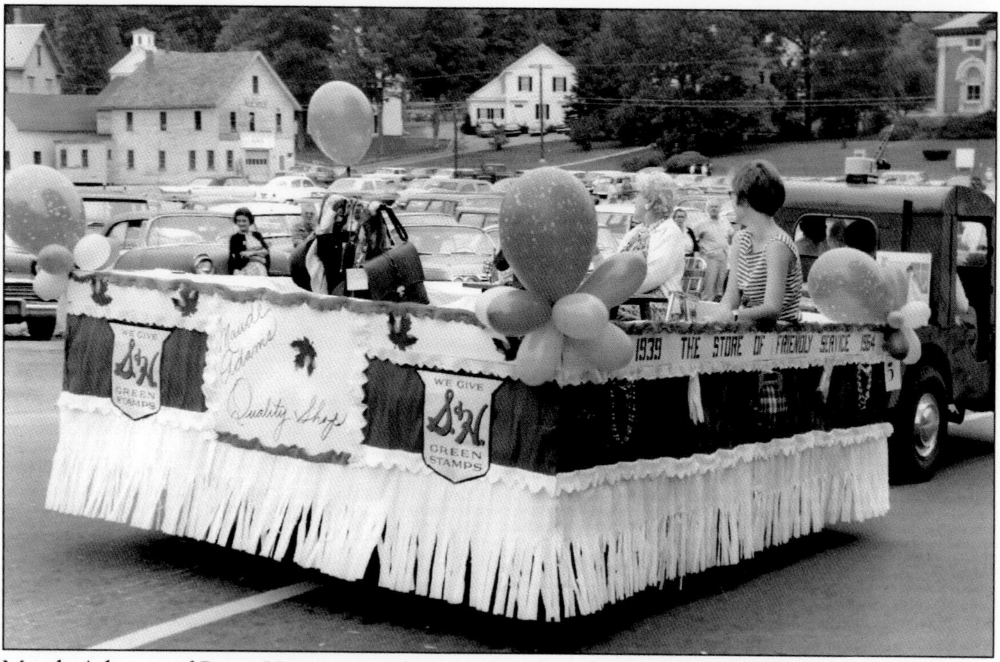

Maude Adams and Peggy Howe were riding the Maude Adams Quality Shop float as it approached Main Street in the 1964 parade. That year, Wilton Old Home Days was celebrated over the course of a three-day weekend. Wilton still celebrates old home week every five years but now has a nine-day celebration. (Courtesy of Dick Putnam.)

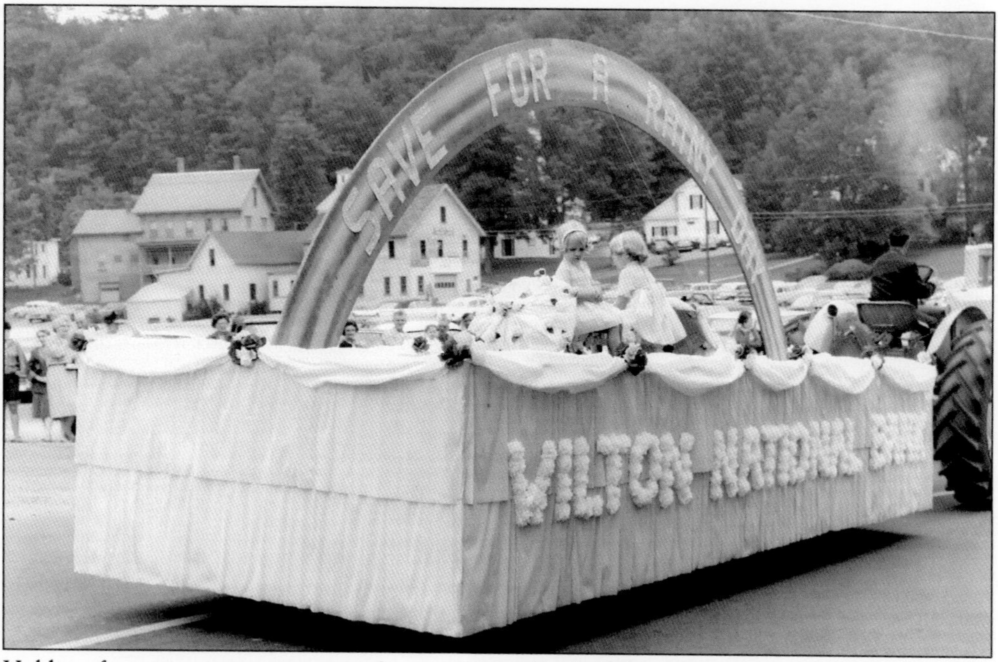

Holding festivities just once every five years, nearly all Wilton businesses make sure to enter floats into the old home days parade. The Wilton National Bank was no exception in 1964. Deborah and Martha Hutchinson were the young savers beneath the financial rainbow in this picture. (Courtesy of Dick Putnam.)

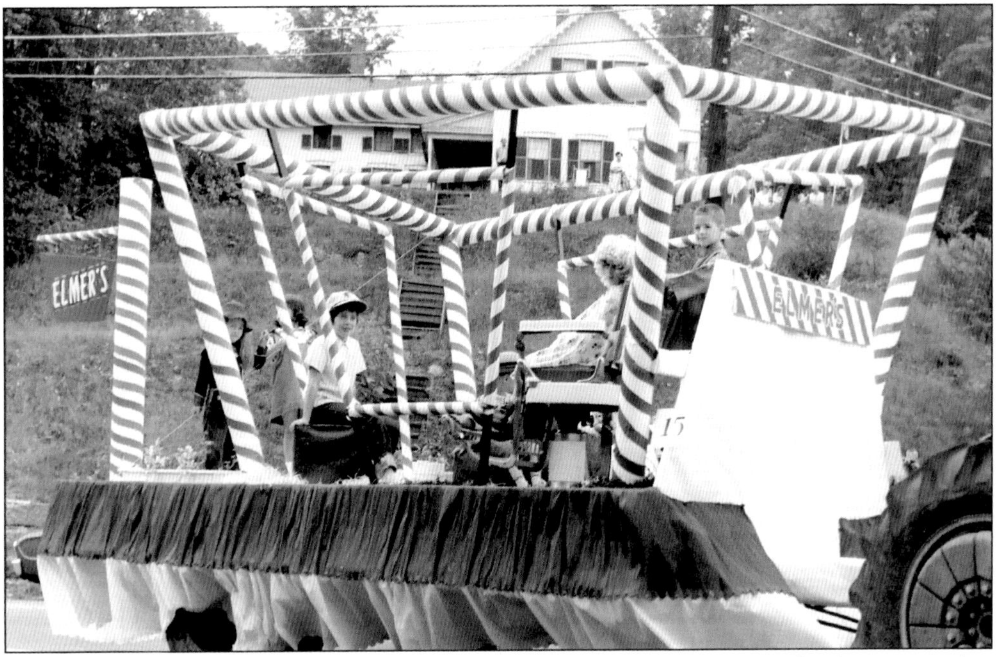

Elmer's barbershop has been providing haircuts on Wilton's Main Street for 50 years and is always represented by one of the best floats in the parade. This 1964 entry was the second of what was to become a long string of Elmer's award-winning floats over the years. (Courtesy of Dick Putnam.)

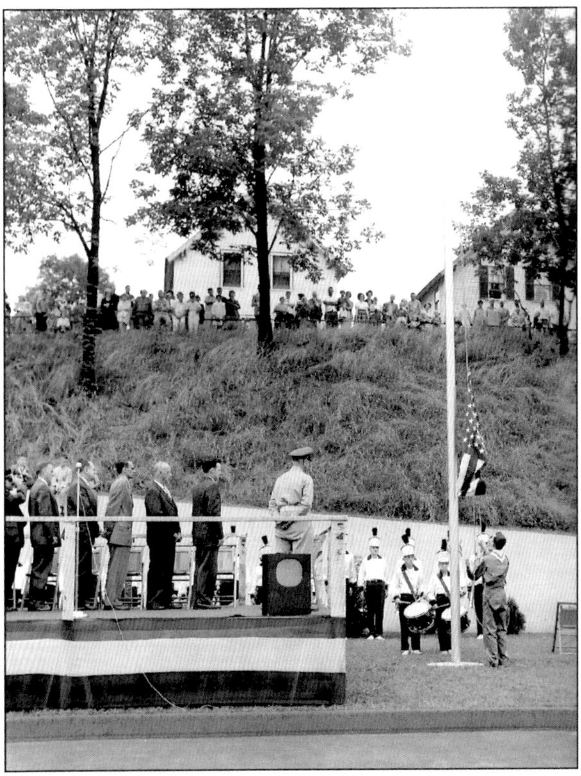

Invited speakers, local officials, and marching bands paused in 1959 to mark Wilton Old Home Days. Boy Scout Jim Nelson is pictured here raising the American flag during ceremonies on the Wilton Fire Station lawn. (Courtesy of Dick Putnam.)

This flyer from 1902 called native sons and daughters home to what was a full menu of activities for Peterborough. A free dinner was offered at Putnam Grove for the entire town and was attended by Gov. Chester B. Jordan. Also marking the holiday was a baseball game pitting Peterborough against Jaffrey. (Courtesy of the Granite State Collection, Sam Allen.)

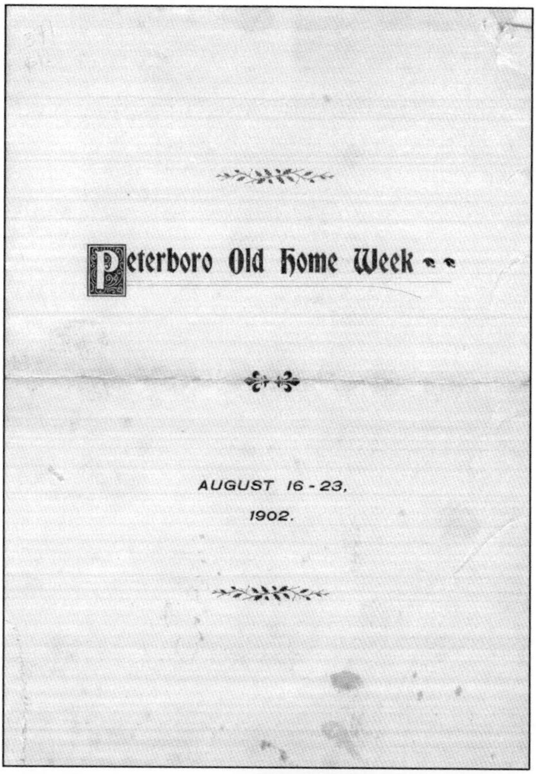

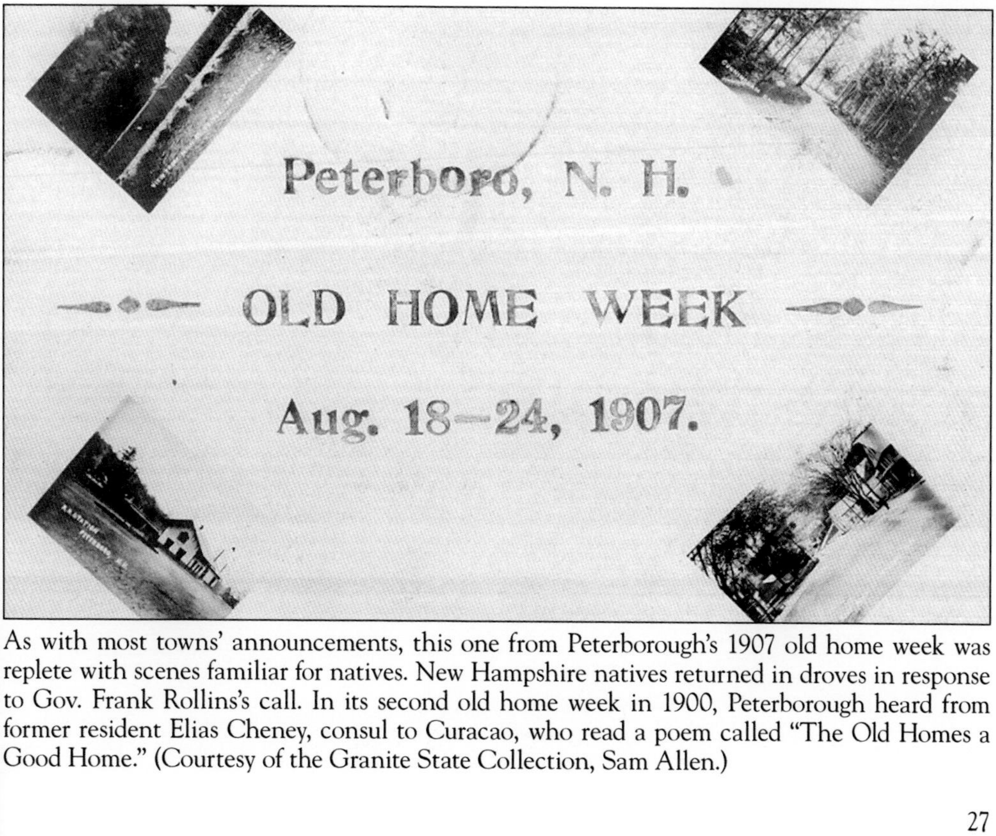

As with most towns' announcements, this one from Peterborough's 1907 old home week was replete with scenes familiar for natives. New Hampshire natives returned in droves in response to Gov. Frank Rollins's call. In its second old home week in 1900, Peterborough heard from former resident Elias Cheney, consul to Curacao, who read a poem called "The Old Homes a Good Home." (Courtesy of the Granite State Collection, Sam Allen.)

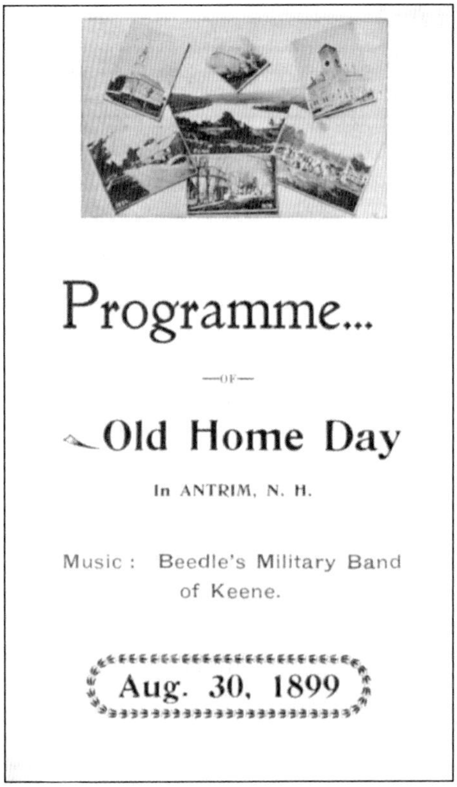
Programme...

—OF—

Old Home Day

In ANTRIM, N. H.

Music : Beedle's Military Band
of Keene.

Aug. 30, 1899

In Antrim, 1899 was a year of firsts. It was the first old home celebration for both the town and the state, as Antrim's sons and daughters answered Gov. Frank Rollins's call to return to the scenes of their youth. It was also the first year in existence for Beedle's Military Band, the main entertainment of the day. (Courtesy of the Granite State Collection, Sam Allen.)

Harrisville Old Home Day

"From across the miles and far away
This little card is on its way
To bid you come and make this day
The Happiest ever!"

Winn's Grove - Saturday, August 27, 1932

Sports, speeches, music and dancing will make the day's entertainment complete.

INVITATION COMMITTEE

This announcement alerted Harrisville residents about a full day of activities at the 1932 old home day celebration. Winn's Grove was the scene of drill demonstrations by the drum corps of the Gordon Bissel American Legion post of Keene. The main speaker for the day was former mayor John J. Landers of Keene. (Author's collection.)

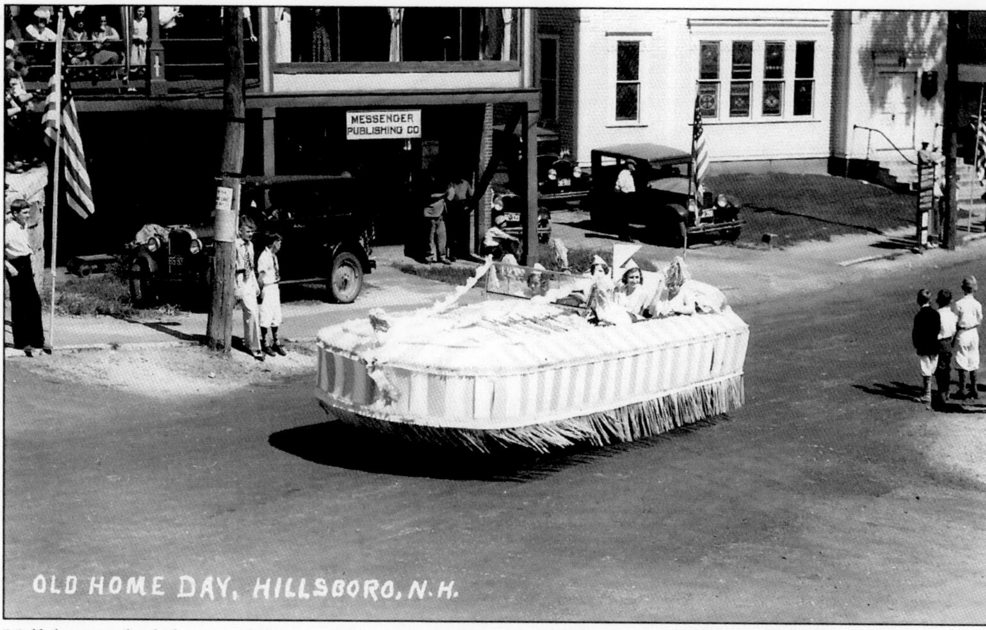

Hillsborough did not celebrate old home week on a regular basis in the early history of the event but did occasionally get in on the fun, as shown here during a parade. As for many towns, the end of World War I and the return of America's soldiers was a cause for old home festivities in 1919. That year, each of Hillsborough's 106 veterans was presented with bronze medals. (Author's collection.)

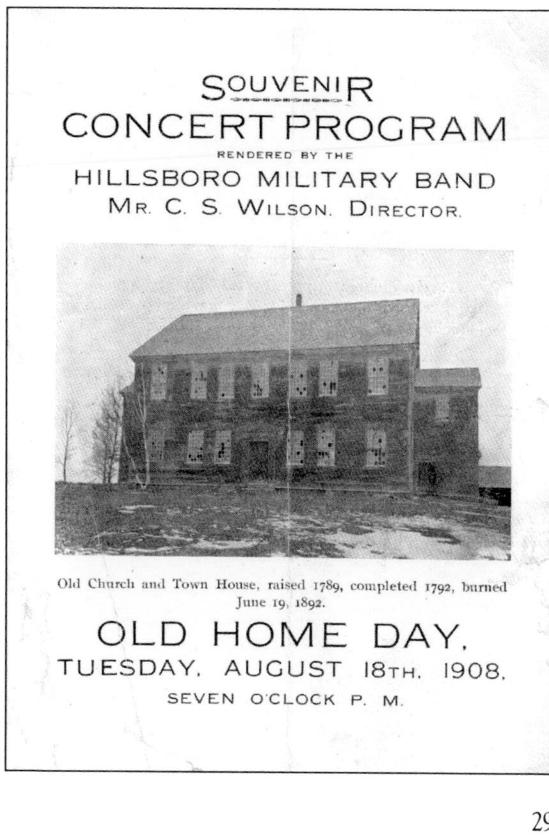

SOUVENIR

CONCERT PROGRAM

RENDERED BY THE

HILLSBORO MILITARY BAND

MR. C. S. WILSON, DIRECTOR.

Old Church and Town House, raised 1789, completed 1792, burned June 19, 1892.

OLD HOME DAY,

TUESDAY, AUGUST 18TH, 1908,

SEVEN O'CLOCK P. M.

The 1908 old home day in Hillsborough was highlighted by an evening performance of the Hillsboro Military Band. Among the selections presented to local concertgoers were a baritone solo of "Down on the Farm" by W. C. Dennison and a closing rendition of "Auld Lang Syne." Immediately following the concert, townspeople were urged not to miss the *Kadet Show* at the Child's Opera House. (Author's collection.)

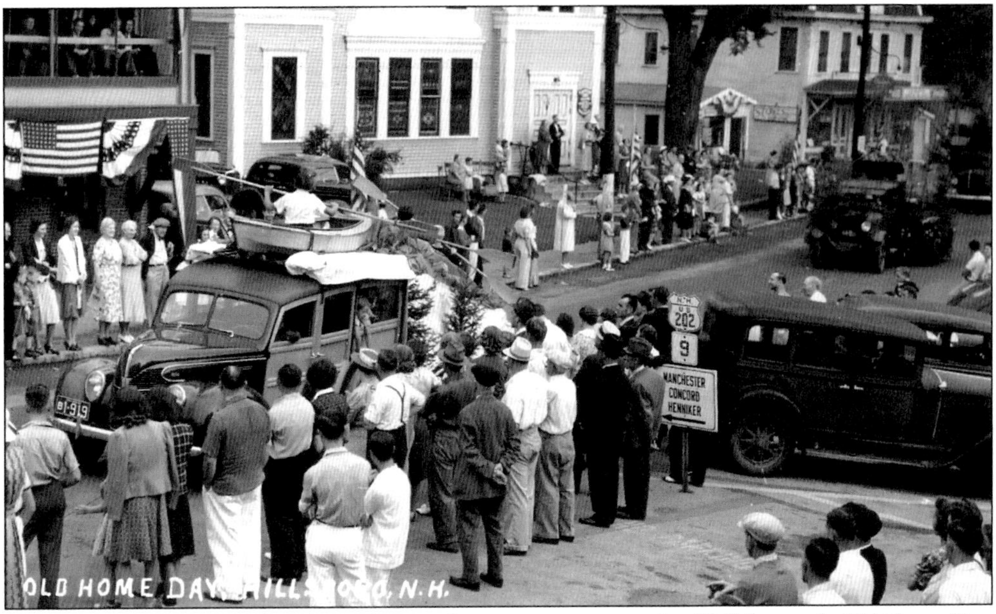

A little humor is always a hit along the parade route as it was on this Hillsborough Old Home Day float. Surrounded by bunting and American flags, residents all seemed to enjoy this Hillsborough beach wagon. The parade traveled the length of Main Street before ending at Grime's Field. (Courtesy of Washington Historical Society.)

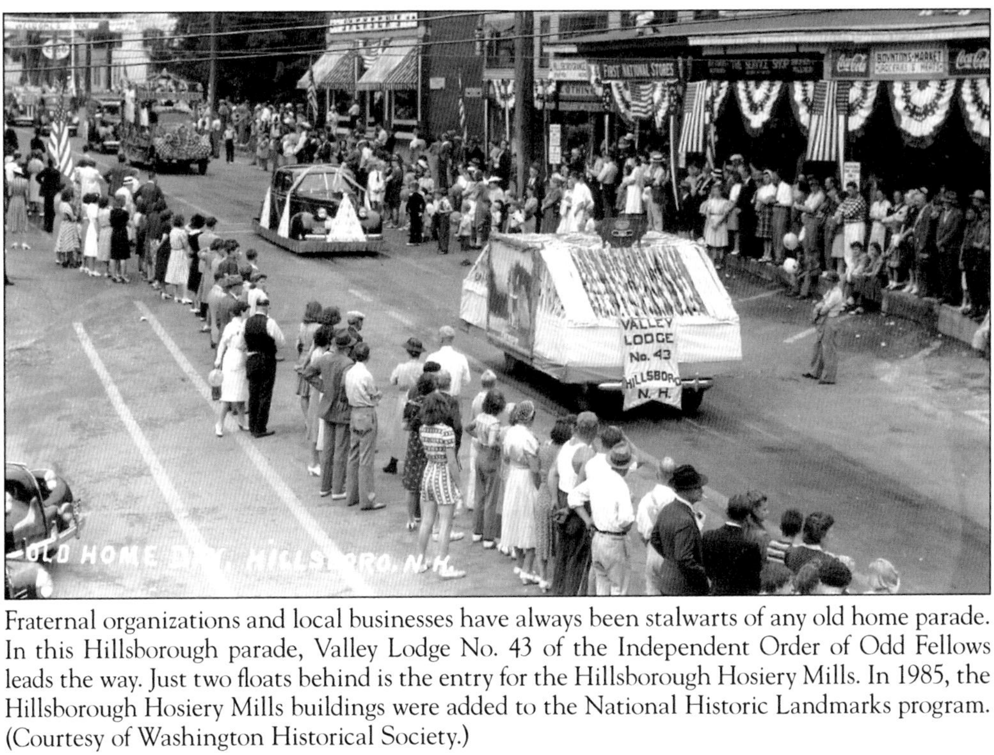

Fraternal organizations and local businesses have always been stalwarts of any old home parade. In this Hillsborough parade, Valley Lodge No. 43 of the Independent Order of Odd Fellows leads the way. Just two floats behind is the entry for the Hillsborough Hosiery Mills. In 1985, the Hillsborough Hosiery Mills buildings were added to the National Historic Landmarks program. (Courtesy of Washington Historical Society.)

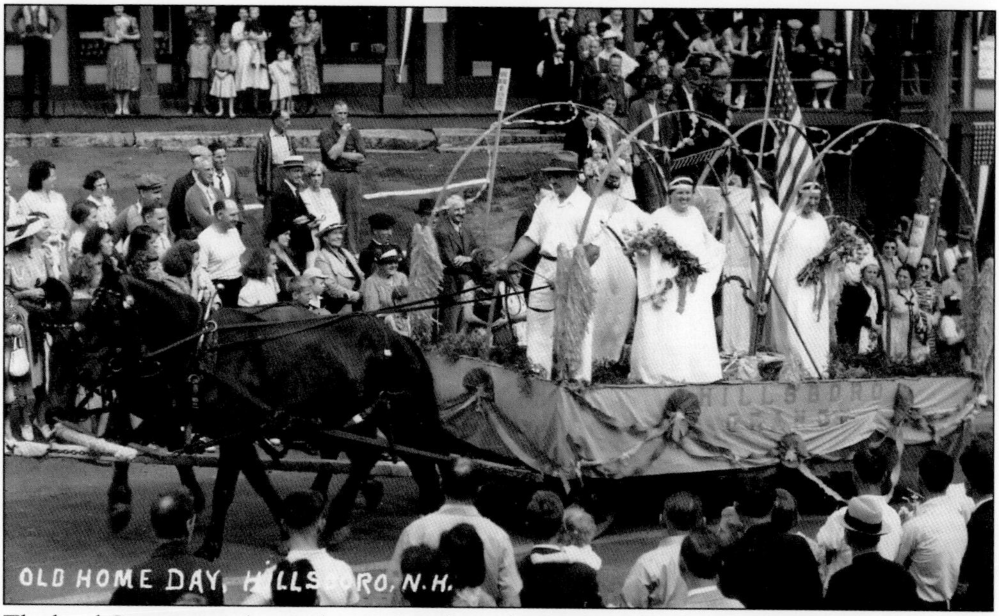

The local Grange was almost always a sure bet to be involved in any town's old home celebration. As well as entering floats like this one in Hillsborough, the Grange was always active on both the state and local level in supporting Gov. Frank Rollins's plans to revitalize the rural landscape of New Hampshire. (Courtesy of Washington Historical Society.)

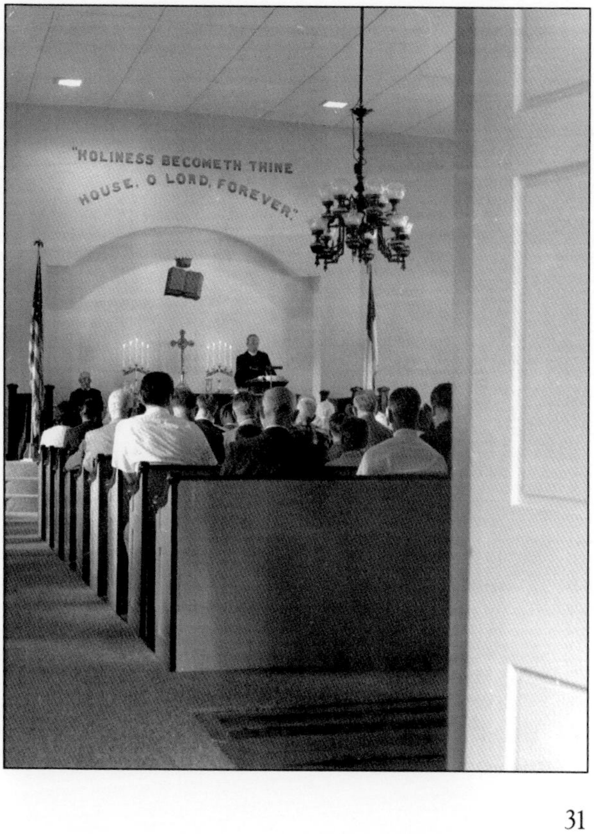

Ecumenical cooperation has always been a feature of old home day observances. In many towns, the celebrations have actually been under the direction of one or more of the churches in town. Here a full crowd is on hand as part of Mason's combined old home day and 200th anniversary in 1968. (Courtesy of Mason Historical Society.)

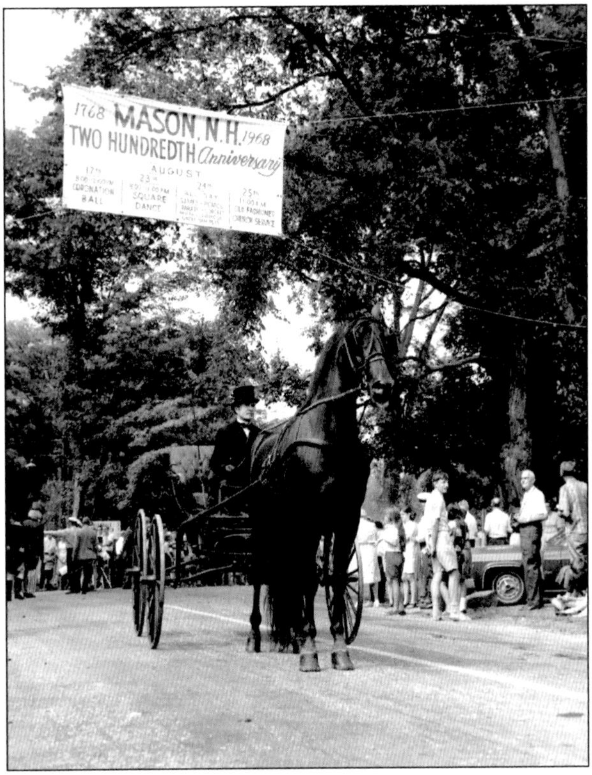

The date of the first settlement of Mason was 1768, and many townspeople got right into character for the events 200 years later. Playing the part quite convincingly in horse and buggy is Mason resident Al Gravlin. A look at the banner behind him shows that the methods of celebrating had not changed too much since the first New Hampshire Old Home Week in 1899. (Courtesy of Mason Historical Society.)

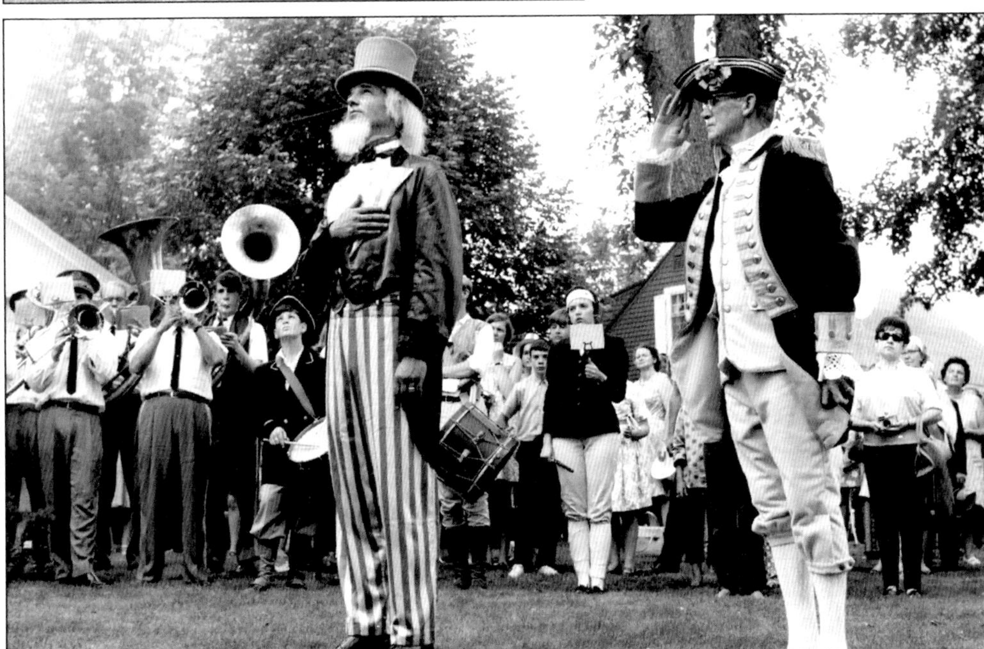

With a local band in the background, it is hard to imagine a more patriotic image than this one from Mason's 1968 old home day/bicentennial. Uncle Sam (played by Arthur French) and the continental officer (played by French's uncle Charles Crathern) pay tribute to Old Glory. (Courtesy of Mason Historical Society.)

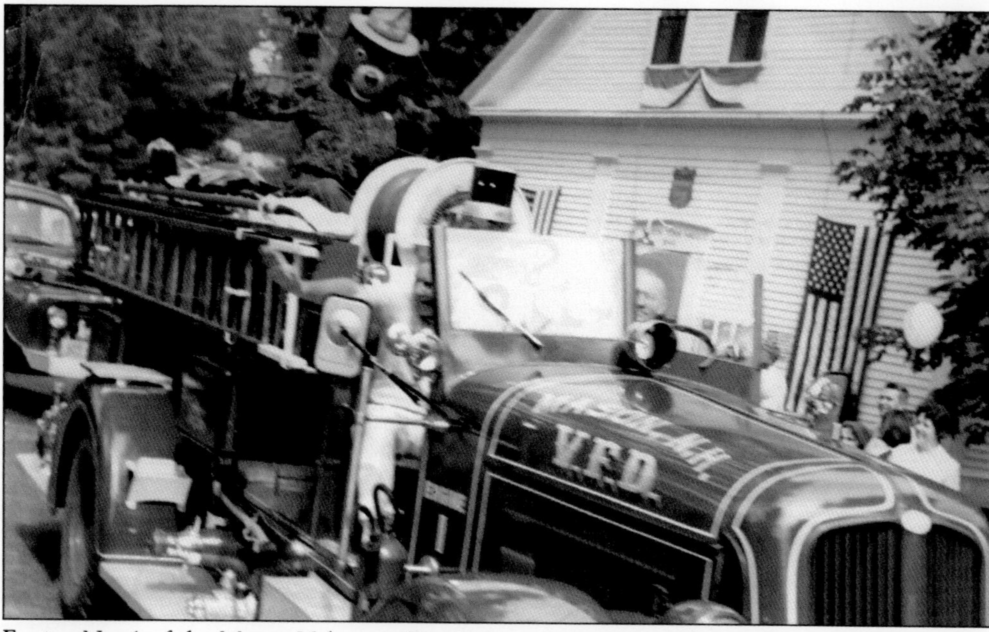

Engine No. 1 of the Mason Volunteer Fire Department gives a ride to a hero almost as famous as Uncle Sam. Driving Smokey along for the 1968 parade is volunteer fireman Burt Jackson. Following the parade, Mason's tribute to its past continued with guided tours of the first meetinghouse, the town cattle pound, and various 18th-century cemeteries. (Courtesy of Mason Historical Society.)

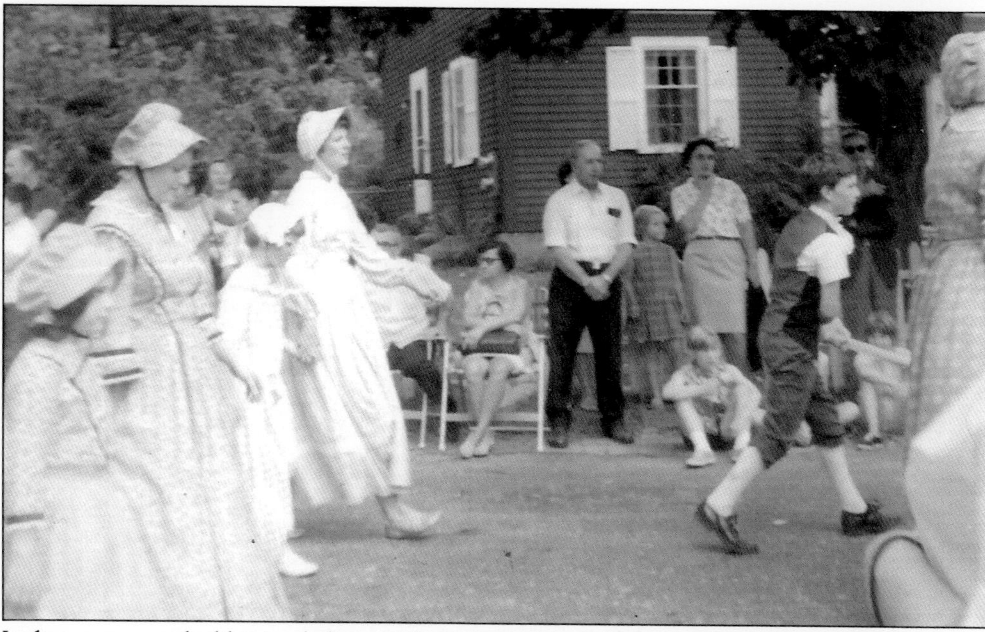

Ladies young and old joined the parade in costume to honor early settlers of Mason at the 1968 old home day/bicentennial. The observance marked the 200th year since the signing of the town's charter. At Mason's old home day in 2008, more local history was recognized with the dedication of a memorial to Bode, an African American who is considered the town's first non-Native American resident. (Courtesy of Mason Historical Society.)

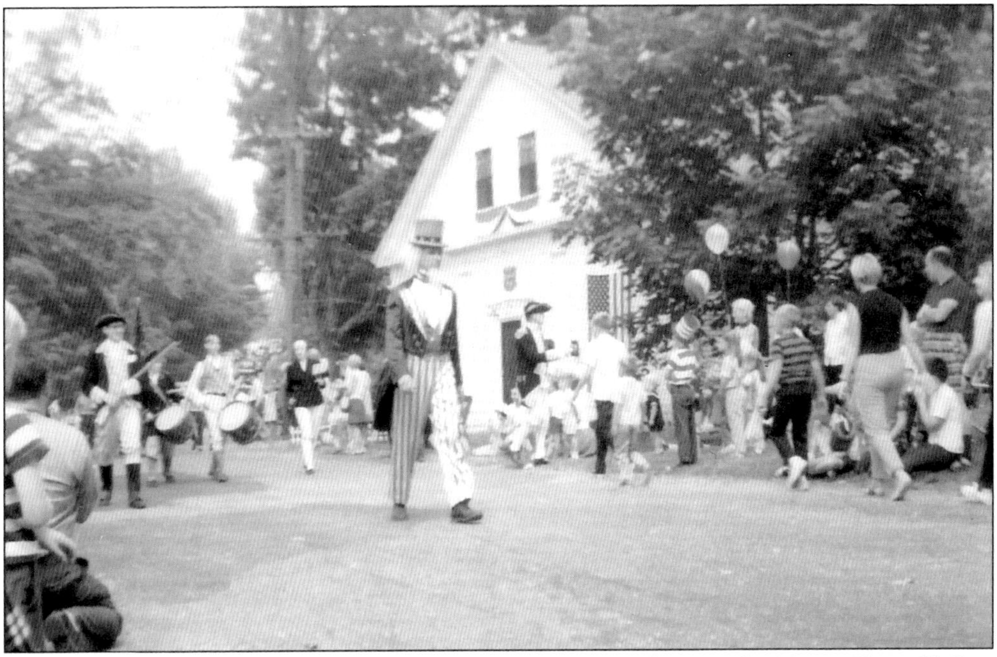

Arthur French, in his celebratory persona of Uncle Sam, strides past the Mason Town Hall at the head of the 1968 parade. "Uncle Sam" Wilson, whose boyhood home was in Mason on Valley Road, was officially declared the real Uncle Sam by the United States Congress. (Courtesy of Mason Historical Society.)

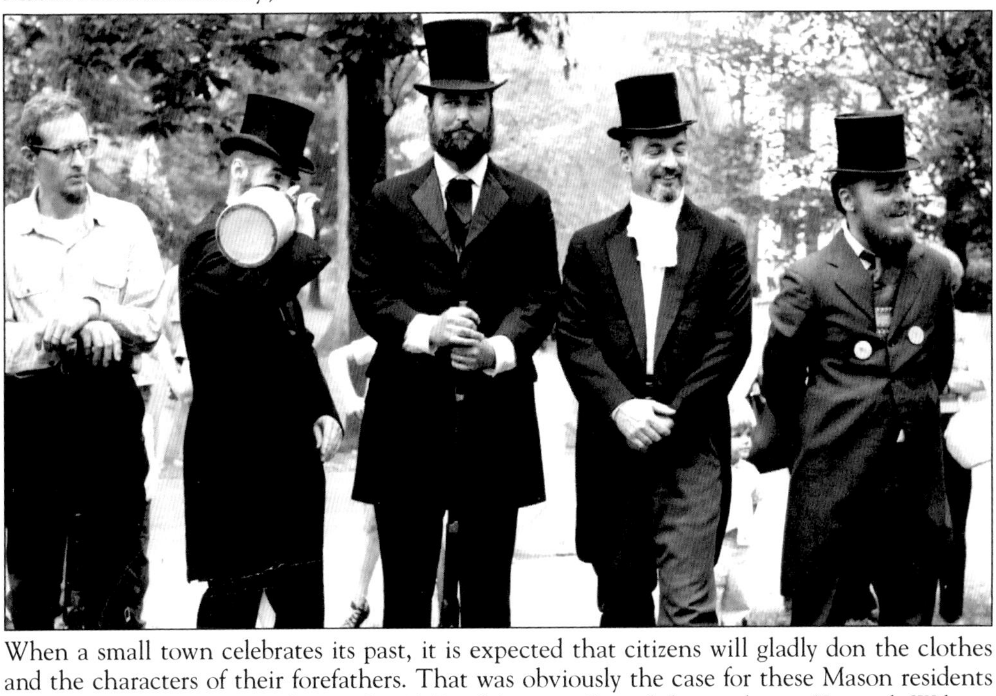

When a small town celebrates its past, it is expected that citizens will gladly don the clothes and the characters of their forefathers. That was obviously the case for these Mason residents who took time out to pose during the 1968 celebration. From left to right are Kenneth Wilson, Roger Trempe, Raymond Parker, Edward McCaffrey, and Robert Russo. (Courtesy of Mason Historical Society.)

Two

SEACOAST REGION

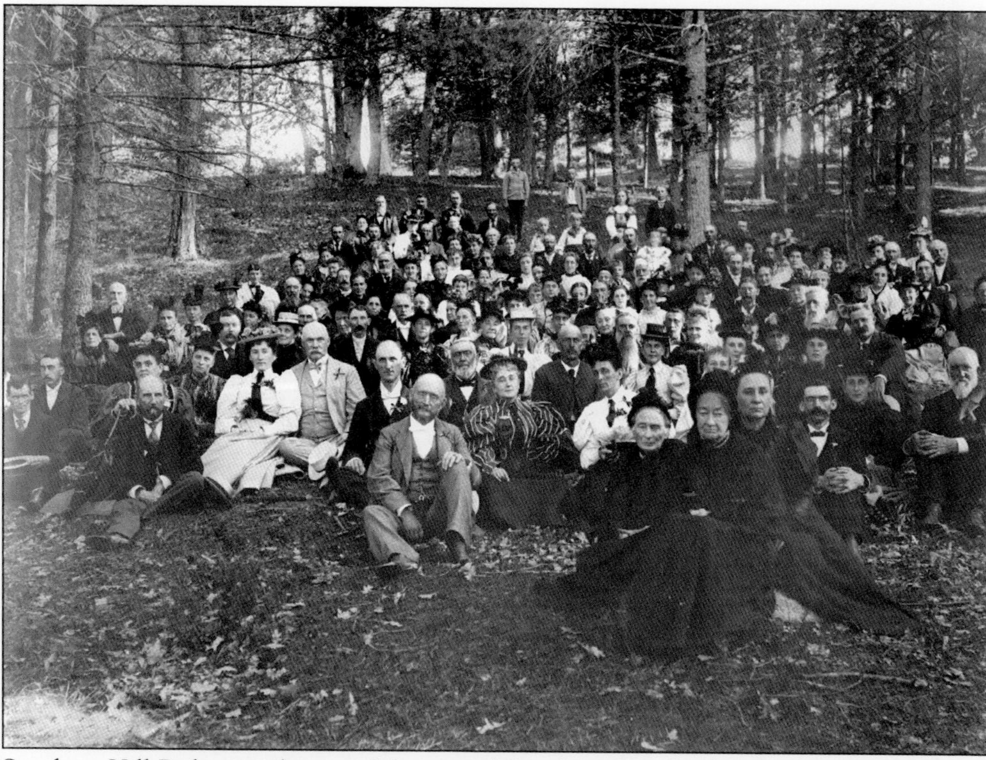

Stratham Hill Park, now the site of the annual Stratham Fair, has long been a gathering spot for town residents. Here celebrants turned out for food and music and posed on the hill during Stratham Old Home Day 1906. This photograph was taken shortly after the 70-acre parcel surrounding the hill was purchased and donated to the town by Edward Tuck. (Courtesy of Stratham Historical Society.)

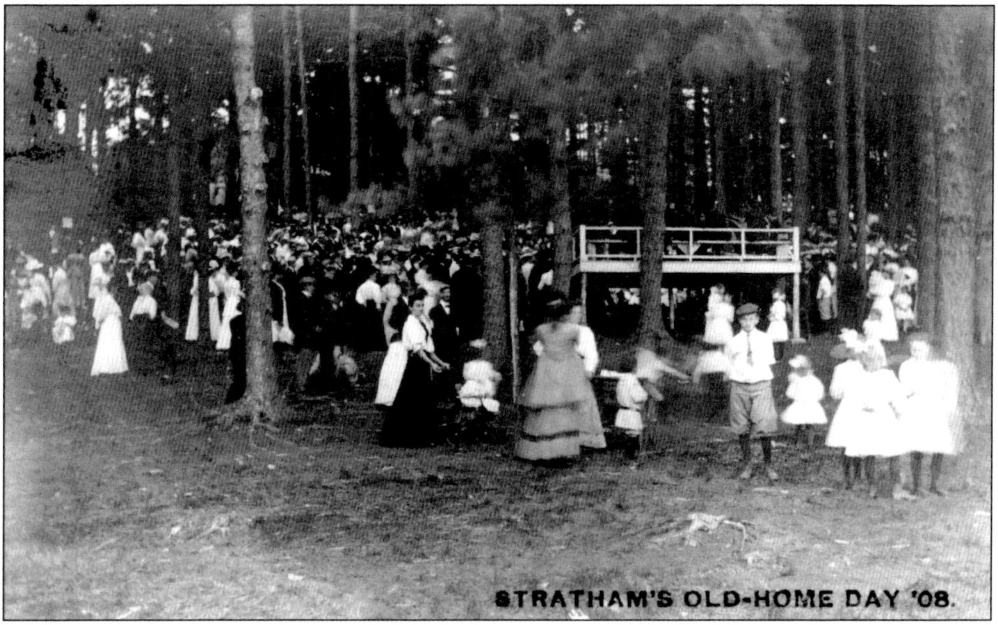

First observed in 1904, old home day in Stratham was also known as the town picnic. Like many New Hampshire towns, Stratham quickly warmed to the idea of joining its annual picnic with the statewide festivities. Stratham Hill Park is the location of this 1906 gathering of both locals and visitors getting together for a picnic and fun. (Courtesy of Stratham Historical Society.)

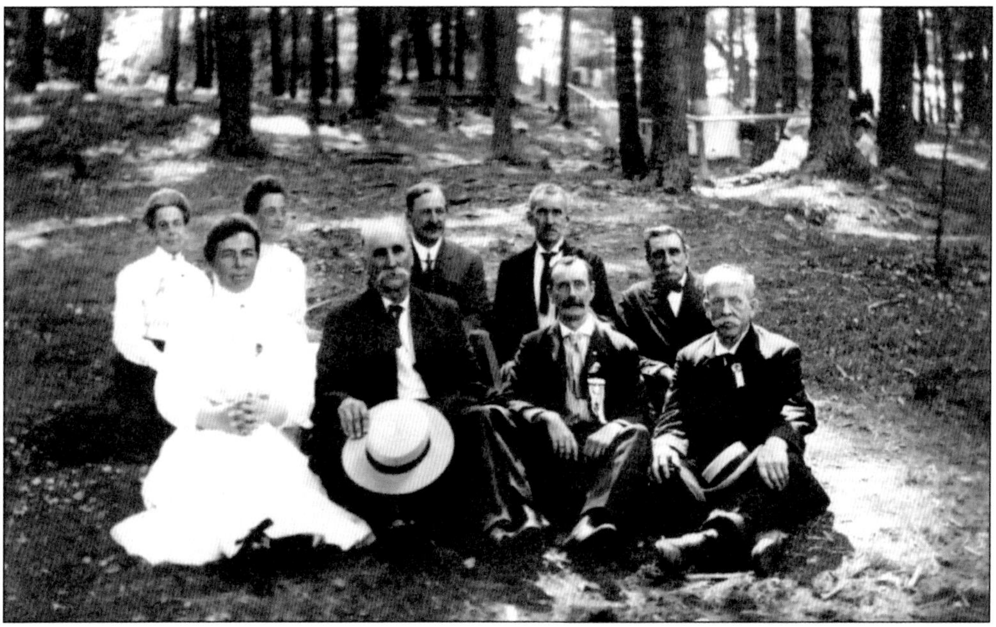

As anyone involved in such events is aware, a lot of planning goes into any town wide event. The same was true for early old home celebrations and groups such as the Stratham Old Home Day planning committee, who were the ones to do the work. From left to right are (first row) Annie Scammon, Isaac S. Wiggin, Fred N. Edwards, and unidentified; (back row) Mrs. J. T. Smart, unidentified, unidentified, Albert C. Lane, and unidentified. (Courtesy of Stratham Historical Society.)

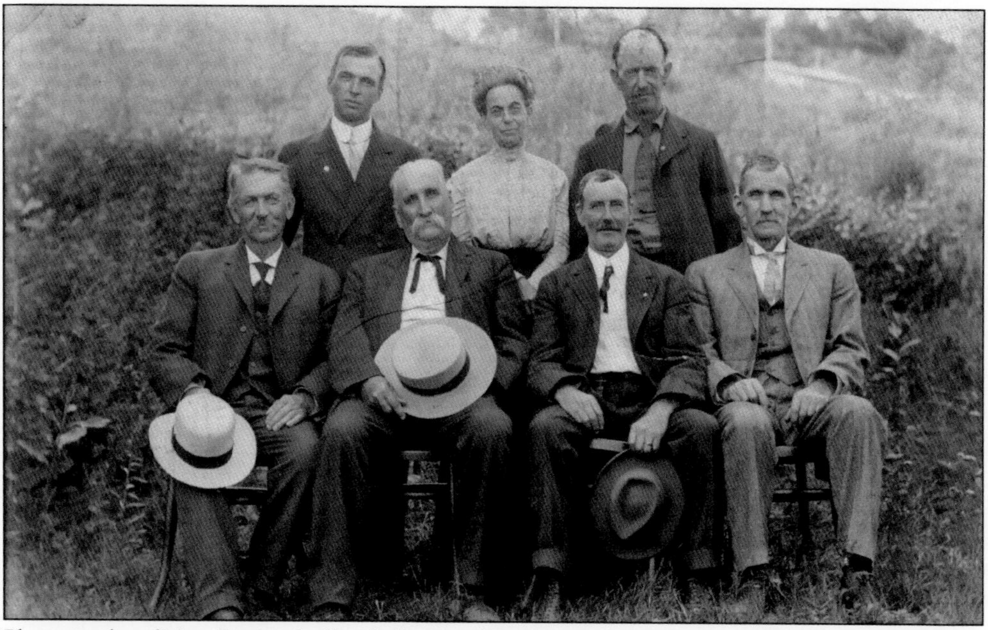

Photographs of New England officials from early in the 20th century usually feature rather stern visages. However, old home days seemed to bring out the smiles even for official photographs such as this from the 1911 Stratham Old Home Day. From left to right are (first row) George E. Gowen, Isaac S. Wiggin, Fred N. Edwards, and Albert C. Lane; (second row) Frank H. Pearson, Mrs. J. T. Smart, and Charles Grant. (Courtesy of Stratham Historical Society.)

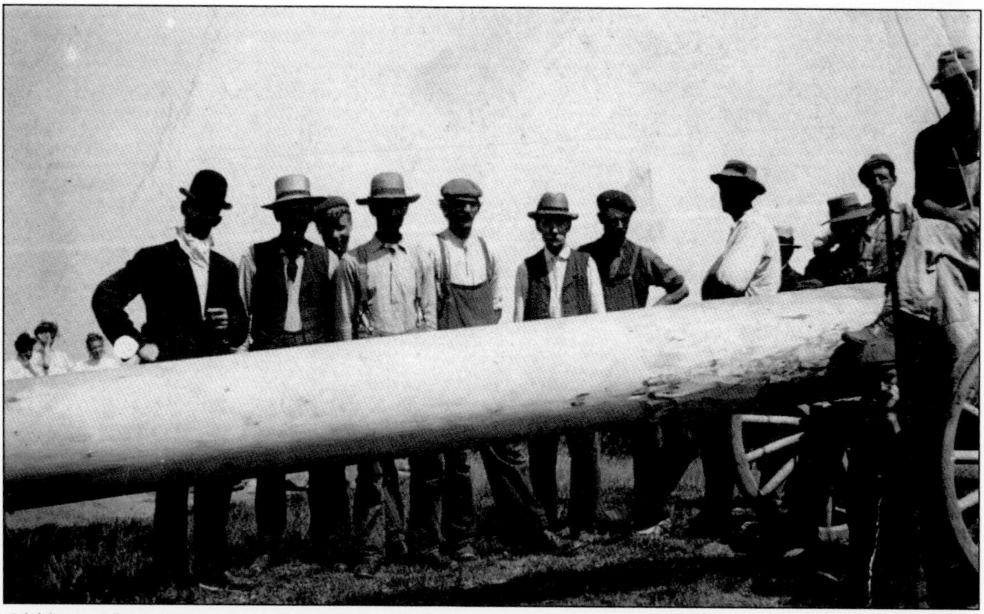

Old home festivities were often used as an opportunity to initiate civic improvements. In August 1908 during Stratham Old Home Day, this flagpole was raised at the base of Stratham Hill Park. Shown posing proudly with the new pole are Bert Burbank, George E. Gowen, Eddie Tuttle, Arthur Jewell, Melvin Stickney, Levi Prentiss Wiggin, J. C. Piper, and Gilbert Thompson. (Courtesy of Stratham Historical Society.)

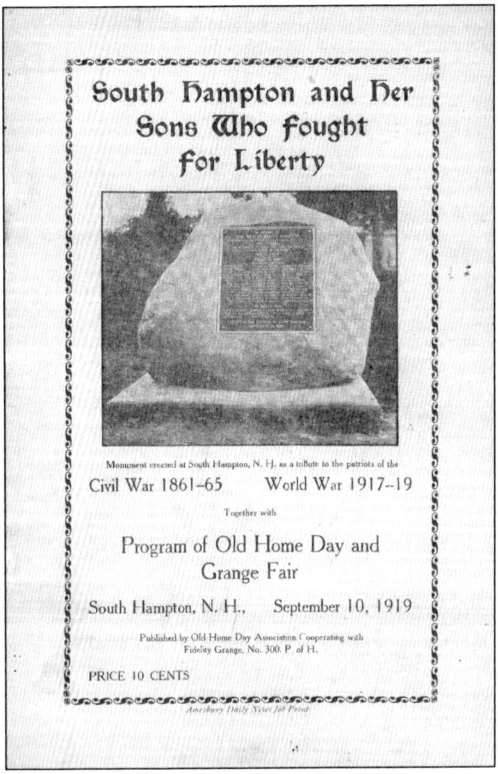

There are no homecomings more poignant or deeply felt than those of soldiers, which made 1919 a special old home day throughout the state. In South Hampton, it was the occasion for dedication of a memorial to veterans who had served in both the Civil War and World War I. (Courtesy of Granite Collection, Sam Allen.)

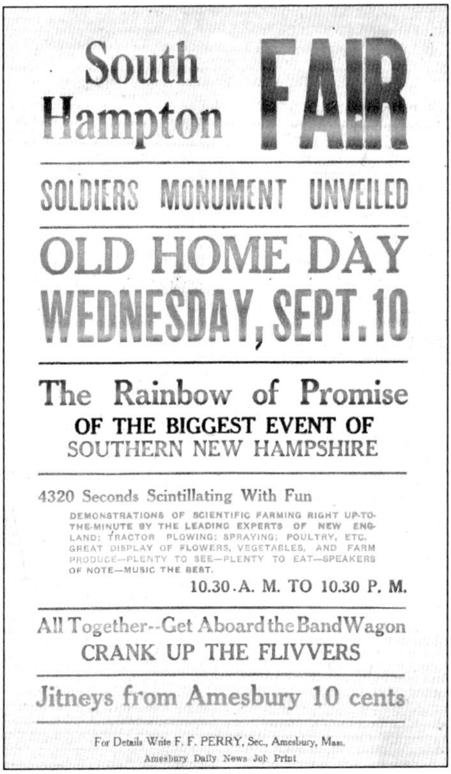

In addition to the dedication of the war memorial, the 1919 South Hampton Old Home Days served as an example of the blending of the holiday with a traditional country fair. For readers 90 years later, this poster might also seem to be partially written in a foreign language. Flivvers were Ford Model Ts, while those 10¢ jitneys were simply shared cabs popular at the time. (Courtesy of the Granite State Collection, Sam Allen.)

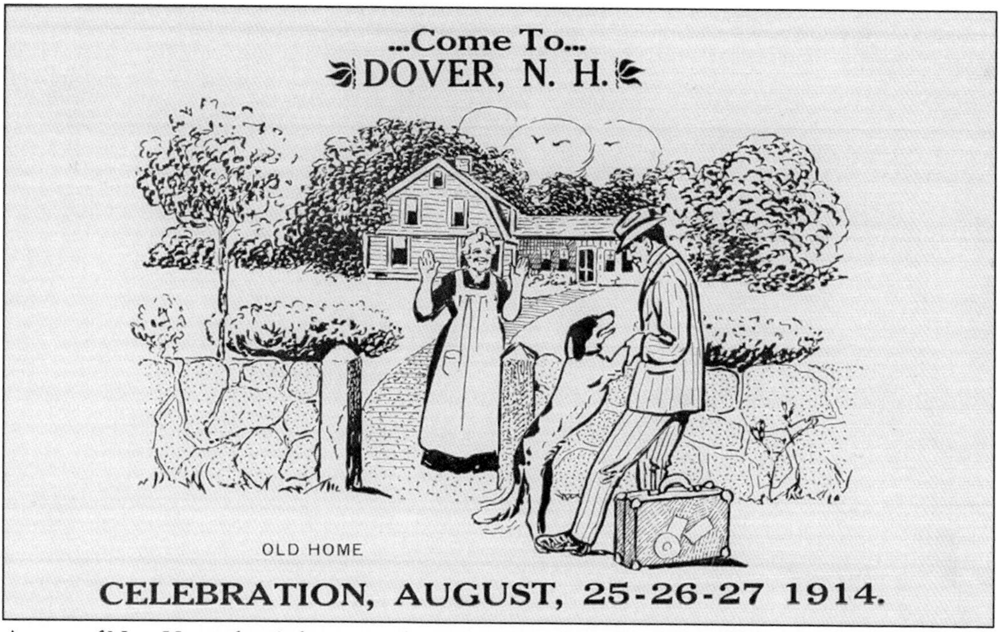

As one of New Hampshire's few coastal communities, Dover took a helping hand from the navy department for its 1914 celebration. During the three nights of Dover Old Home Day, the search light from the battleship *Montana*, on loan from the navy, lit up the night sky from the Sawyer Observatory on Garrison Hill. (Courtesy of the Granite State Collection, Sam Allen.)

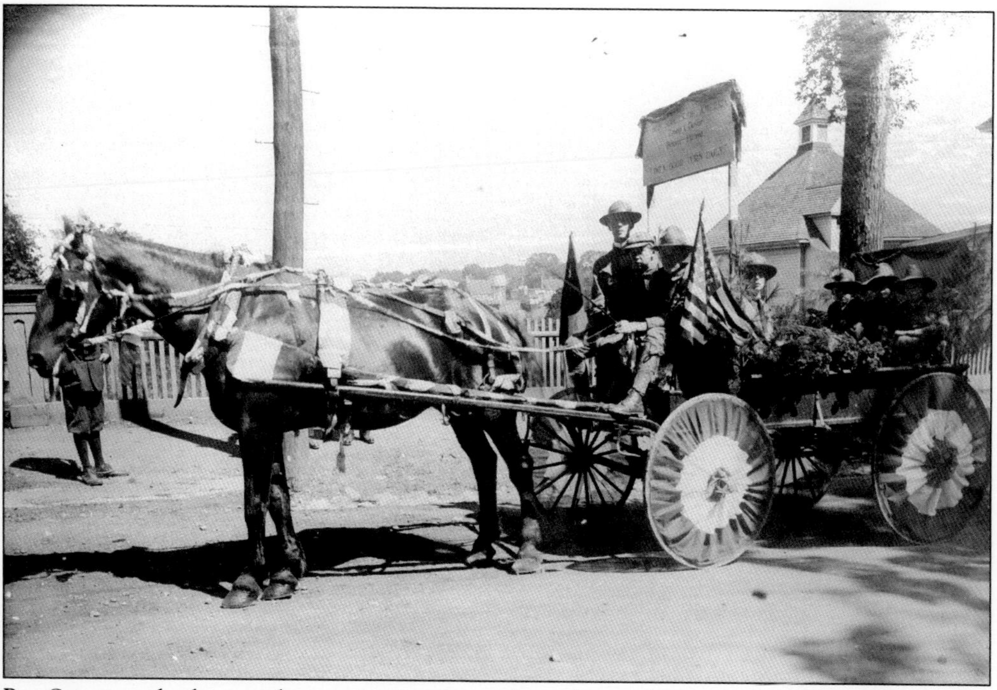

Boy Scouts and other youth organizations have always been a big part of old home days in New Hampshire. Exhorting members to "Do a good turn daily," this float was part of Dover's huge 1914 celebration. (Courtesy of Dover Public Library.)

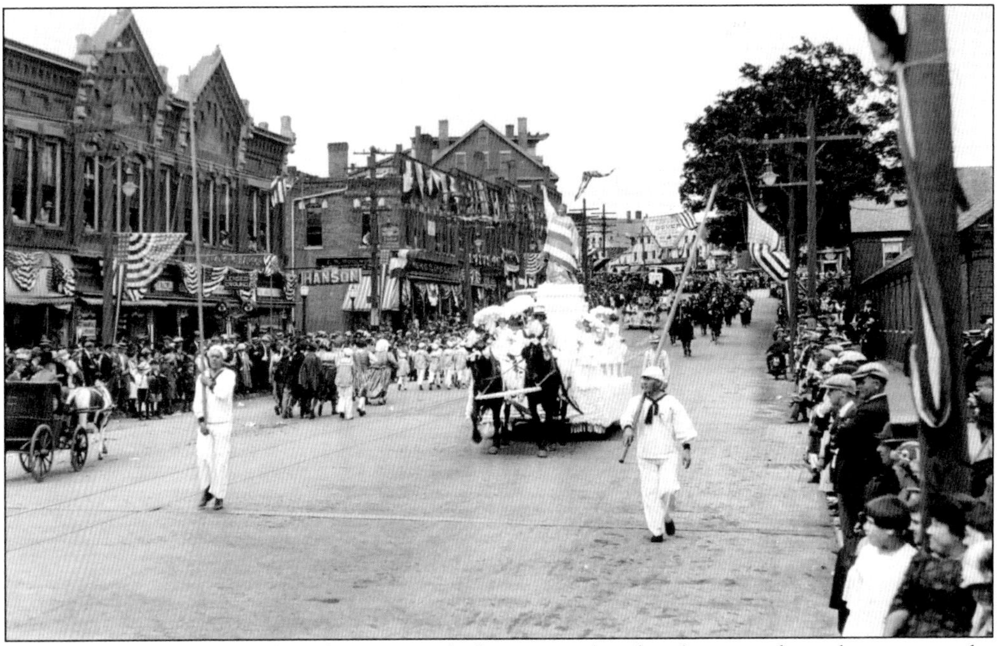

Dedicated just 28 years earlier, the Statue of Liberty was already a favorite of parade organizers by the time of Dover's 1914 old home day. It was estimated at the time that over 30,000 spectators lined the five-mile parade route for the celebration. (Courtesy of Dover Public Library.)

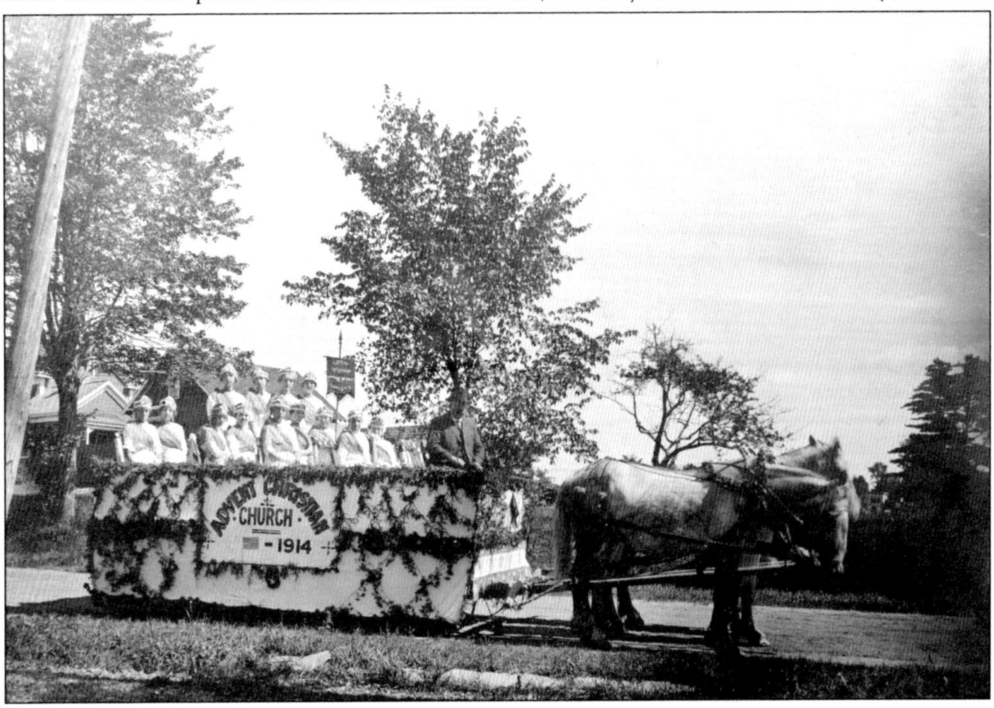

Organized in 1882, the Advent Christian Church of Dover was just one of several religious organizations in town to take part in the 1914 old home parade. Local churches are still often used for opening and closing ceremonies for many old home observances. (Courtesy of Dover Public Library.)

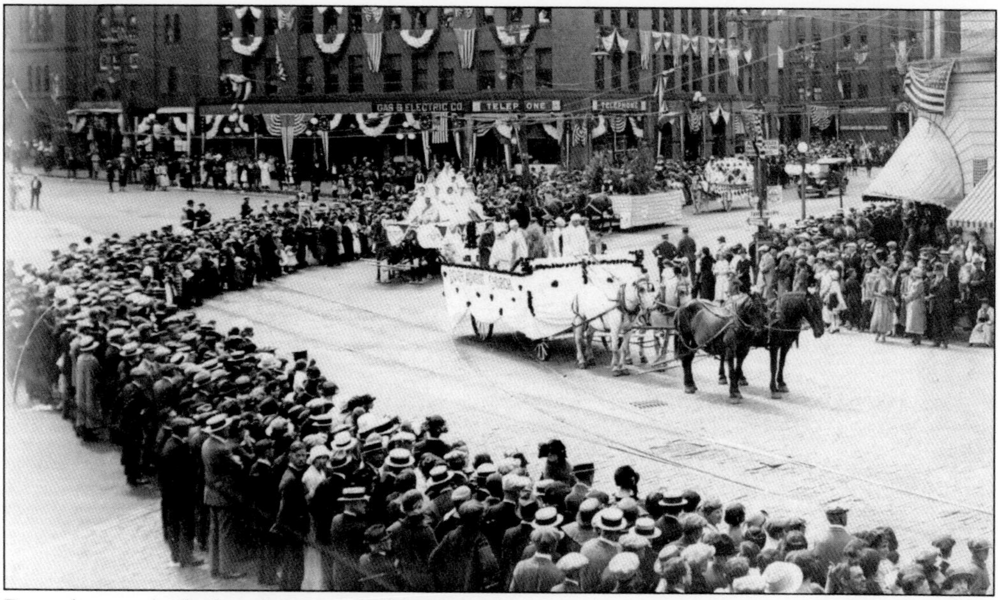

Dover has not had a long history of celebrating old home days, but it went all out in 1914. Heading the festivities and serving as president of the Dover Old Home Day committee was former mayor Alonzo Foss. Buildings and streets were decorated throughout the city. The parade consisted of three divisions, each nearly one mile in length. (Courtesy of Dover Public Library.)

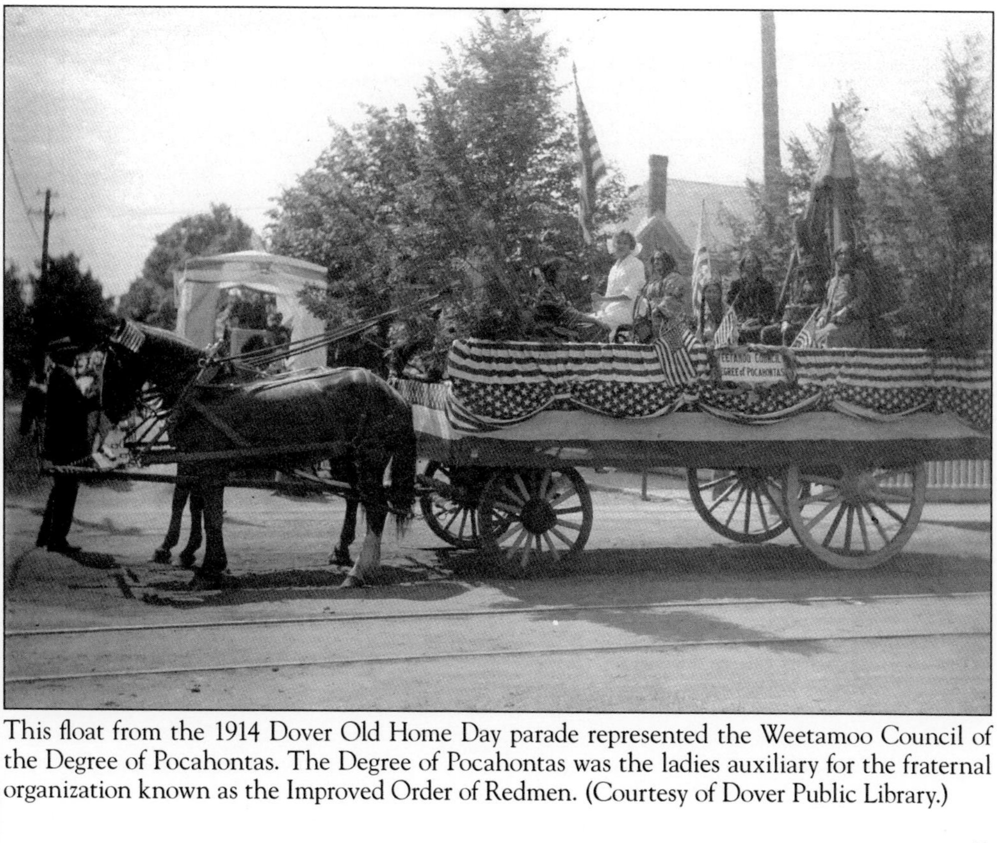

This float from the 1914 Dover Old Home Day parade represented the Weetamoo Council of the Degree of Pocahontas. The Degree of Pocahontas was the ladies auxiliary for the fraternal organization known as the Improved Order of Redmen. (Courtesy of Dover Public Library.)

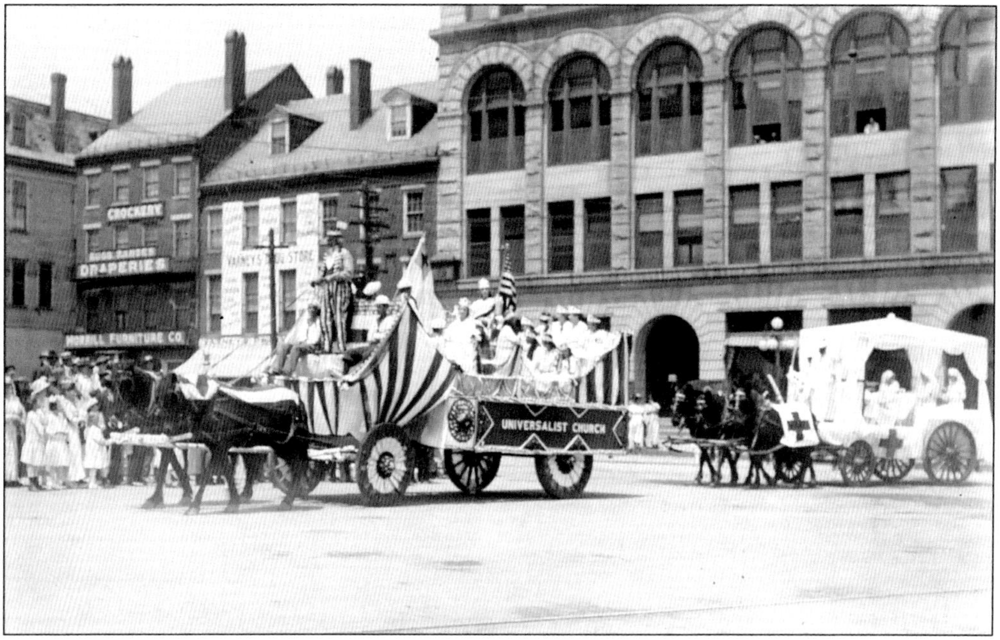

The three divisions of Dover's huge 1914 parade included a marching division, automobiles, and of course one made up of floats and decorated teams. The float division had over 100 entries, including the two pictured here from the Universalist Church and the Red Cross. (Courtesy of Dover Public Library.)

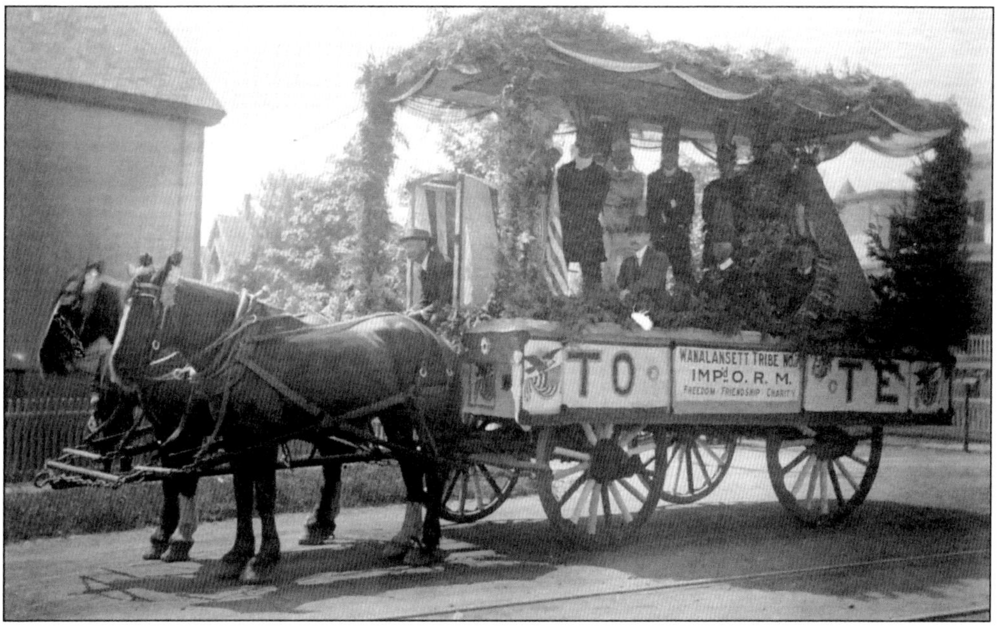

The Wanalansett Tribe No. 7 of the Improved Order of Red Men was on hand for the 1914 Dover Old Home Day festivities. The Improved Order of Red Men is a fraternal organization founded in 1834 whose membership has dwindled greatly since the end of World War II. In the early 1900s, however, its float entries could be found in old home parades throughout the state. (Courtesy of Dover Public Library.)

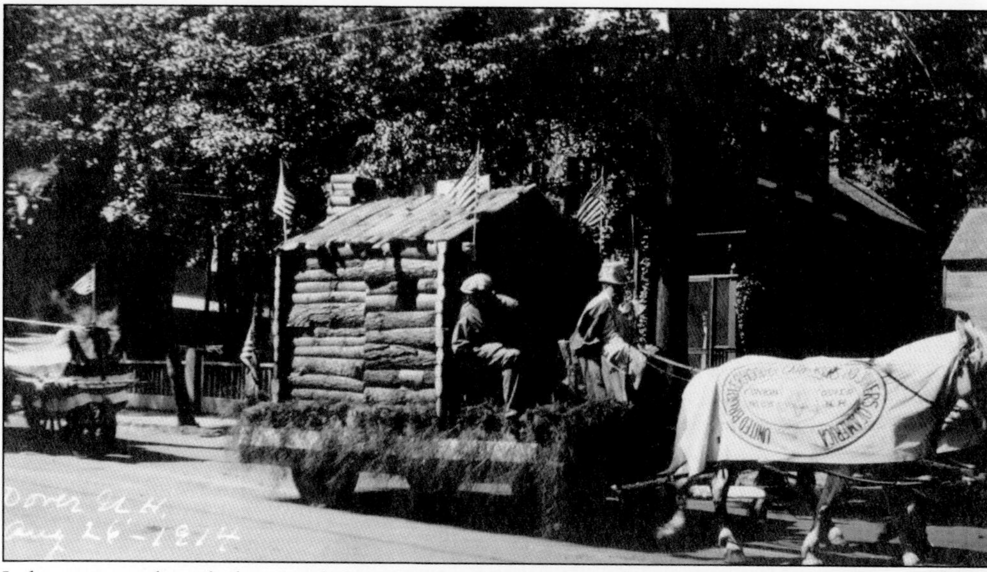

Labor was on board along with many other organizations for the 1914 Dover Old Home Day parade. This rather rustic example of the building trade was presented on the float of the United Brotherhood of Carpenters and Joiners. The parade route stretched five miles through Dover. (Courtesy of Dover Public Library.)

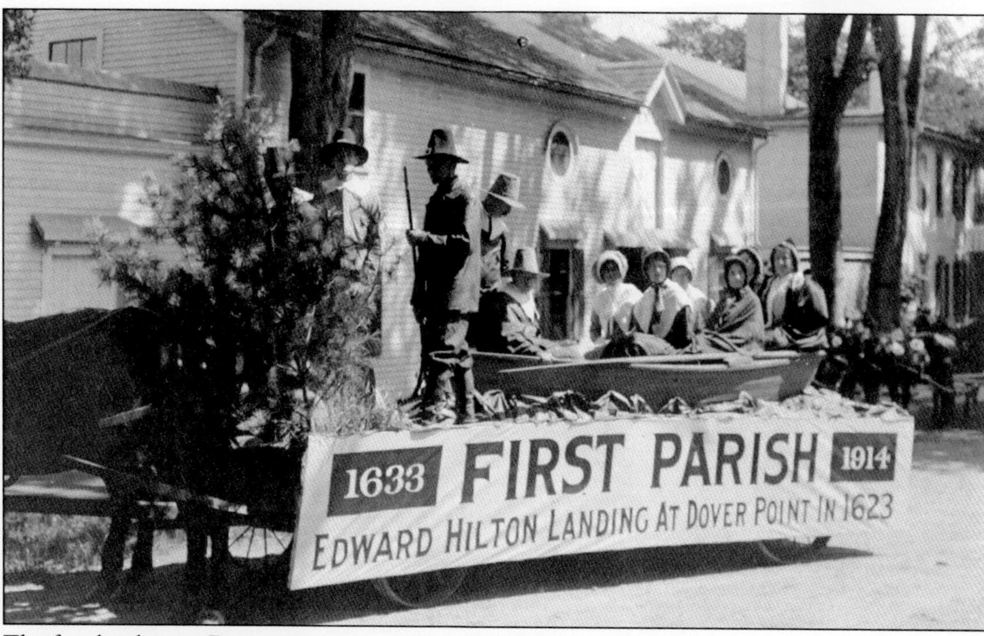

The first landing in Dover is represented on this 1914 float. The reenactment depicts the landing of Edward Hilton in the area that came to be known as Dover. Dover was originally known as Hilton's Point. The site of this first landfall can still be seen at Hilton Park on Dover Point Road. (Courtesy of Dover Public Library.)

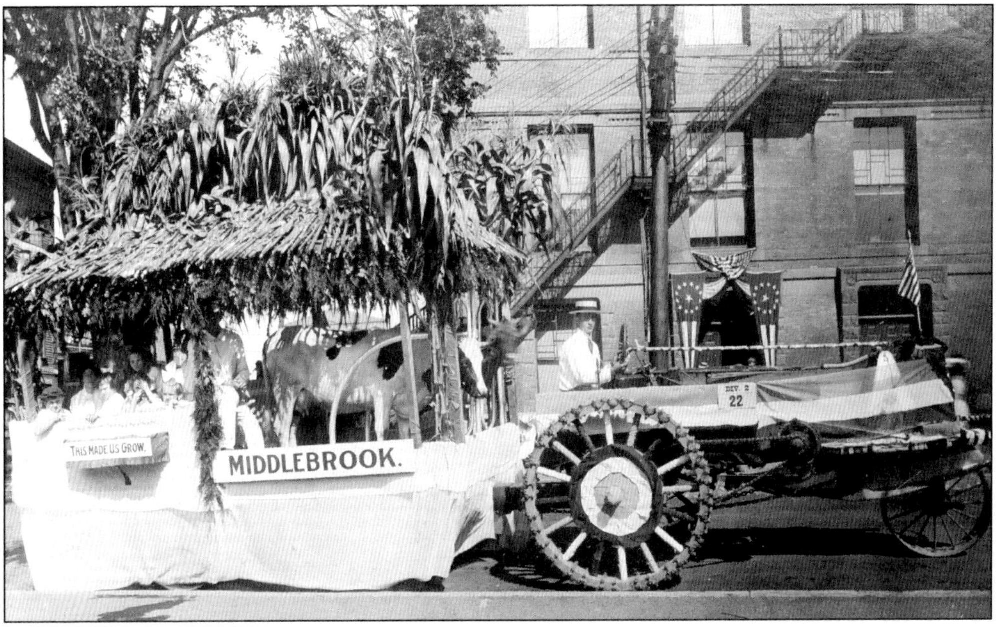

Healthy living, courtesy of Middlebrook Farm, was the message of this Dover Old Home Day float. Middlebrook Farm was a major supplier of milk for the area up until World War II. On Tuesday during the 1914 Dover Old Home Day, a pageant called "Little Boy Blue" was staged at Middlebrook Farm under the direction of Marion W. Seavey. (Courtesy of Dover Public Library.)

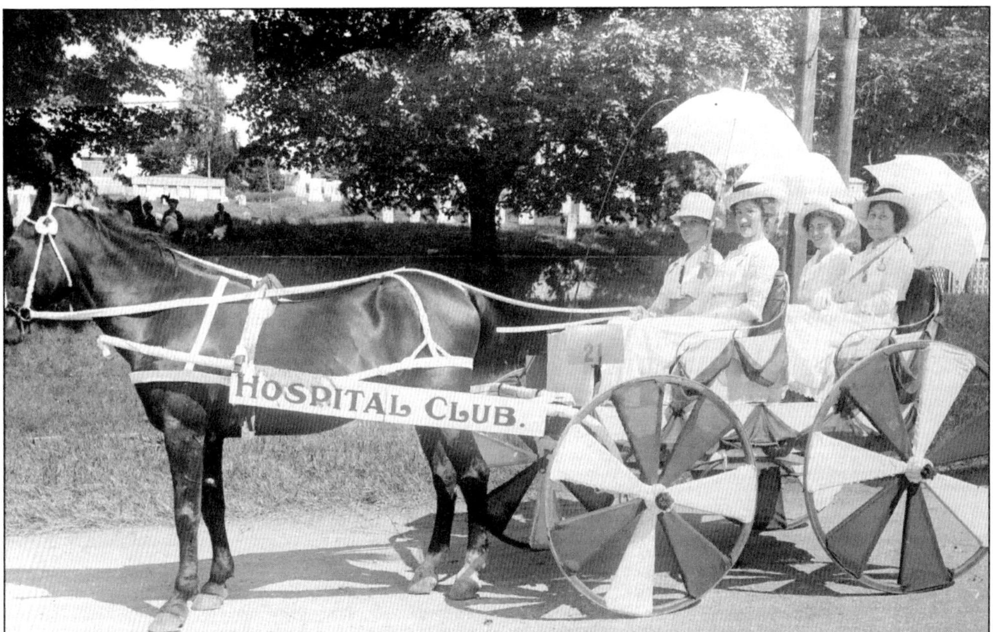

One of the many entries of decorated teams in the 1914 parade was that of the Hospital Club of Dover. The appearance of many parade floats was not the only sign of the times in the 1914 celebration. The elaborate festivities that took place over three days received an appropriation of a mere $500 from the Dover treasury. (Courtesy of Dover Public Library.)

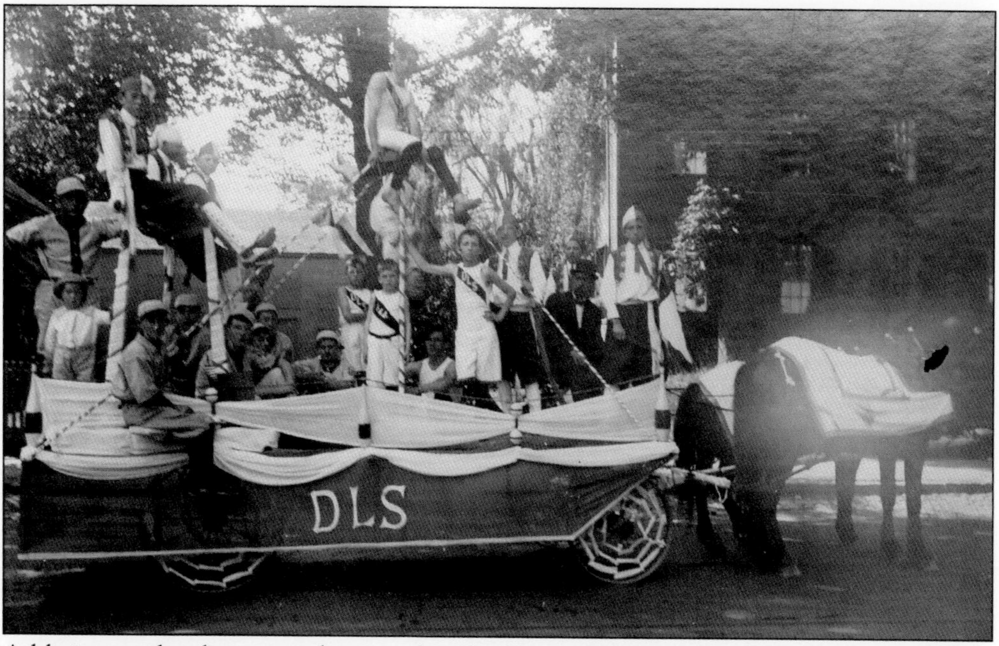

Athletics was the obvious emphasis on this 1914 Dover Old Home Day float. Sports were a large part of the celebration in general. Thursday, the final day of old home revelries, was dedicated in large part to athletic contests. Also included in the final day's events were balloon ascensions, band concerts, and fireworks. (Courtesy of Dover Public Library.)

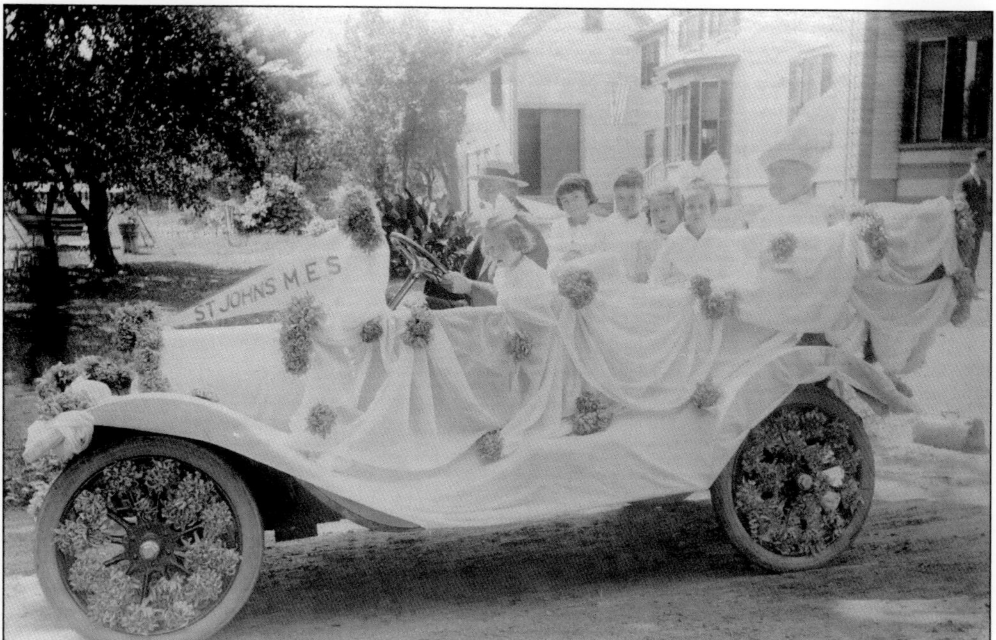

St. John's Parish in Dover chose a decorated motorcar for its entry in 1914's parade. Because of the growing popularity of the horseless carriage in 1914, there were enough automobiles in the city for an entire division of the parade to be dedicated to them. (Courtesy of Dover Public Library.)

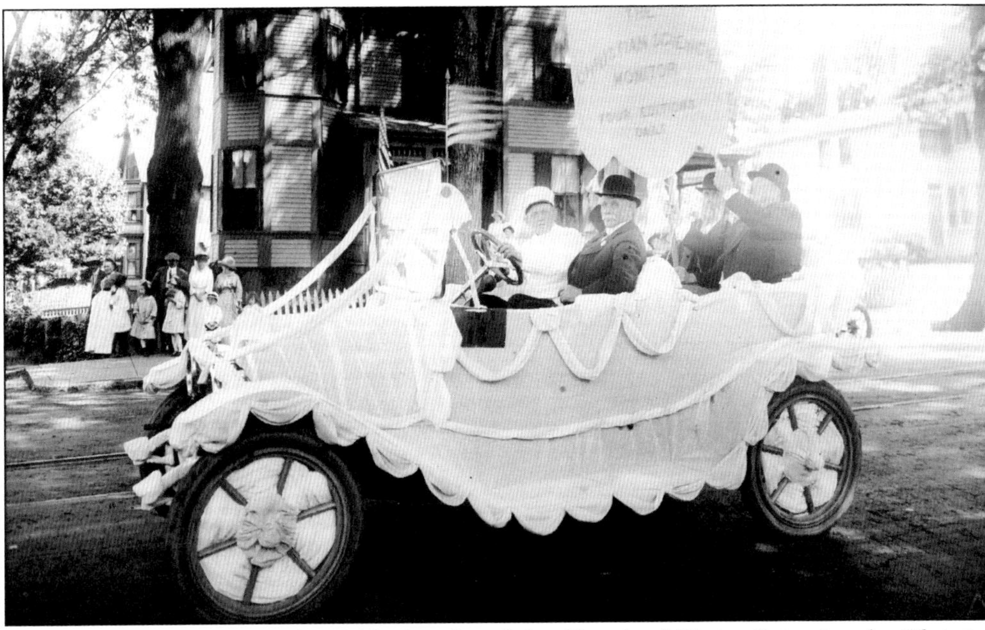

Started in 1908 by Mary Baker Eddy, founder of the Church of Christ, Scientist, the *Christian Science Monitor* is heralded on this 1914 float as "A Daily Newspaper for the Home." Along with thousands of other spectators on the parade route, the floats were reviewed by New Hampshire governor Samuel D. Felker and Mayor Charles H. Foss of Dover. (Courtesy of Dover Public Library.)

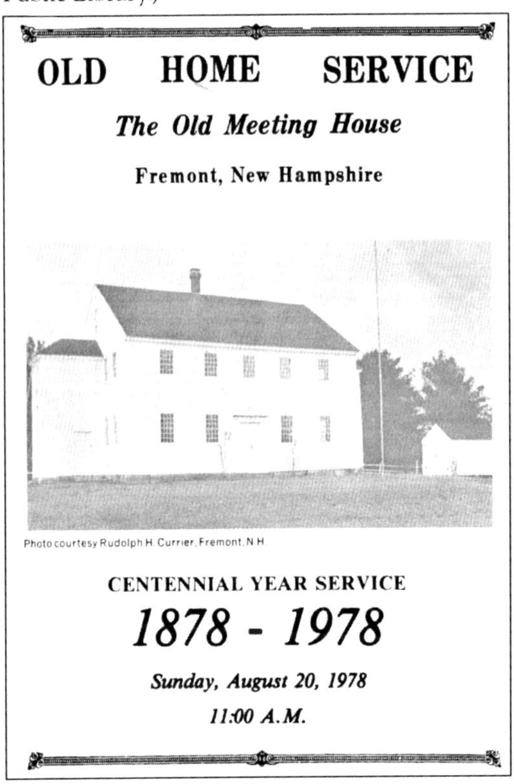

OLD HOME SERVICE

The Old Meeting House

Fremont, New Hampshire

Photo courtesy Rudolph H. Currier, Fremont, N.H.

CENTENNIAL YEAR SERVICE

1878 - 1978

Sunday, August 20, 1978

11:00 A.M.

The Universalist Society of Fremont continues a long tradition of old home day observances up to the present day. The guest speaker at this 1978 service was Congressman Norman D'Amours. Almost 30 years earlier in 1949, Congressman Chester Merrow highlighted the program. The other speaker in 1949 was Rev. Arthur Webster of the First Universalist Church of Salem, Massachusetts. (Author's collection.)

Three

White Mountains and Great North Woods

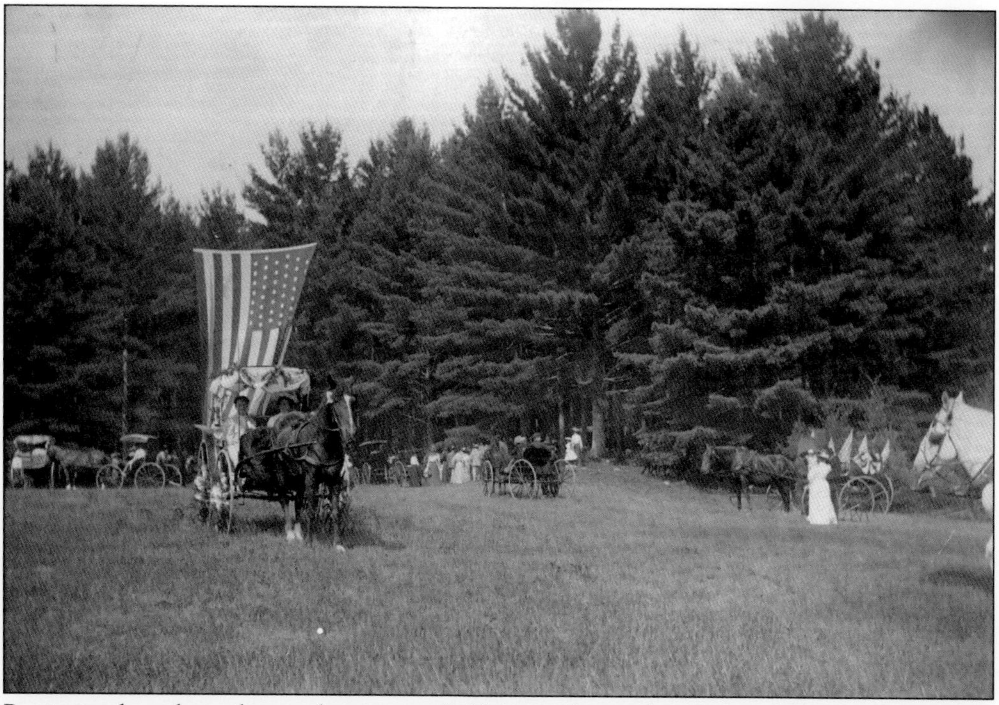

Patriotism has always been a large part of old home day, and it was no different in Campton in 1905. Sisters Mrs. Henry Fifield and Laura Foss are pictured here in front of an impressive American flag. This Campton Old Home Day gathering probably took place in a field at the corner of Cross Street (now Osgood Street) and Mad River Road. (Courtesy of Campton Historical Society.)

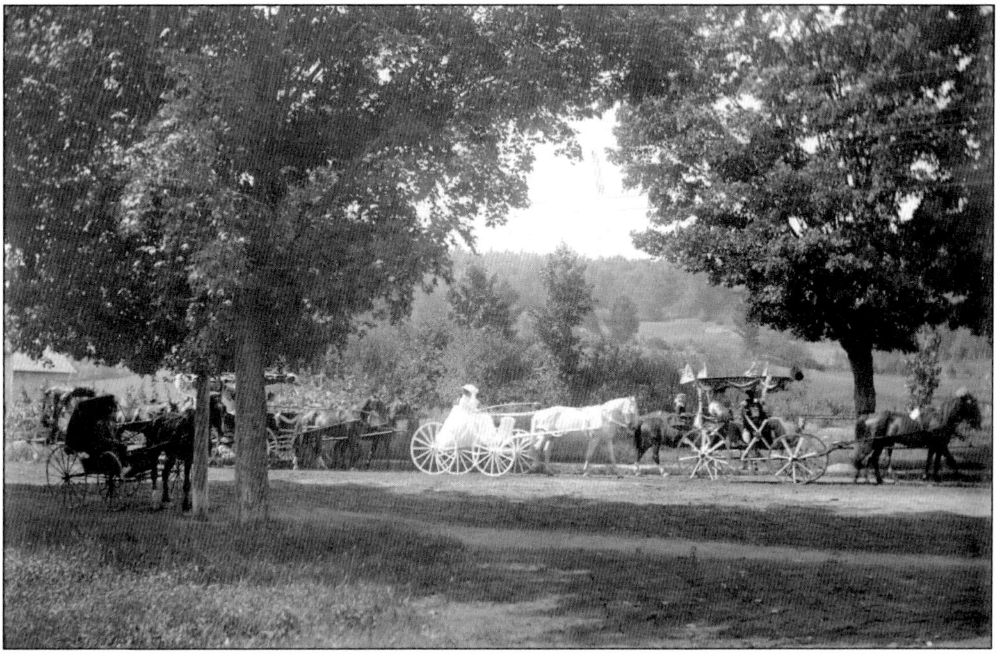

Moody Dole is in the lead vehicle in this 1905 Campton Old Home Day carriage procession. Alongside the procession is Olive Dole, riding Old John. The horse was the property of Webb and John Little. For many years, Campton Old Home Days were held under the auspices of the Pemigewasset Valley Pomona Grange. (Courtesy of Campton Historical Society.)

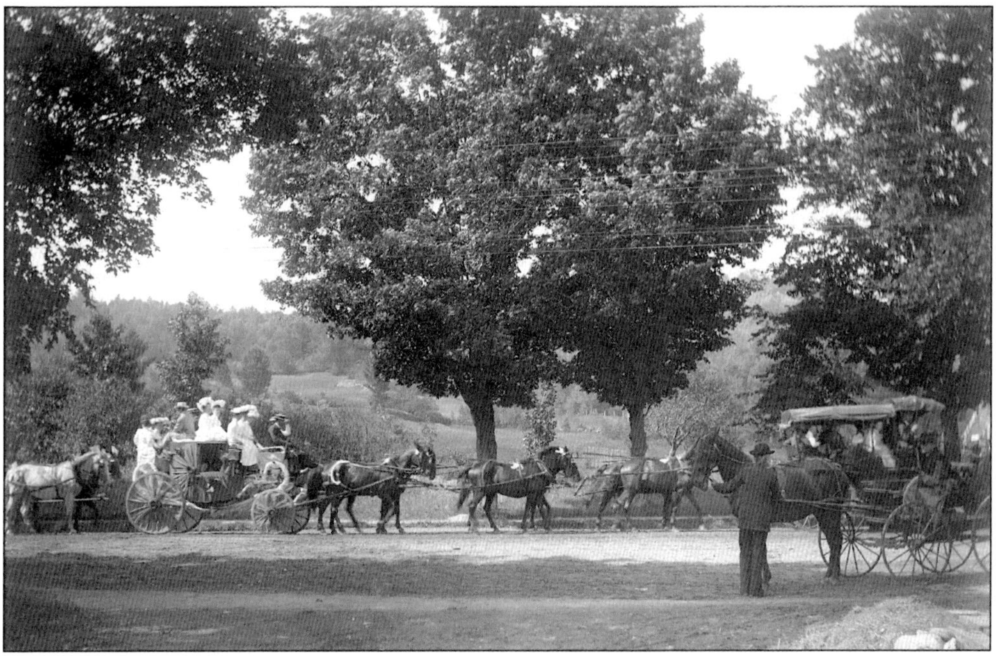

Old stagecoaches and old home days just seem to go together. This coach, decorated and loaded with passengers for Campton Old Home Day, was originally used to run the route out of Plymouth to Woodstock in the days before the Pemigewasset Valley Railroad was built. (Courtesy of Campton Historical Society.)

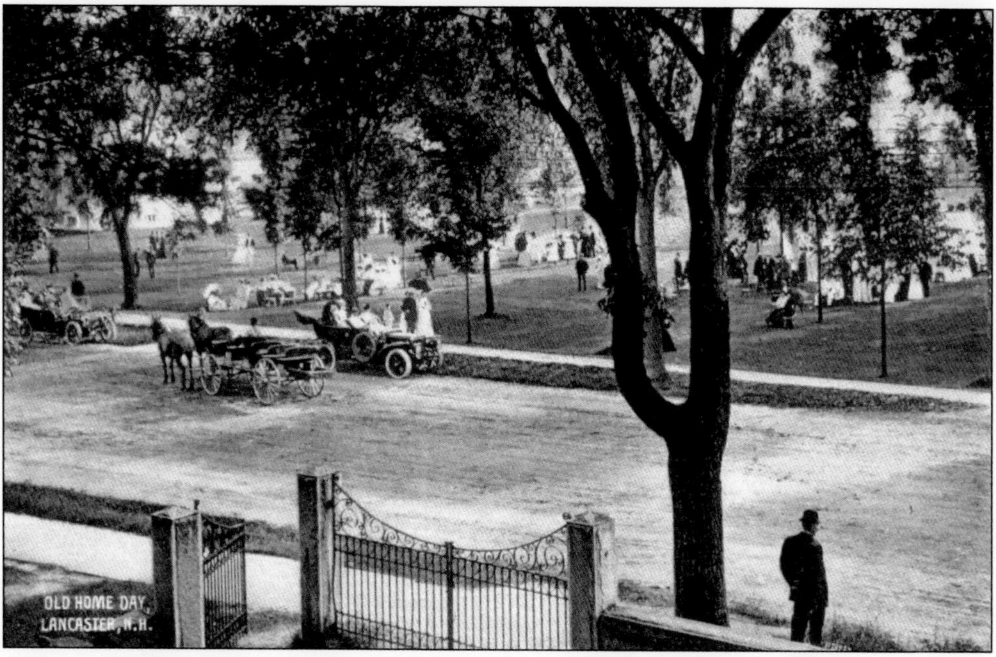

As late as 1964, Lancaster held a combined old home day/bicentennial celebration, although the yearly Lancaster Fair is the main event in town each Labor Day weekend. As this scene from about 1900 shows, however, Lancaster was part of the New Hampshire Old Home Week movement at one time. (Courtesy of the Granite State Collection, Sam Allen.)

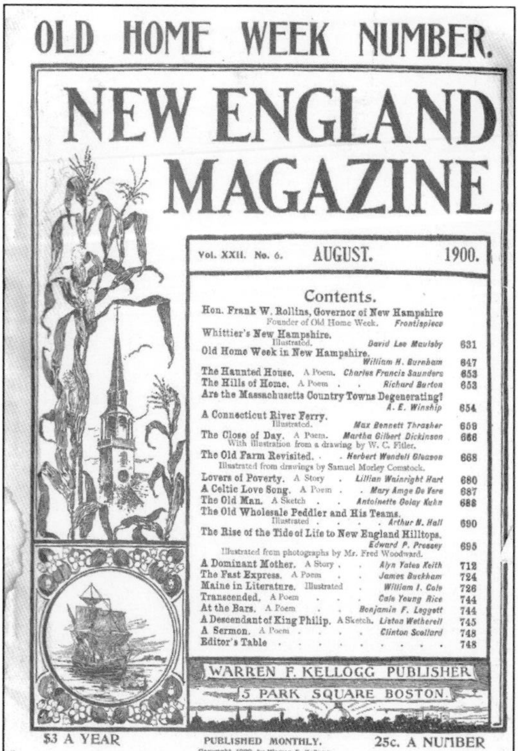

OLD HOME WEEK NUMBER.

NEW ENGLAND MAGAZINE

Vol. XXII. No. 6. AUGUST. 1900.

Contents.

Hon. Frank W. Rollins, Governor of New Hampshire
Founder of Old Home Week. *Frontispiece*
Whittier's New Hampshire. Illustrated. *David Lee Maulsby* 631
Old Home Week in New Hampshire. *William H. Burnham* 647
The Haunted House. A Poem. *Charles Francis Saunders* 653
The Hills of Home. A Poem . . *Richard Burton* 653
Are the Massachusetts Country Towns Degenerating? *A. E. Winship* 654
A Connecticut River Ferry. Illustrated. *Max Bennett Thrasher* 659
The Close of Day. A Poem. *Martha Gilbert Dickinson* 666
With illustration from a drawing by W. C. Fitler.
The Old Farm Revisited. . . *Herbert Wendell Gleason* 668
Illustrated from drawings by Samuel Morley Comstock.
Lovers of Poverty. A Story . *Lillian Wainright Hart* 680
A Celtic Love Song. A Poem . . *Mary Amge De Vere* 687
The Old Man. A Sketch . . *Antoinette Golay Kuhn* 688
The Old Wholesale Peddler and His Teams. Illustrated . . . . *Arthur N. Hall* 690
The Rise of the Tide of Life to New England Hilltops. *Edward P. Pressey* 695
Illustrated from photographs by Mr. Fred Woodward.
A Dominant Mother. A Story . . *Alyn Yates Keith* 712
The Fast Express. A Poem . . *James Buckham* 724
Maine in Literature. Illustrated . *William I. Cole* 726
Transcended. A Poem . . . *Cale Young Rice* 744
At the Bars. A Poem . . *Benjamin F. Leggett* 744
A Descendant of King Philip. A Sketch. *Liston Wetherell* 745
A Sermon. A Poem . . . . *Clinton Scollard* 748
Editor's Table 748

WARREN F. KELLOGG PUBLISHER
5 PARK SQUARE BOSTON.

$3 A YEAR PUBLISHED MONTHLY. 25c. A NUMBER

Copyright, 1900, by Warren F. Kellogg.
Entered at Boston Post Office as Second Class Mail Matter.

Gov. Frank Rollins admitted from the beginning that his idea for old home celebrations was an advertisement to encourage investment. The idea quickly caught on with both the press and neighboring states. This August 1900 edition of *New England Magazine* was dedicated to the governor's successful promotion. Also in this issue was an article on the denigration of the Massachusetts countryside. Massachusetts and the rest of New England quickly followed suit. (Author's collection.)

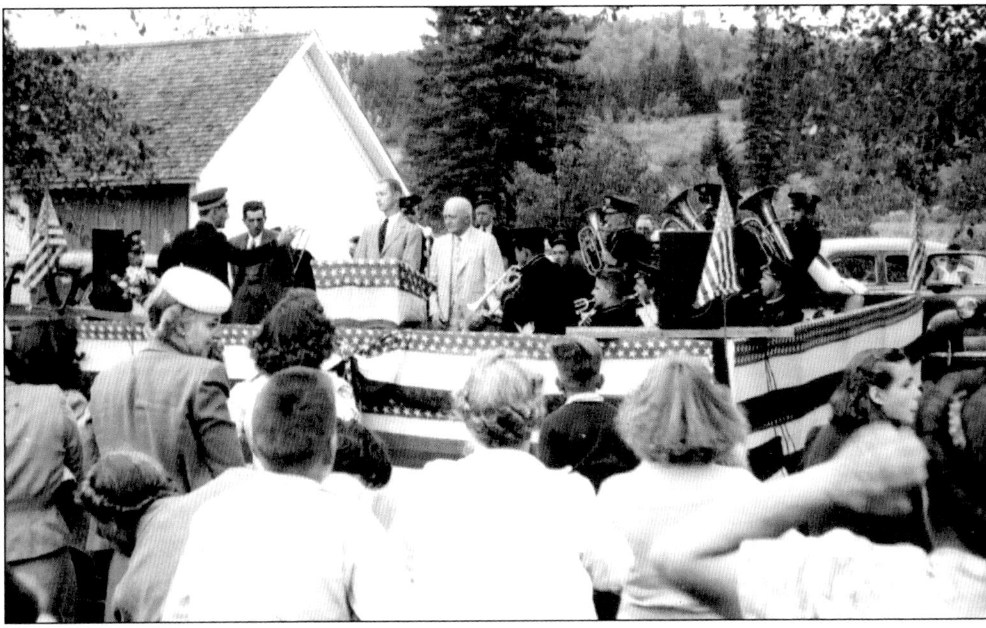

Surrounded by bands and bunting and a large crowd, the Reverend Curtis Smith is at the podium to kick off a Pittsburg Old Home Day sometime in the 1940s. Religion and rural concerns played a large role in Pittsburg Old Home Day celebrations, as they did throughout the state. The Aurora Grange was always one of the backers of the day in Pittsburg. (Courtesy of Pittsburg Historical Society.)

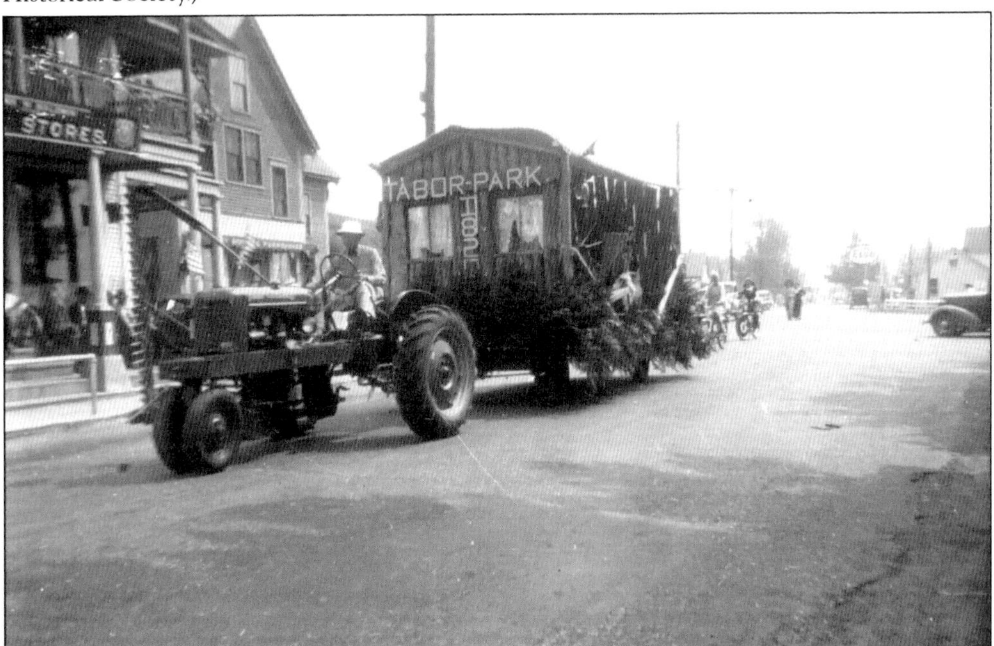

The 1942 Pittsburg parade featured this float from Tabor Park. The park was named after the first Tabor who lived in Pittsburg in the 1820s. There was plenty of space then as there is now in New Hampshire's largest town by area. Pittsburg now celebrates every year on the third Saturday in August. (Courtesy of Pittsburg Historical Society.)

Small-town parades always welcome neighbors, and this 1940s Pittsburg Old Home Day celebration was no exception. American Legionnaire Orville Trask of Colebrook is seen here riding the horse Carney. While Trask was a visitor, Carney was a local, belonging to Pittsburg's Harry Haynes. (Courtesy of Pittsburg Historical Society.)

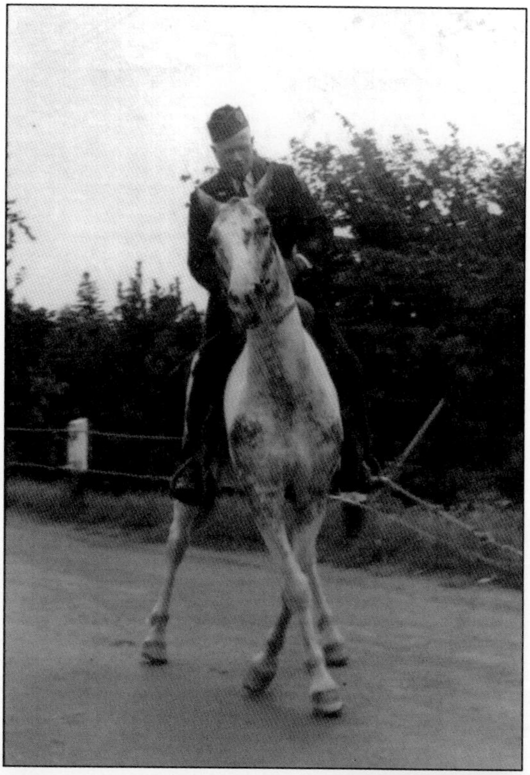

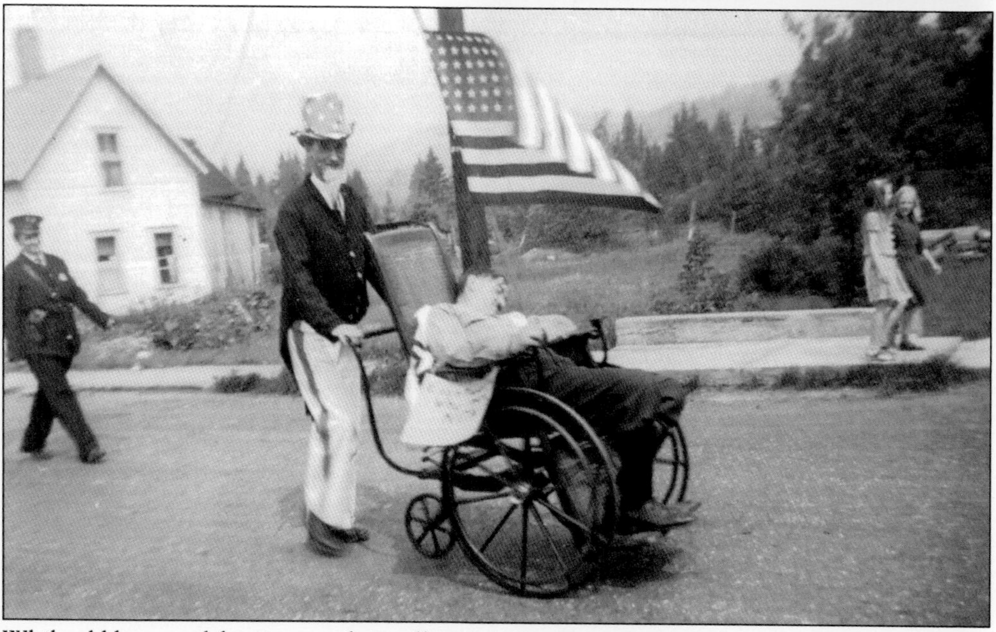

While old home celebrations traditionally are an opportunity to pause and look back at earlier times, current events often are parade subjects. Such was obviously the case in the 1942 parade, as Pittsburg natives made their opinions of Adolph Hitler very clear. Roger Fissette was Uncle Sam, while Norman Young was cast as the ailing Hitler. Viola Bumford is looking on dressed in a police uniform. (Courtesy of Pittsburg Historical Society.)

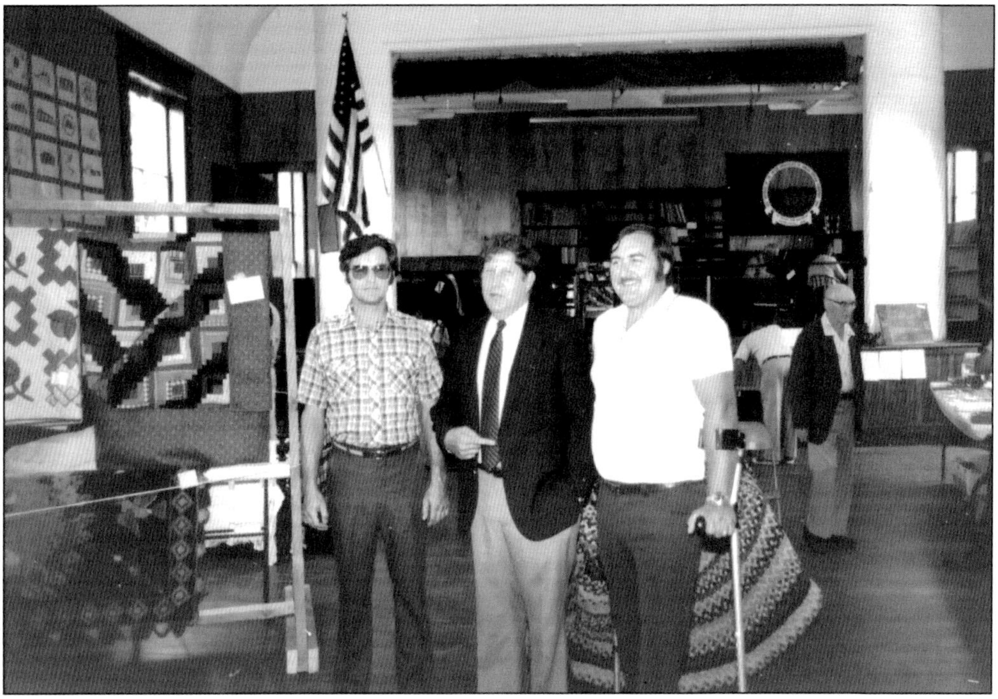

The Pittsburg Historical Society was the scene of this old home day picture taken in the 1980s. Seen flanking a young Gov. John H. Sununu are Sheriden Roderick (left) and Lesley Covell. Many communities open their historical society rooms for extended hours during old home celebrations. (Courtesy of Pittsburg Historical Society.)

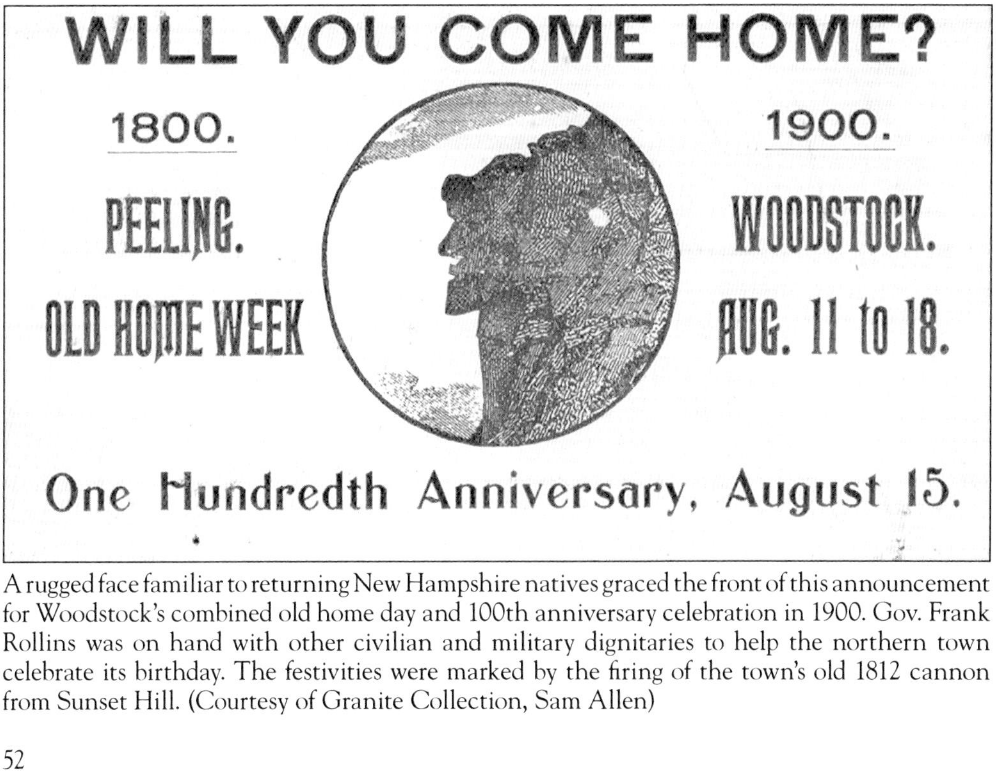

A rugged face familiar to returning New Hampshire natives graced the front of this announcement for Woodstock's combined old home day and 100th anniversary celebration in 1900. Gov. Frank Rollins was on hand with other civilian and military dignitaries to help the northern town celebrate its birthday. The festivities were marked by the firing of the town's old 1812 cannon from Sunset Hill. (Courtesy of Granite Collection, Sam Allen)

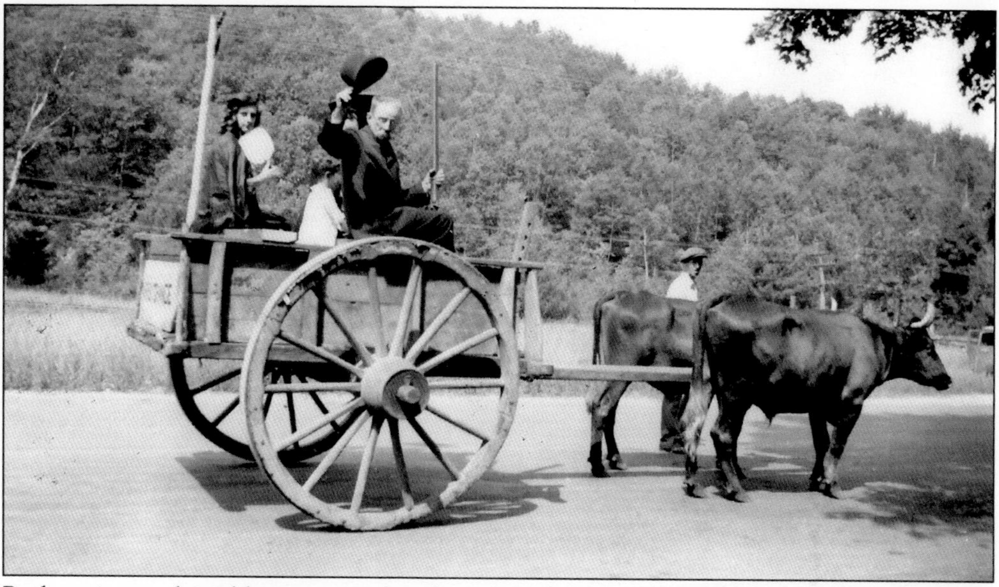

Both natives and neighbors were on hand in 1941 when Warren celebrated old home day along with the 175th anniversary of the town's founding. Pictured here tipping his cap is Herbert Robie of Bristol, who brought his oxen along for the parade. (Courtesy of Warren Historical Society.)

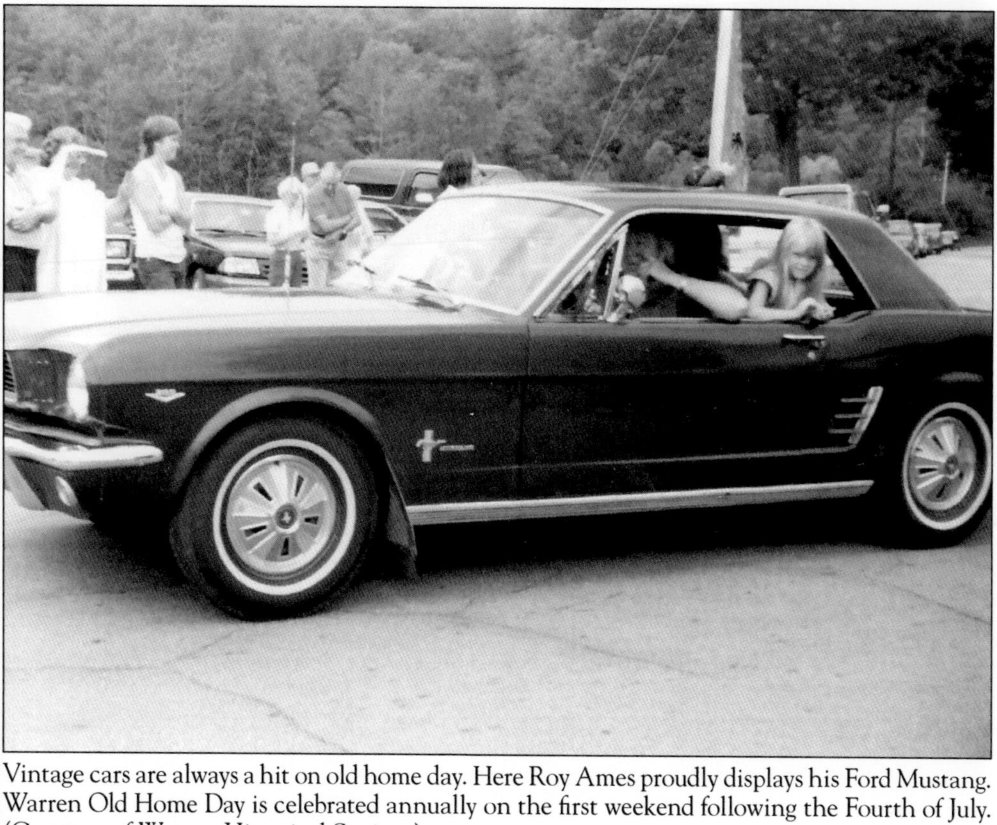

Vintage cars are always a hit on old home day. Here Roy Ames proudly displays his Ford Mustang. Warren Old Home Day is celebrated annually on the first weekend following the Fourth of July. (Courtesy of Warren Historical Society.)

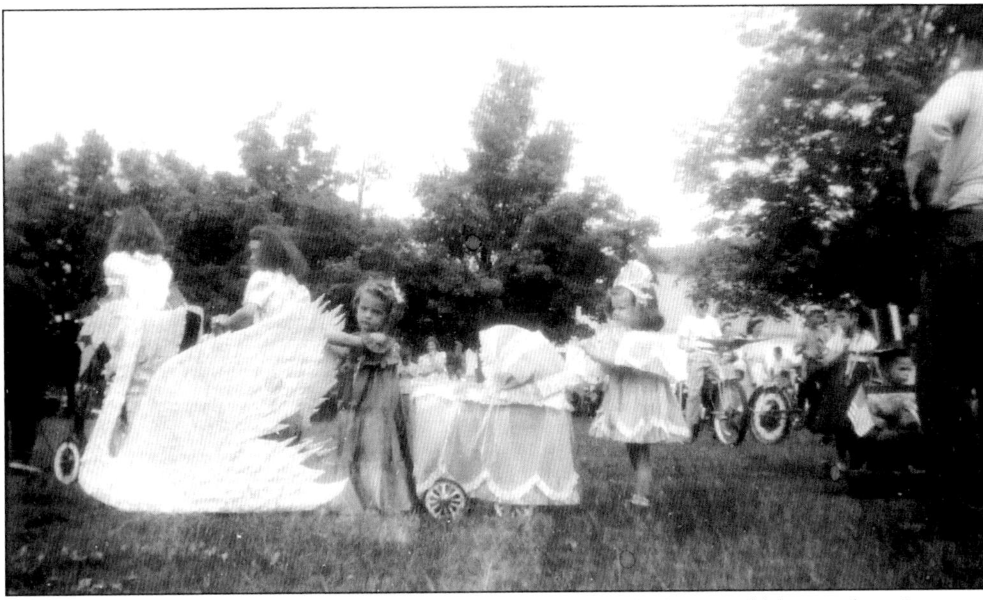

Adult floats are not the only ones that require a lot of work during old home days. Lorraine Ball is the young lady pushing this beautiful swan carriage at an early Warren celebration. Longtime resident and historical society member Jan Sackett says she can remember her mother spending hours constructing the swan out of cardboard and crepe paper. (Courtesy of Warren Historical Society.)

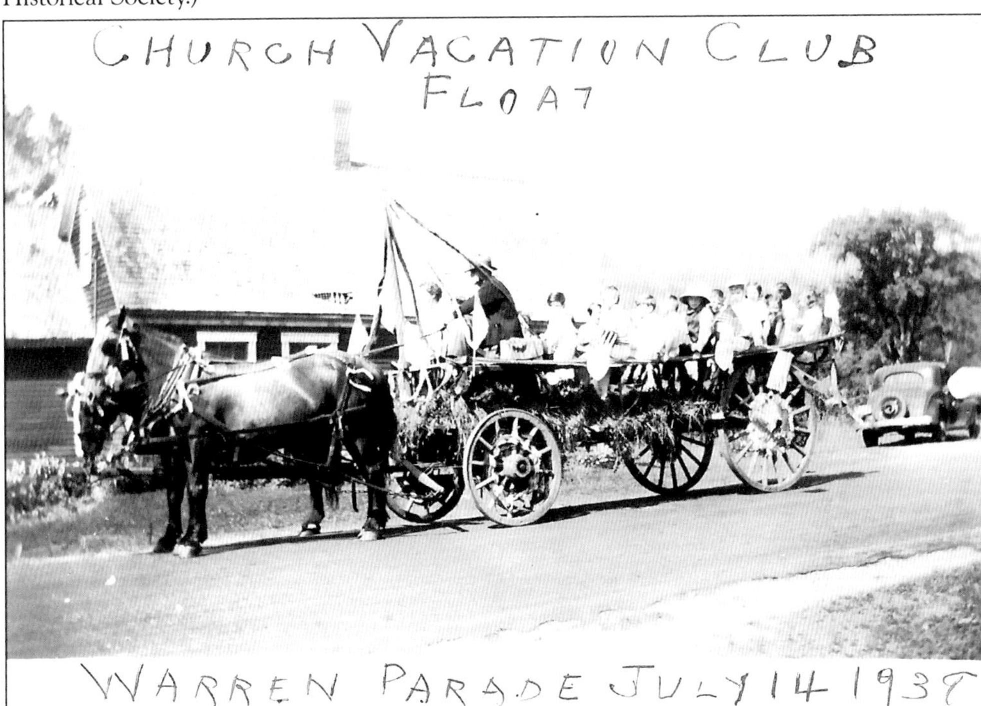

Local churches have always been highly involved in the old home day movement, and festivities in Warren are no different. This heavily populated float from 1938 was an entry from the Church Vacation Club. (Courtesy of Warren Historical Society.)

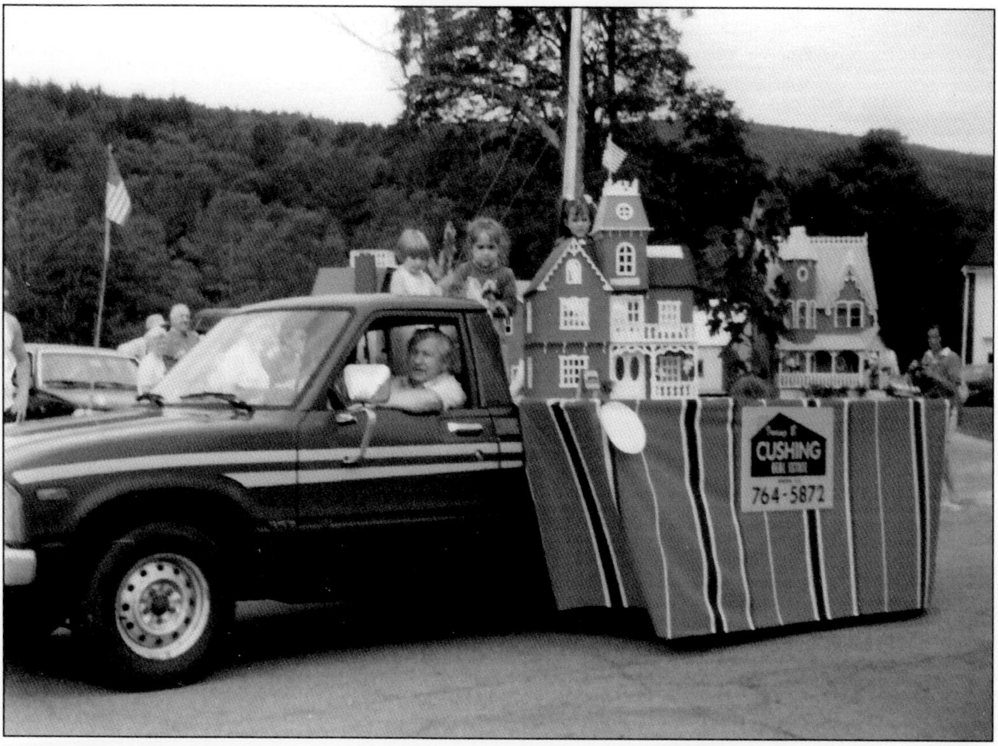

Re-creating a local business is the surest way to a successful if small float. This Warren real estate company has reproduced an impressive array of real estate right in the back of a pickup truck for the Warren Old Home Day parade. (Courtesy of Warren Historical Society.)

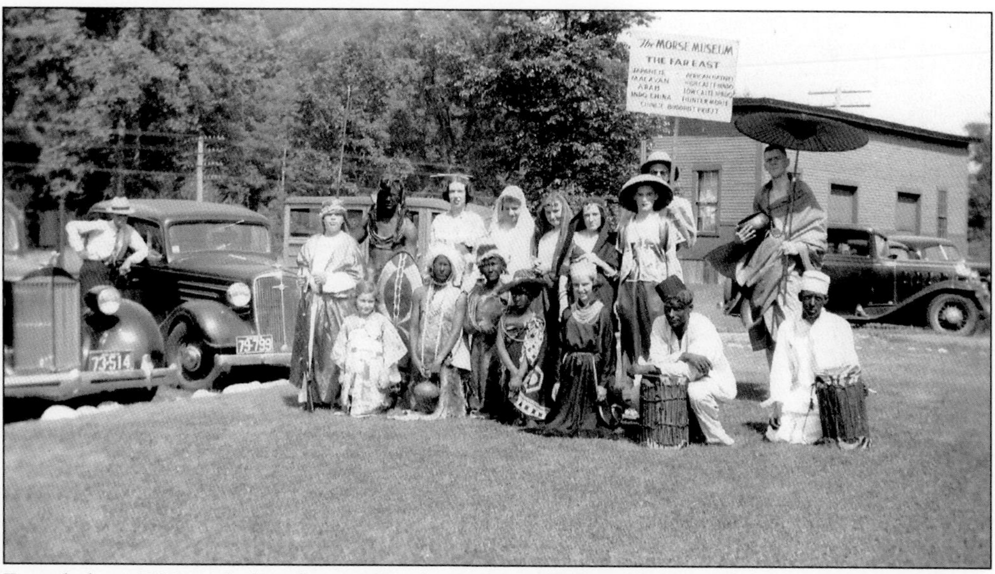

Founded in 1928 and closed in 1992, the Morse Wildlife Museum was a longtime landmark in Warren. It was also an integral part of the community and Warren Old Home Day. This group representing the museum was part of the 1938 celebration. (Courtesy of Warren Historical Society.)

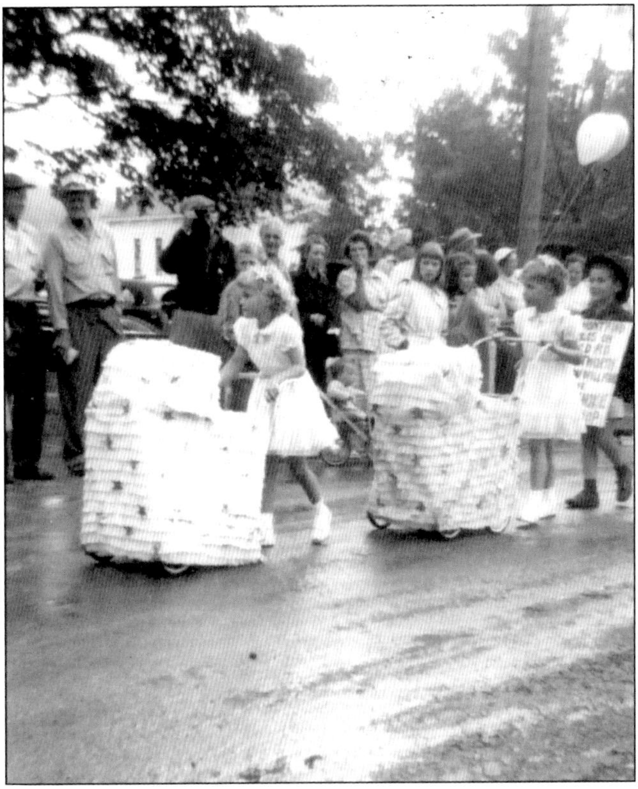

The involvement of a community's children in old home days has been one of the factors in keeping the tradition alive. The always-popular children's parade is a fixture in many towns. Here in Warren's 1954 parade, Dale Ramsey's girls are a hit with their baby carriages. (Courtesy of Warren Historical Society.)

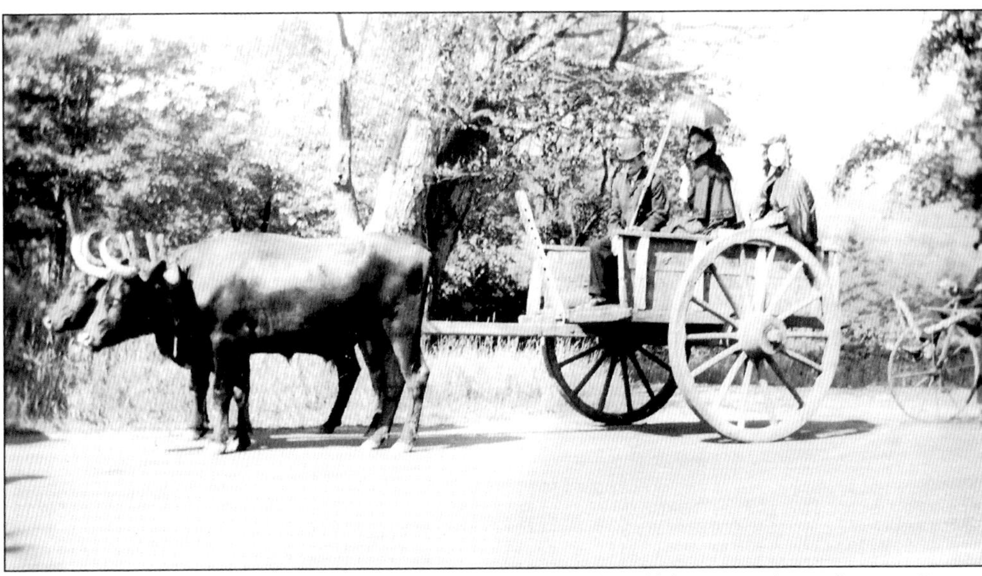

Agriculture was still an important factor in 1899 when the old home tradition began. Grange organizations throughout the state were active participants and supporters of the movement from its beginnings. Here the Warren Grange float is on hand for the town's 1938 parade. (Courtesy of Warren Historical Society.)

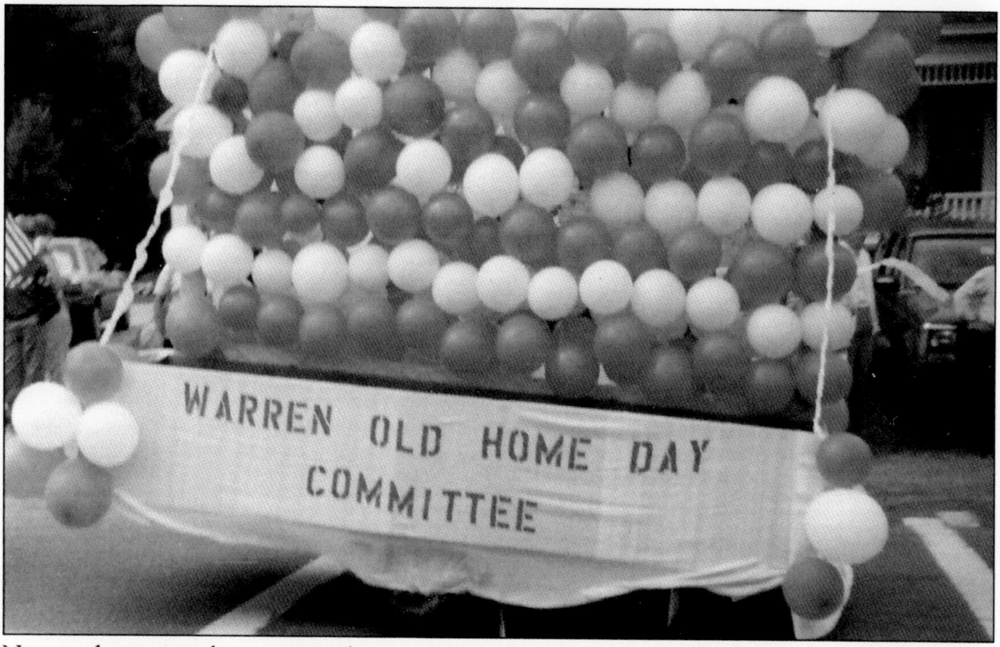

No one deserves to be recognized more during old home day than the folks who put the whole thing together. In Warren, there are three days of fun every year, including Friday night fireworks and Saturday's parade. Shown here is the float representing the committee that makes it all happen. (Courtesy of Warren Historical Society.)

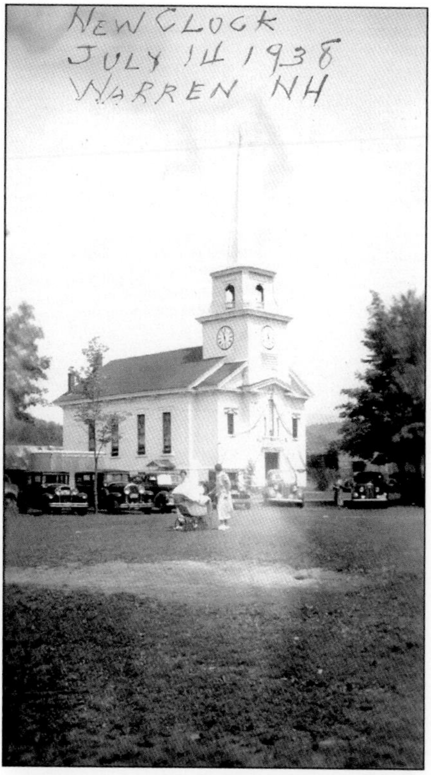

The dedication of the new clock in the center of town was the occasion for this Warren Old Home Day photograph from 1938. Like many communities, Warren has used old home day to dedicate various town landmarks or additions. During Warren Old Home Day in 1971, the town dedicated the famous Mercury Redstone Missile that graces the green in front of the historical society. (Courtesy of Warren Historical Society.)

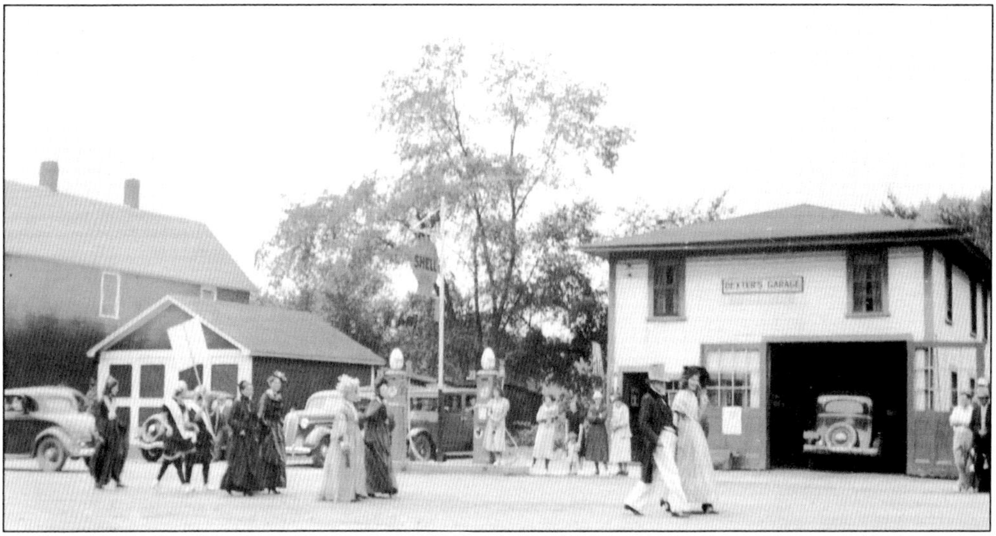

Striding past Dexter's garage, these participants in the children's parade are part of Bath Old Home Day in the 1930s. Bath still celebrates the holiday today, and parades are still a mainstay of the event. While Bath does not observe the holiday every year, it is a full-town effort when a celebration is held. (Courtesy of Bath Historical Society.)

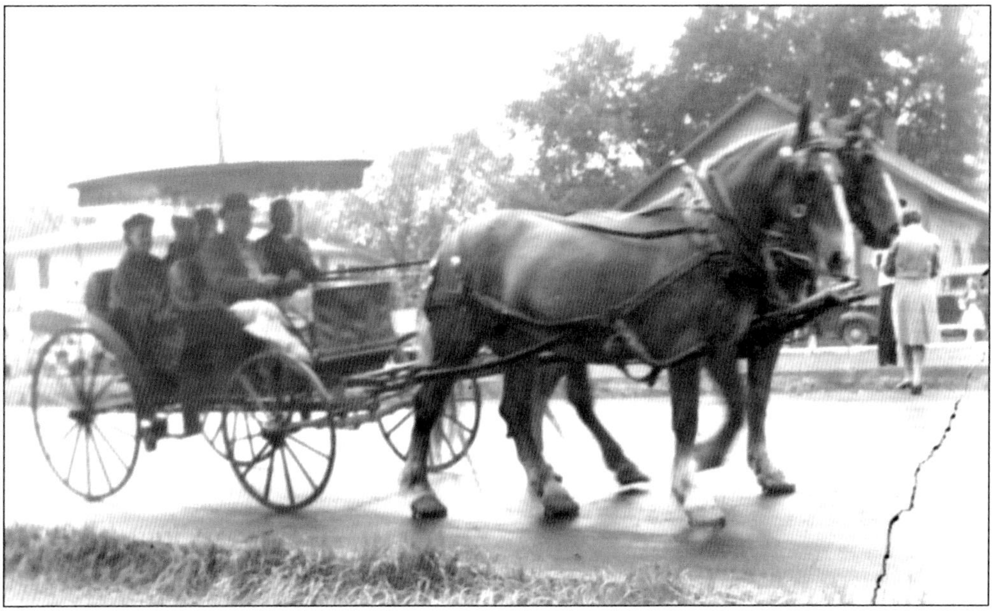

This foursome was part of a Bath Old Home Day in the 1930s. Like most New Hampshire towns, Bath held old home celebrations in conjunction with military homecomings. In August 1946, World War II veterans were guests of honor for the day. Mrs. Roger Reed of West Bath was in charge of the day, which included a dinner for all veterans served at the Colonial Inn. (Courtesy of Bath Historical Society.)

Four

DARTMOUTH–LAKE SUNAPEE REGION

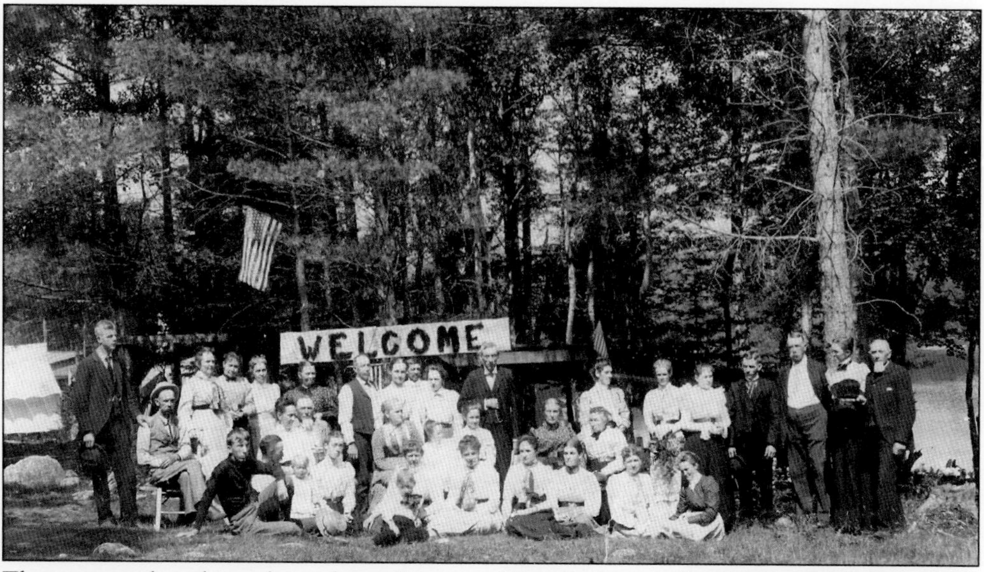

This group gathered to welcome home former residents at the very first Canaan Old Home Week in 1899. Two of the most popular traditions throughout the state were the lighting of hilltop bonfires and torch-lit parades. Canaan's 1899 procession ended atop Cardigan Mountain where the town's old cannon was fired three times and a bonfire was lit that was visible from Canaan village. (Courtesy of Donna Zani-Dunkerton.)

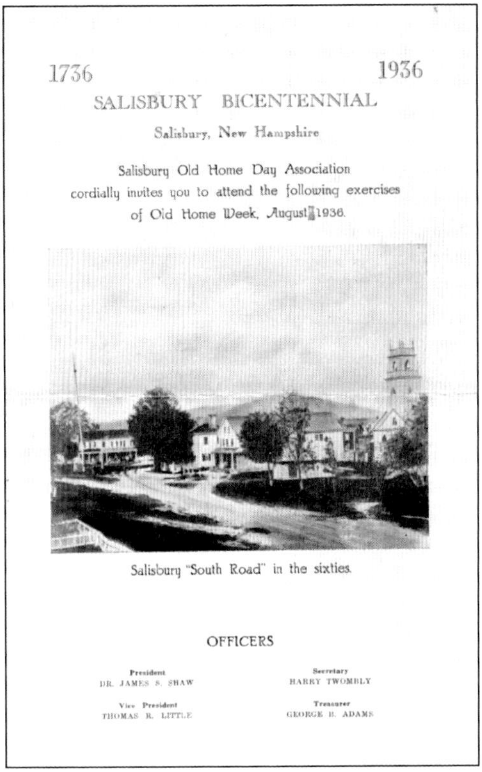
1736 1936

SALISBURY BICENTENNIAL

Salisbury, New Hampshire

Salisbury Old Home Day Association
cordially invites you to attend the following exercises
of Old Home Week, August [illegible] 1936.

Salisbury "South Road" in the sixties.

OFFICERS

President
DR. JAMES S. SHAW

Secretary
HARRY TWOMBLY

Vice President
THOMAS R. LITTLE

Treasurer
GEORGE B. ADAMS

A picture of Salisbury South Road from the 1860s appeared on the cover of this 1936 program. Salisbury celebrated both its bicentennial and old home week with many events. One of the highlights was Salisbury's "Little World Series" in which the Sand Crabs took on the Sand Fleas in a game of baseball. (Courtesy of Salisbury Historical Society.)

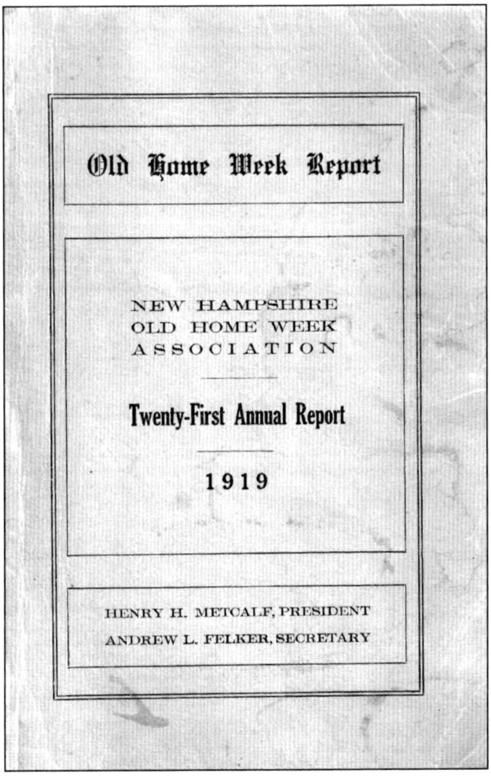
Old Home Week Report

NEW HAMPSHIRE
OLD HOME WEEK
ASSOCIATION

Twenty-First Annual Report

1919

HENRY H. METCALF, PRESIDENT
ANDREW L. FELKER, SECRETARY

The year 1919 was one of the high-water marks of the New Hampshire Old Home Week movement. Towns reported to the state, and the state issued yearly reports like this one, until the early 1950s. The return of World War I soldiers sparked interest in the homecoming holiday in all sections of the state. Dartmouth–Lake Sunapee region towns celebrating the doughboys return included Canaan, Goshen, Grafton, Langdon, Lempster, Plainfield, Warner, Webster, and Wilmot. (Author's collection.)

Pride in local accomplishment was evident on this 1902 announcement from Salisbury Old Home Week. Salisbury Academy was where statesman and orator Daniel Webster received his schooling. Many events were held at Sen. Jacob Gallinger's Grove next to the Salisbury Baptist Church. (Courtesy of Salisbury Historical Society.)

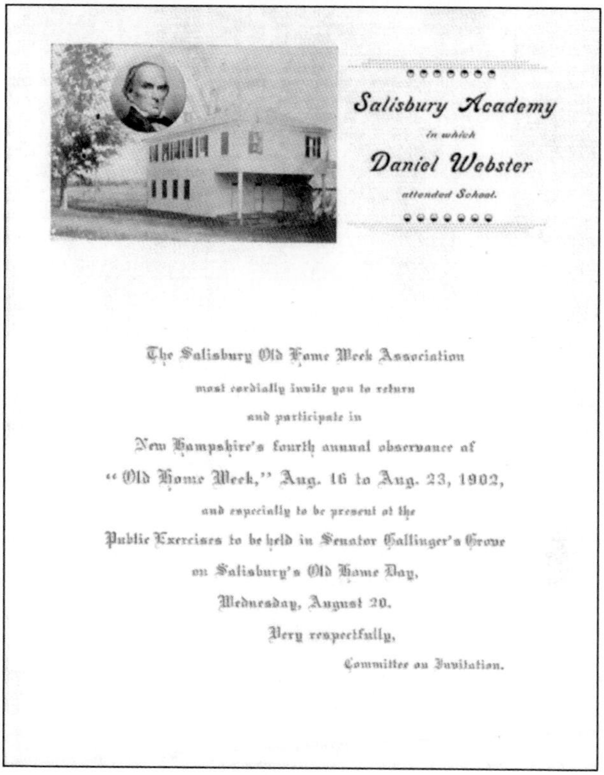

Salisbury Academy
in which
Daniel Webster
attended School.

The Salisbury Old Home Week Association
most cordially invite you to return
and participate in
New Hampshire's fourth annual observance of
"Old Home Week," Aug. 16 to Aug. 23, 1902,
and especially to be present at the
Public Exercises to be held in Senator Gallinger's Grove
on Salisbury's Old Home Day,
Wednesday, August 20.
Very respectfully,
Committee on Invitation.

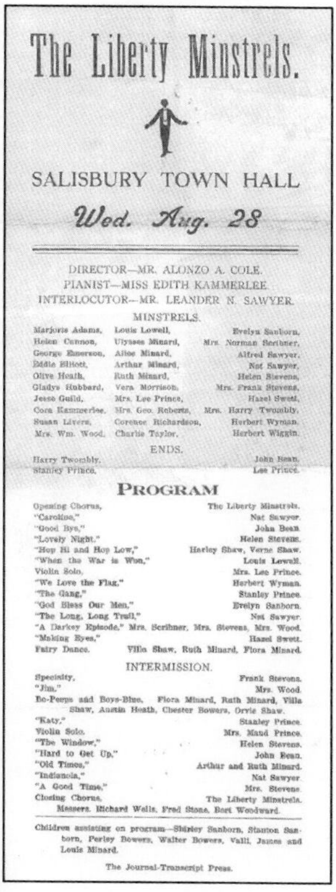

The Liberty Minstrels.

SALISBURY TOWN HALL

Wed. Aug. 28

DIRECTOR—MR. ALONZO A. COLE.
PIANIST—MISS EDITH KAMMERLEE.
INTERLOCUTOR—MR. LEANDER N. SAWYER.

MINSTRELS.

Marjorie Adams,	Louis Lowell,	Evelyn Sanborn,
Helen Cannon,	Ulysses Minard,	Mrs. Norman Scribner,
George Emerson,	Alice Minard,	Alfred Sawyer,
Eddie Elliott,	Arthur Minard,	Nat Sawyer,
Olive Heath,	Ruth Minard,	Helen Stevens,
Gladys Hubbard,	Vera Morrison,	Mrs. Frank Stevens,
Jesse Guild,	Mrs. Lee Prince,	Hazel Swett,
Cora Kammerlee,	Mrs. Geo. Roberts,	Mrs. Harry Twombly,
Susan Livers,	Corence Richardson,	Herbert Wyman,
Mrs. Wm. Wood,	Charlie Taylor,	Herbert Wiggin.

ENDS.

Harry Twombly,	John Bean,
Stanley Prince,	Lee Prince.

PROGRAM

Opening Chorus,	The Liberty Minstrels.
"Caroline,"	Nat Sawyer.
"Good Bye,"	John Bean.
"Lovely Night,"	Helen Stevens.
"Hop Hi and Hop Low,"	Harley Shaw, Verne Shaw.
"When the War is Won,"	Louis Lowell.
Violin Solo,	Mrs. Lee Prince.
"We Love the Flag,"	Herbert Wyman.
"The Gang,"	Stanley Prince.
"God Bless Our Men,"	Evelyn Sanborn.
"The Long, Long Trail,"	Nat Sawyer.
"A Darkey Episode,"	Mrs. Scribner, Mrs. Stevens, Mrs. Wood.
"Making Eyes,"	Hazel Swett.
Fairy Dance,	Villa Shaw, Ruth Minard, Flora Minard.

INTERMISSION.

Specialty,	Frank Stevens.
"Jim,"	Mrs. Wood.
Bo-Peeps and Boys-Blue,	Flora Minard, Ruth Minard, Villa Shaw, Austin Heath, Chester Bowers, Orvie Shaw.
"Katy,"	Stanley Prince.
Violin Solo,	Mrs. Maud Prince.
"The Window,"	Helen Stevens.
"Hard to Get Up,"	John Bean.
"Old Times,"	Arthur and Ruth Minard.
"Indianola,"	Nat Sawyer.
"A Good Time,"	Mrs. Stevens.
Closing Chorus,	The Liberty Minstrels.

Messers. Richard Wells, Fred Stone, Bert Woodward.

Children assisting on program—Shirley Sanborn, Stanton Sanborn, Perley Bowers, Walter Bowers, Valli, James and Louis Minard.

The Journal-Transcript Press.

Minstrel shows were popular early in the 20th century. Salisbury Old Home Week in 1918 was the setting for this production of the *Liberty Minstrels*, directed by summer resident A. A. Cole of Boston. (Courtesy of Salisbury Historical Society.)

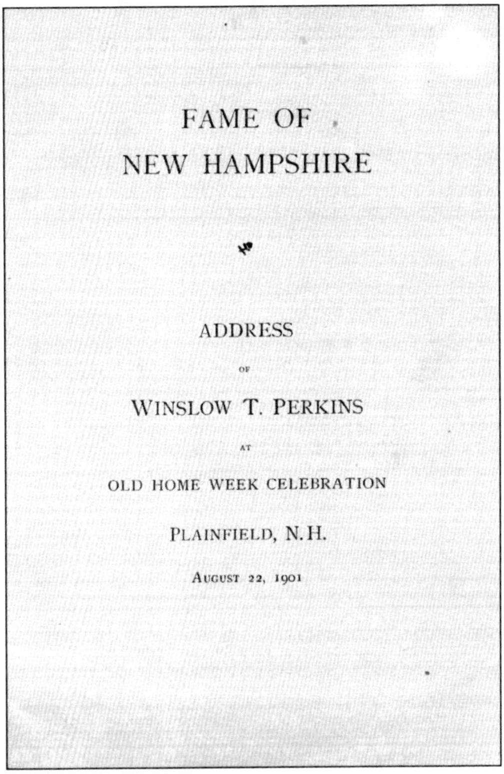

FAME OF
NEW HAMPSHIRE

ADDRESS
OF
WINSLOW T. PERKINS
AT
OLD HOME WEEK CELEBRATION
PLAINFIELD, N.H.
AUGUST 22, 1901

Picnic lunches, orchestra music, and poetry recitations were all part of the ceremonies at Plainfield in 1902. In one of the greatest homecoming celebrations of the century in 1919, those were still the staples of the festivities. Speeches were delivered by returning World War I veterans Rev. Chester Jenney, Rev. Ray E. Jenney, Lt. Leon Hadley, and Hall Peterson. (Courtesy of the Granite State Collection, Sam Allen.)

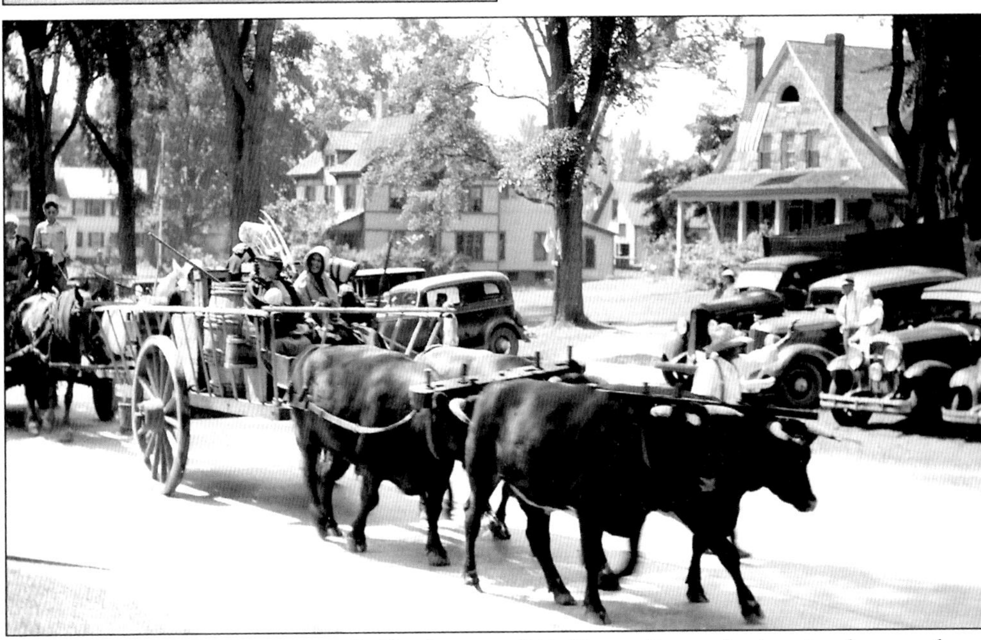

Dressing in costume was part of Charlestown Old Home Days whether in the parade, as pictured here, or on the stage. One musical skit put on in the 1940s was "The Butcher Boy" with Mrs. George Parks as the charming daughter, Mrs. Carl Brown as the sympathetic mother, Horace Bascom as the cruel father, and starring Robert Laffin as the Butcher Boy. (Courtesy of Charlestown Historical Society.)

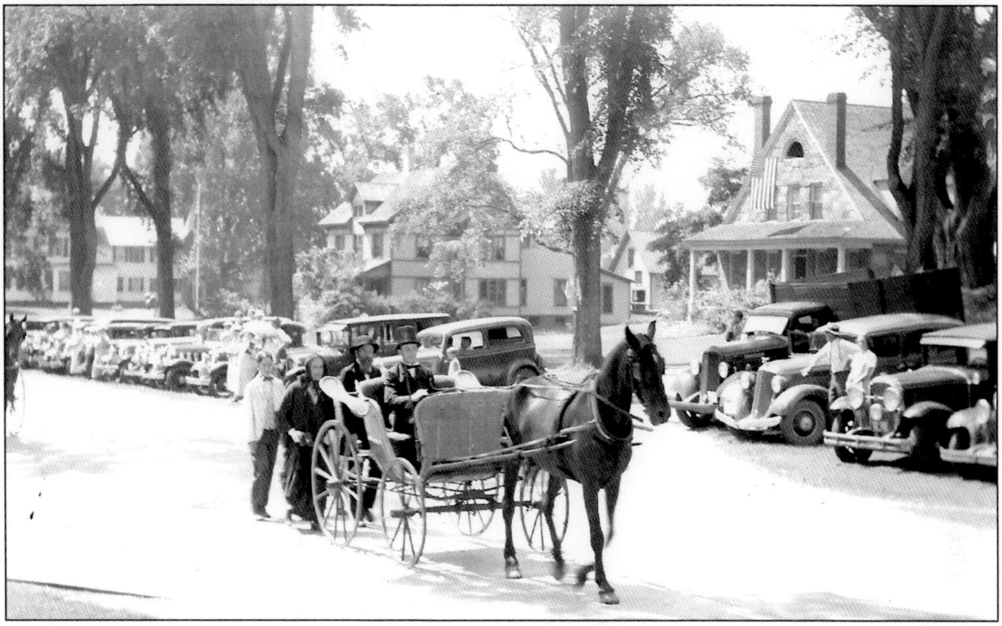

Charlestown got on board with their old home day celebrations starting in 1902. One of the biggest celebrations came in 1935 as the town celebrated the 200th anniversary of the granting of the town charter. That year a crowd of over 3,000 watched a parade that was followed by lunch and supper under the supervision of Winnie Parks. (Courtesy of Charlestown Historical Society.)

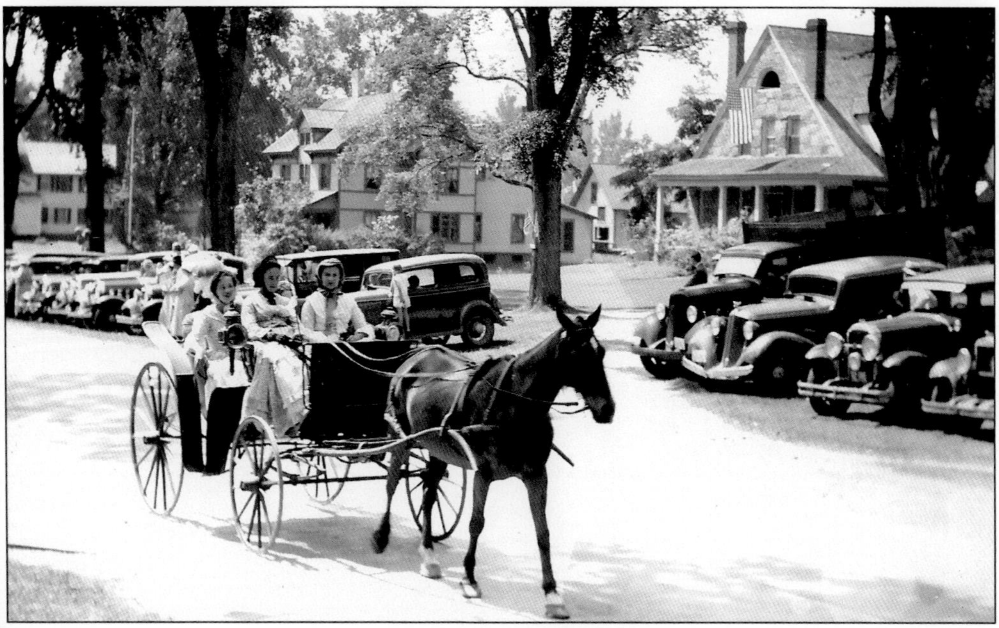

The ladies taking a buggy ride are actually part of a 1930s Charlestown Old Home Day parade on the town's historic Main Street. The buggy driver is Veronica Soucy. Pride in local history is always on display during old home celebrations. In Charlestown, it can be just a matter of a stroll down the Main Street parade route where 63 buildings are on the National Register of Historic Places. (Courtesy of Charlestown Historical Society.)

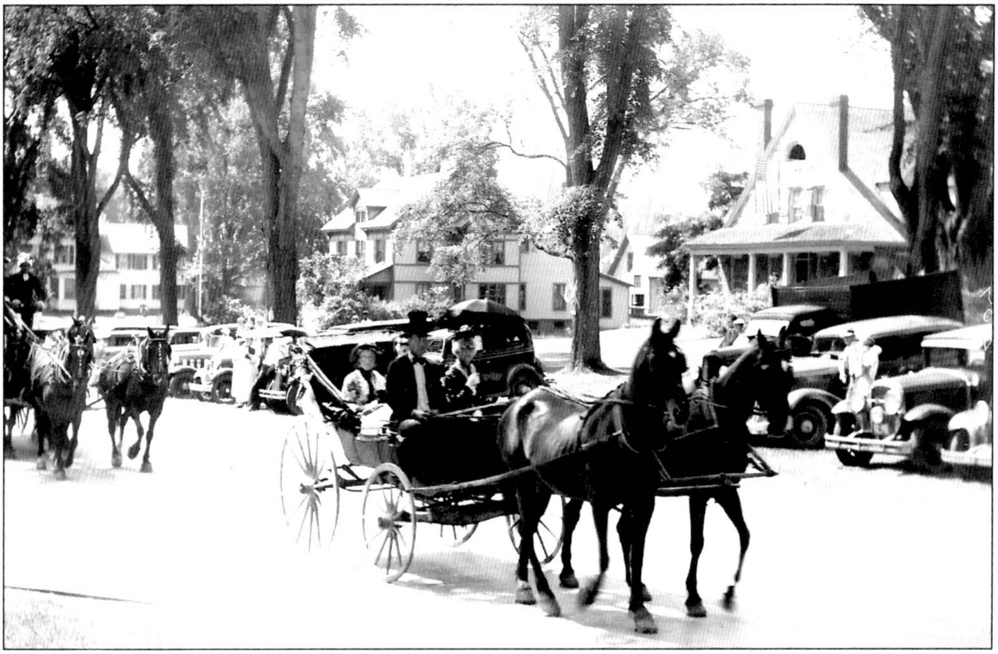

Older residents always get special treatment, as is the case with these riders in an early Charlestown Old Home Day parade. The parade route passes by the historic Charlestown Town Hall, which was designed by New Hampshire's preeminent post–Civil War architect Edward Dow. (Courtesy of Charlestown Historical Society.)

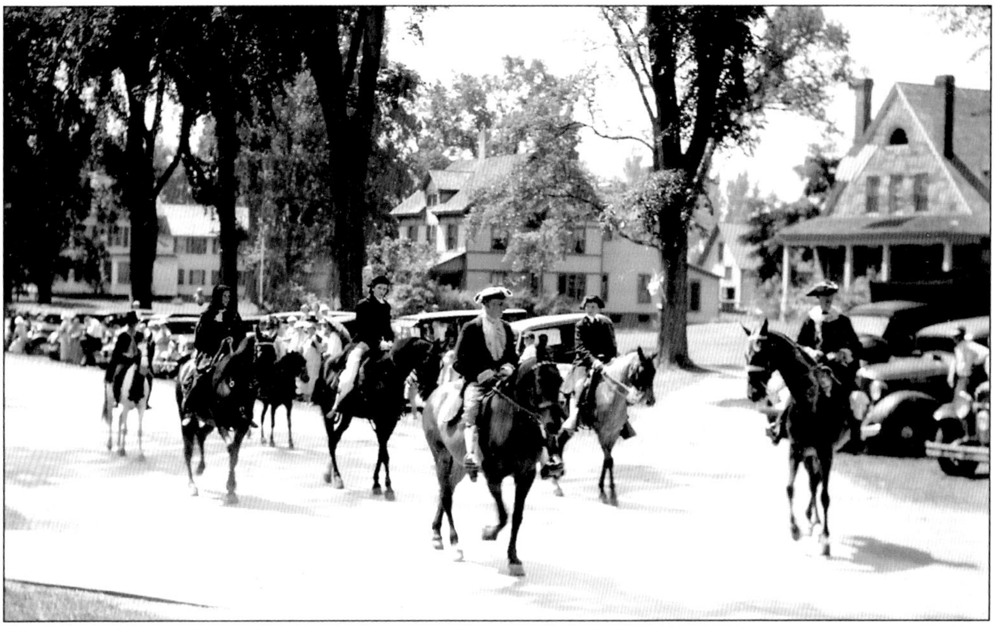

Horseback riders in Colonial uniforms are not an unusual sight at any old home day parade. They hold special significance for Charlestown, as they did when they appeared in this old home day parade. Charlestown is the site of the re-creation of the Fort at No. 4, which was the northernmost New Hampshire settlement along the Connecticut River. (Courtesy of Charlestown Historical Society.)

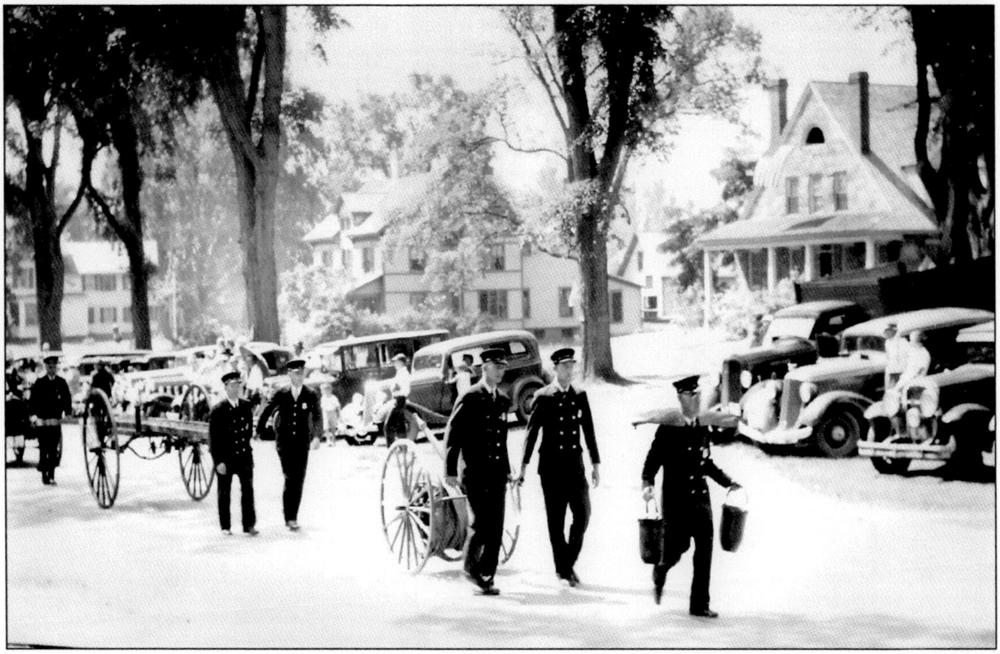

Volunteerism is what usually gets old home celebrations off the ground, and in New Hampshire, no group represents the spirit of volunteerism more than the local fire department. In this Charlestown Old Home Day parade, department marchers demonstrate how fires were fought in the very early days of firefighting. (Courtesy of Charlestown Historical Society.)

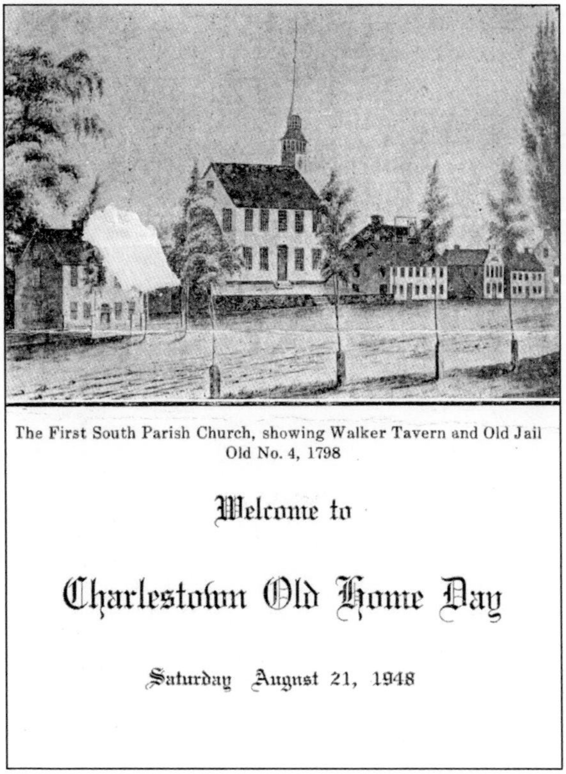

The First South Parish Church, showing Walker Tavern and Old Jail
Old No. 4, 1798

Welcome to

Charlestown Old Home Day

Saturday August 21, 1948

Scenes of historic local buildings were common on programs like this one from Charlestown's 1948 old home days. A baseball game as part of the 1948 festivities saw the Charlestown Merchants defeat the Claremont Collegiates 3-2 in extra innings. General chairman for the day was Cecil Fisk. (Courtesy of Charlestown Historical Society.)

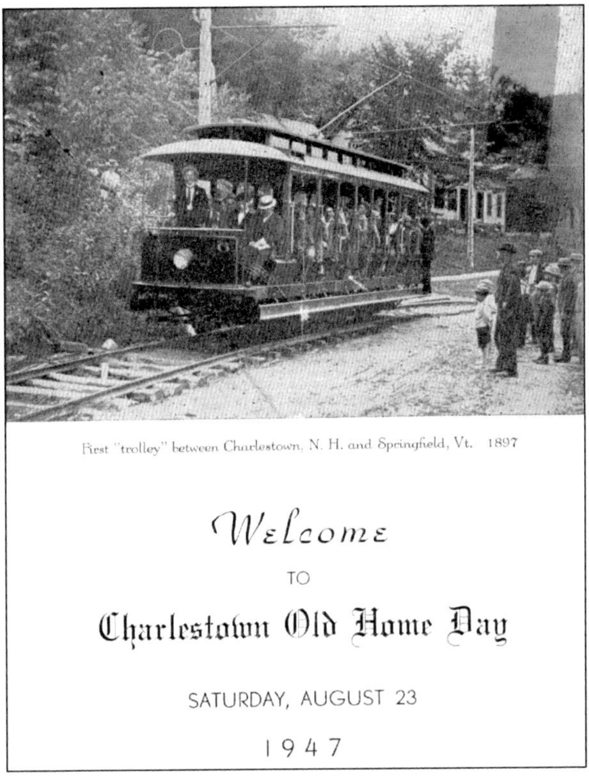

Pride in past accomplishments has always been a staple of the old home spirit, as it was in Charlestown in 1947. Honored on the front of the program was the first trolley to make the trip between Charlestown and Springfield, Vermont. Following the popularity of the New Hampshire Old Home Week movement, neighboring Vermont and the rest of New England soon joined in with observances of their own. (Courtesy of Charlestown Historical Society.)

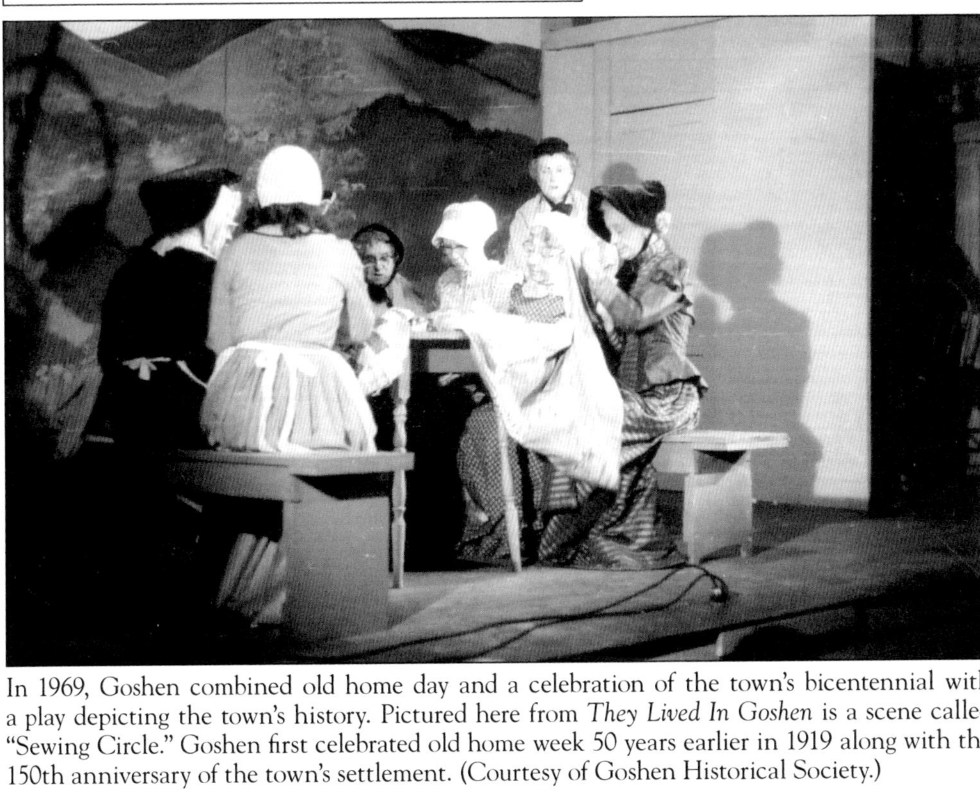

In 1969, Goshen combined old home day and a celebration of the town's bicentennial with a play depicting the town's history. Pictured here from *They Lived In Goshen* is a scene called "Sewing Circle." Goshen first celebrated old home week 50 years earlier in 1919 along with the 150th anniversary of the town's settlement. (Courtesy of Goshen Historical Society.)

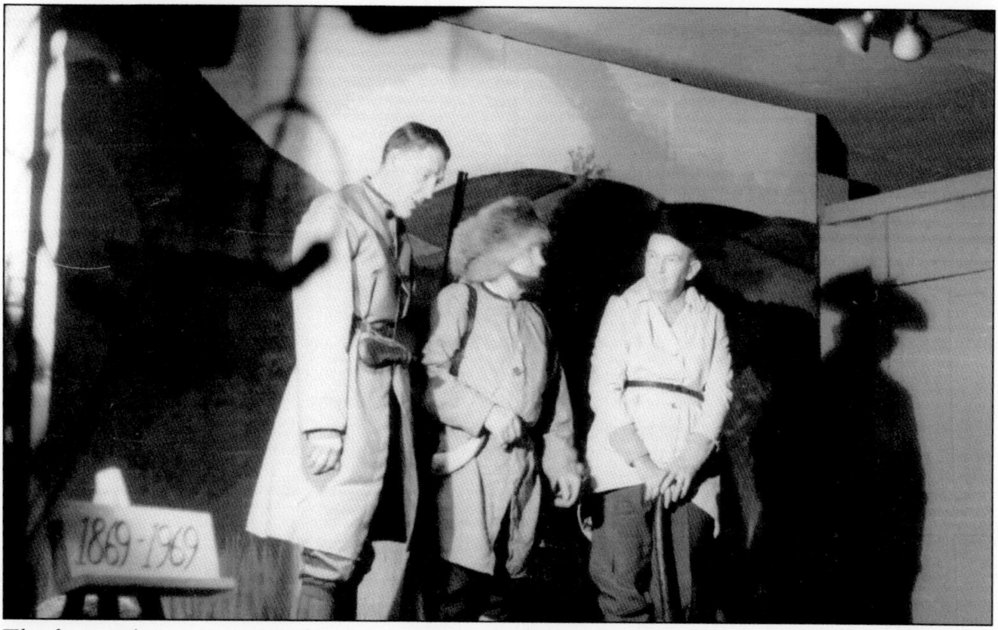

The first settlers to come to what is now the town of Goshen arrived in an area known as Savillie at the time. Here a few of those early arrivals in what was to become Goshen are depicted in a scene from the play *They Lived in Goshen*. At the town's 1919 celebration, the final event was also a historical pageant presented by the girls of Camp Soangetaha. (Courtesy of Goshen Historical Society.)

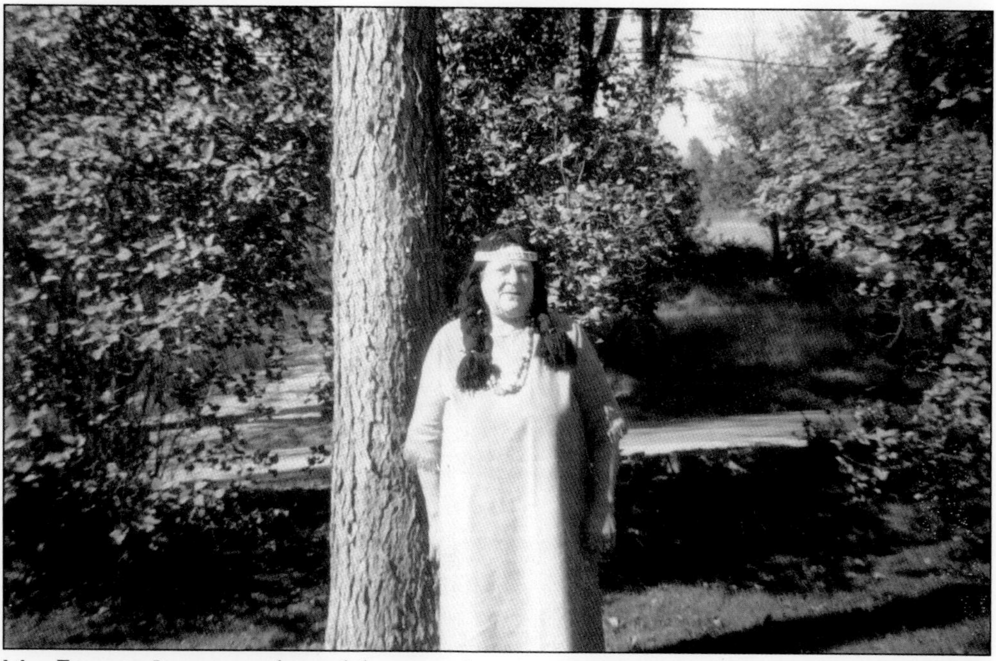

Mrs. Emerson Lewis was chair of the general committee in 1969 and also an active participant in the re-creation of the town's history. She is pictured here in her historical persona of Princess Busy Beaver. Arthur W. Nelson chaired the committee 50 years earlier. (Courtesy of Goshen Historical Society.)

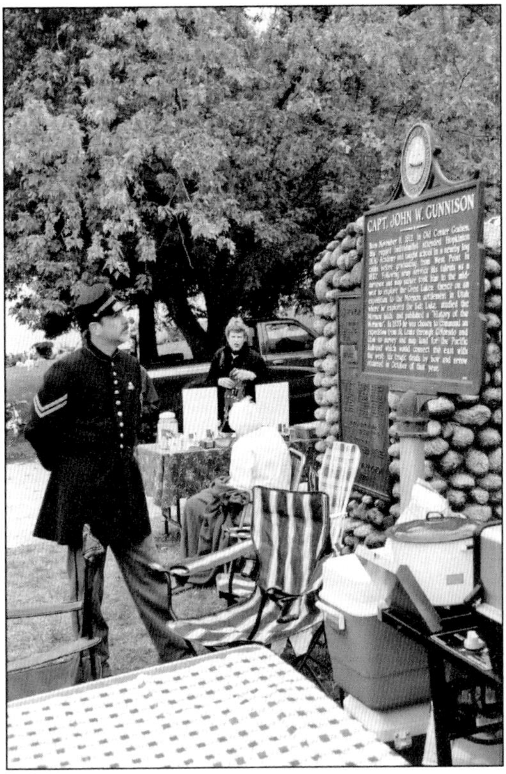

History is always a big part of Goshen Old Home Day. Here a Civil War reenactor peruses the historic plaque that recounts the story of Capt. William Gunnison. Gunnison was born in Goshen in 1812 and lost his life at the hand of Pahvant Indians in the controversial Gunnison-Beckworth Massacre in Utah Territory. (Courtesy of Goshen Historical Society.)

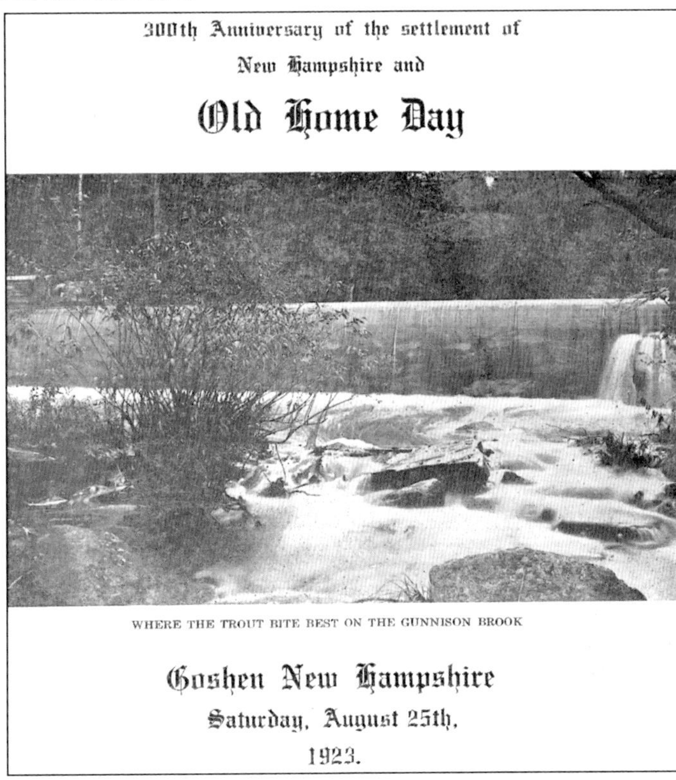
300th Anniversary of the settlement of

New Hampshire and

Old Home Day

WHERE THE TROUT BITE BEST ON THE GUNNISON BROOK

Goshen New Hampshire

Saturday, August 25th,

1923.

The 300th anniversary of the settlement of New Hampshire and another Goshen Old Home Day was celebrated in 1923. Townspeople presented a four-act play titled *Valley Farm*. As usual, athletics were on the schedule, with a 10:00 a.m. tug-of-war pitting Mill Village against Goshen Corner followed by a 1:00 p.m. showdown on the baseball diamond between Unity and Goshen. (Author's collection.)

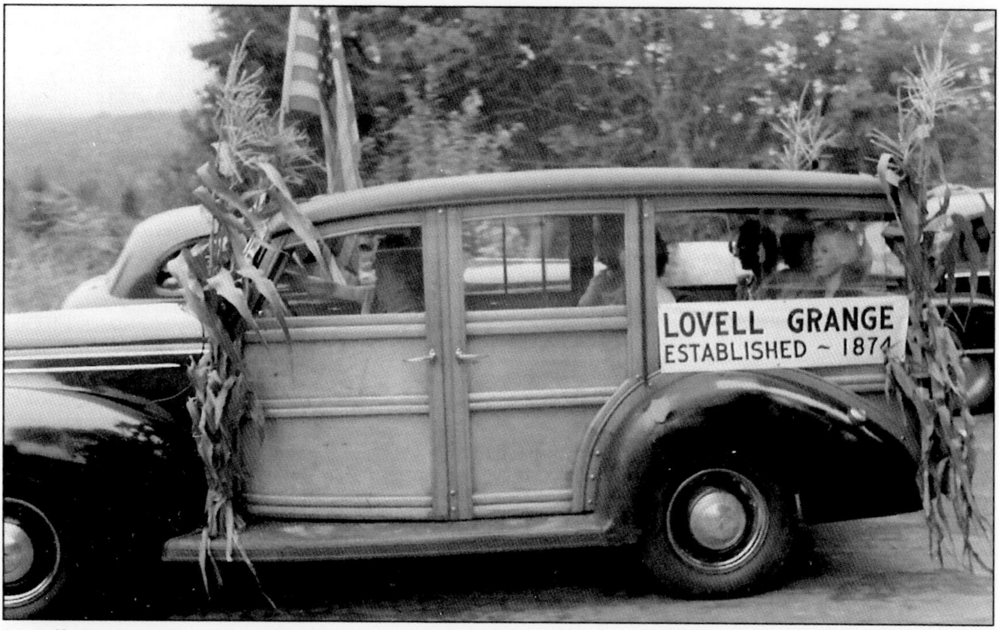

Lovell Grange No. 178 of Washington was represented by a simple entry in this Washington Old Home Day parade. Washington was the nation's first town to be named after the first American president. During the 1900 old home day, Washington residents filled the old town house, built in 1789, and were entertained by a band concert and the recitation of original poetry. (Courtesy of Washington Historical Society.)

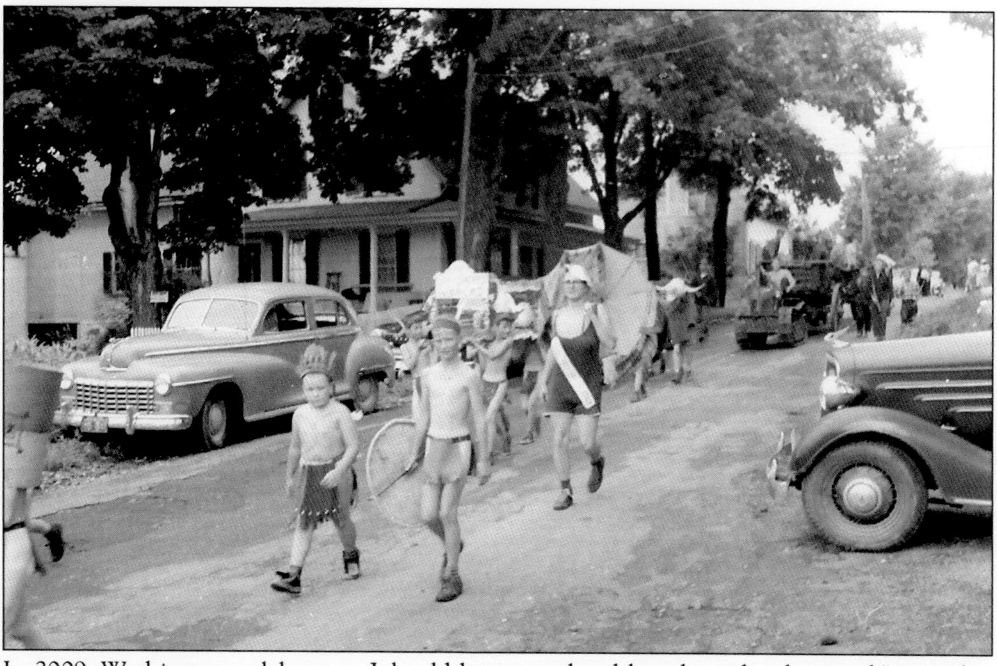

In 2009, Washington celebrates a July old home weekend based on the theme of "remember when." Remembering when was on the mind of these young marchers as they portrayed Native Americans in this early Washington Old Home Day parade. (Courtesy of Washington Historical Society.)

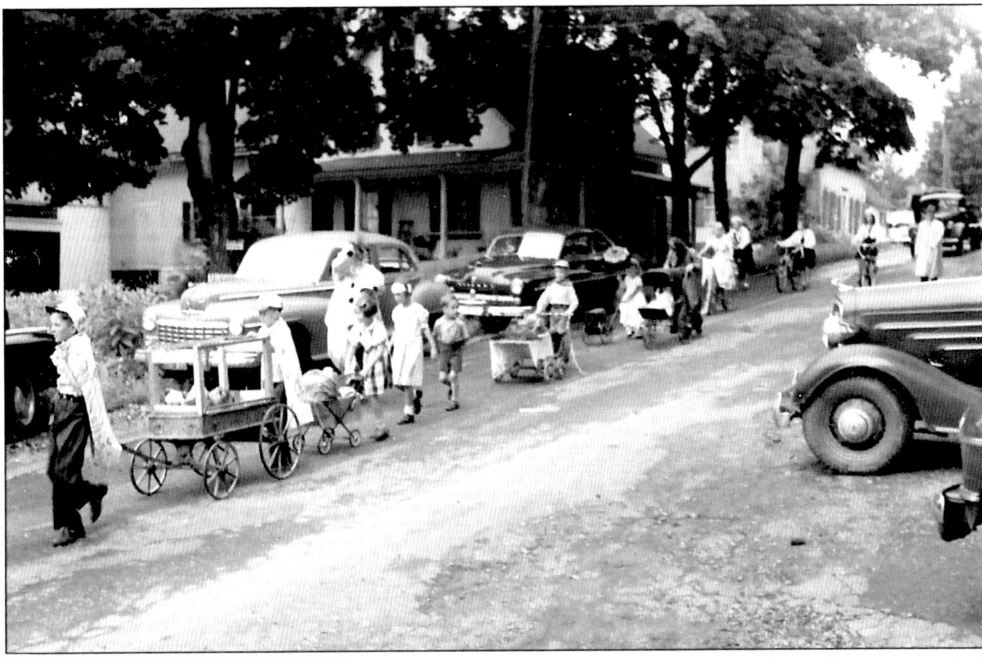

This children's parade from Washington Old Home Day is typical of similar events held throughout the state. It is hoped that many of those who have the memories of such old home happenings go on to help keep the tradition of New Hampshire's homegrown holiday alive. (Courtesy of Washington Historical Society.)

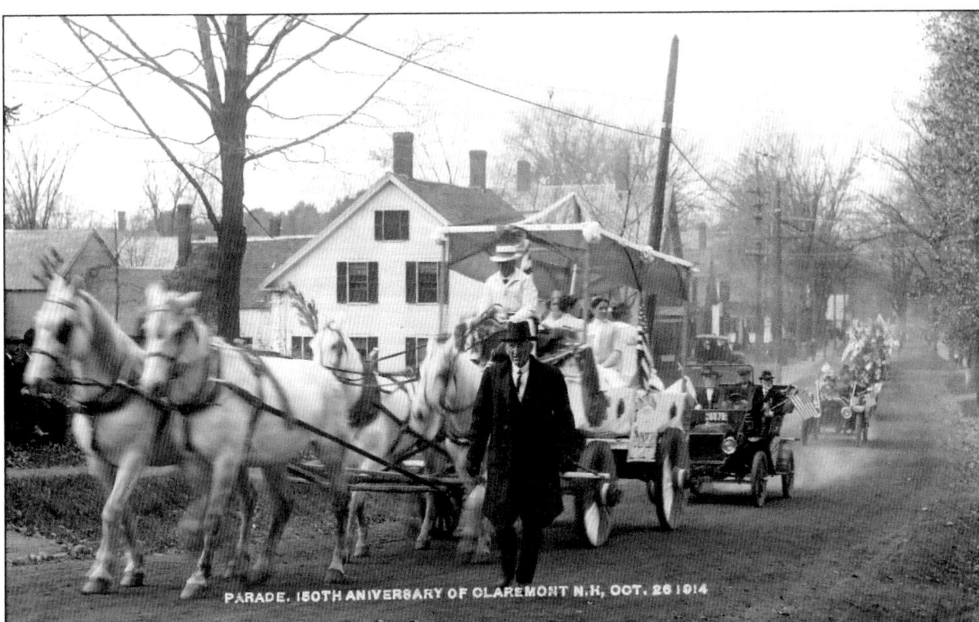

Claremont was another town that combined an anniversary of the town's founding with its old home festivities. Here parade marchers and floats honor Claremont's 150th birthday. Notice the Civil War veterans in the car behind the float that were also being honored. (Courtesy of Washington Historical Society.)

Five

Lakes Region

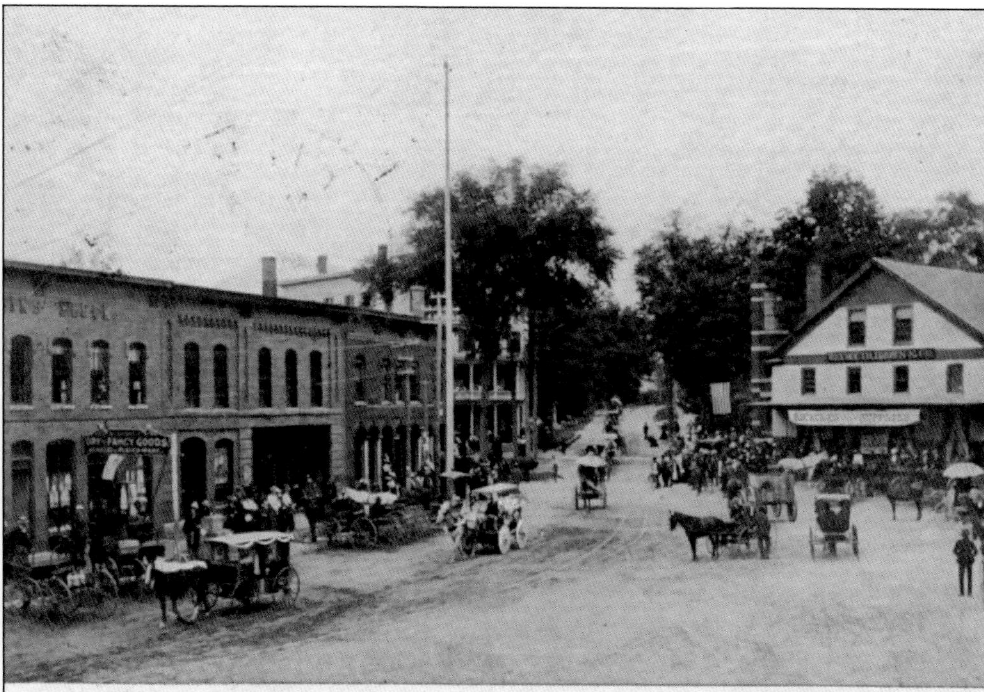

Bristol returned to celebrating old home day in the late 1990s, but it was also one of the very first towns to celebrate in 1899. Here the old home day parade wends its way through the west side of central square for the town's second old home celebration in 1900. (Courtesy of the Granite State Collection, Sam Allen.)

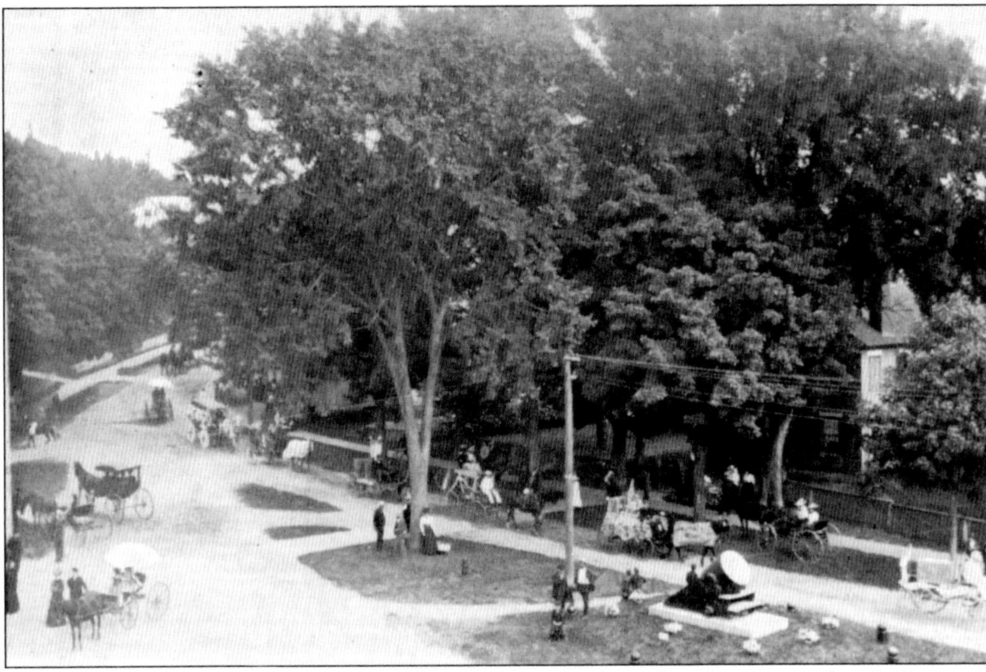

The 1900 old home day parade went all around in Bristol. In the afternoon, a baseball contest matched the "Up-to Dates" against the "Old-Timers." Later in the day, the town band gave a concert on the square, and a gala ball at the Hotel Bristol concluded the day's activities. (Courtesy of the Granite State Collection, Sam Allen.)

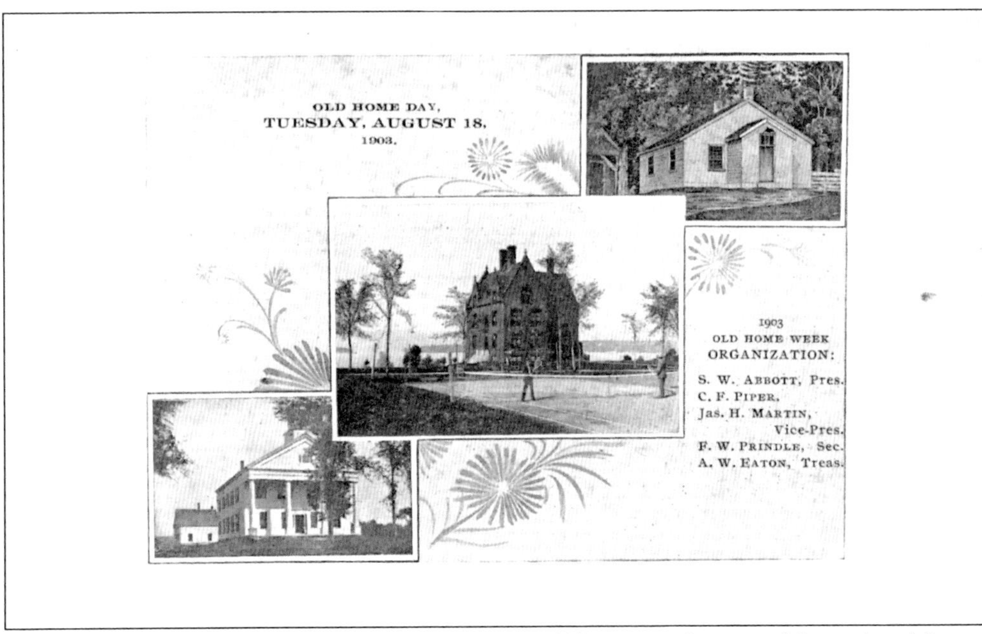

Known as the "oldest summer resort in America," Wolfeboro was also one of the early celebrants of old home days. This public invitation to the 1903 event beckoned residents to a parade that ended up having 5,000 spectators, as well as athletic events, including bicycle races, boat races, and baseball contests. (Author's collection.)

While parades have always been a highlight of old home festivities, religious services were also integral from the beginning. Events were often run under the auspices of area churches with opening and closing ceremonies as well as other events held there. In Wolfeboro in 1903, all area clergy took part in the opening ceremonies for the week. (Courtesy of the Granite State Collection, Sam Allen.)

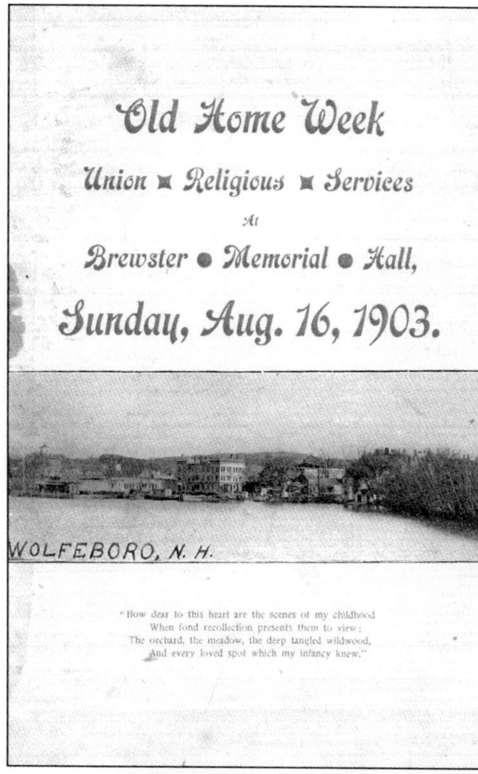

Old Home Week

Union ✖ Religious ✖ Services

At

Brewster • Memorial • Hall,

Sunday, Aug. 16, 1903.

WOLFEBORO, N. H.

"How dear to this heart are the scenes of my childhood
When fond recollection presents them to view;
The orchard, the meadow, the deep tangled wildwood,
And every loved spot which my infancy knew."

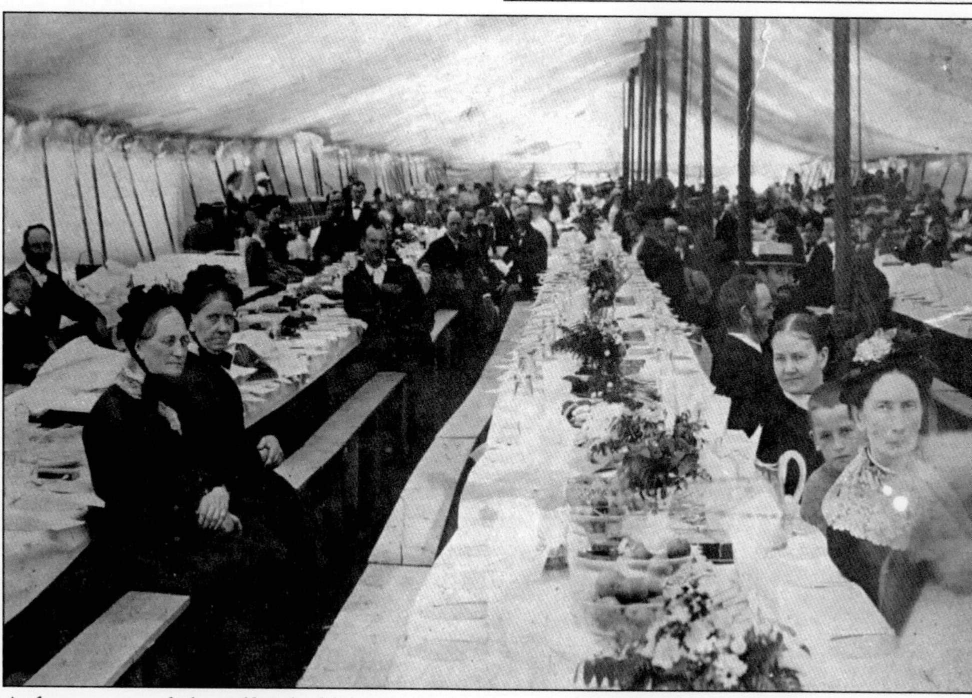

A forerunner of the official old home programs was the annual Lyme celebration honoring the town's older residents. Pictured here are some of the hundreds who gathered on the town common for the annual event in 1885. (Courtesy of Lyme Historians.)

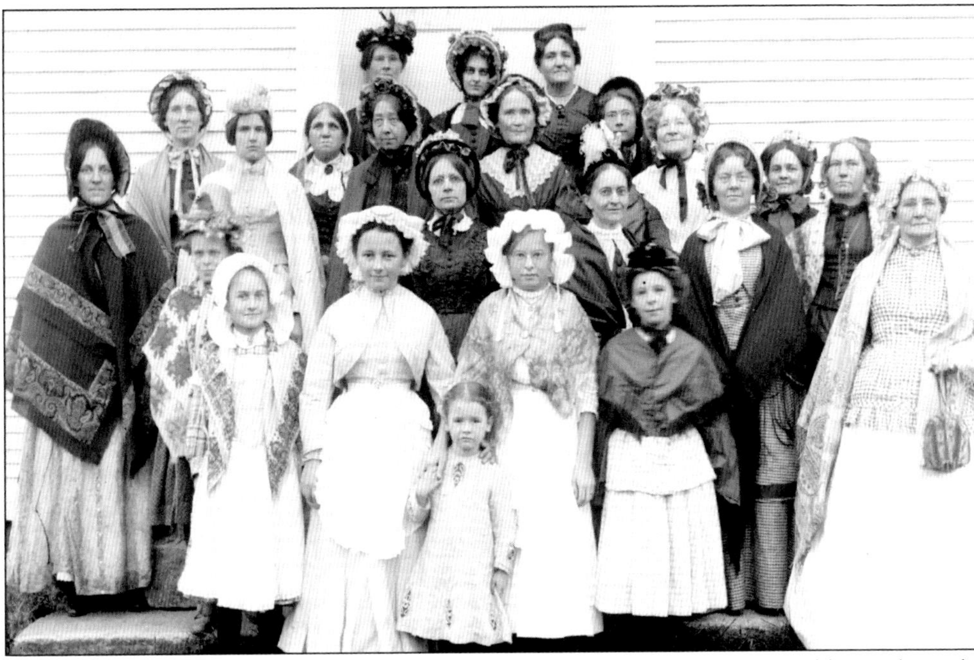

Old home day celebrations have always been an opportunity to both teach and learn about the past in a community. As part of a more recent celebration in Lyme, these ladies dressed in period costumes to re-create what life and fashions were like in the early days of the holiday. (Courtesy of Lyme Historians.)

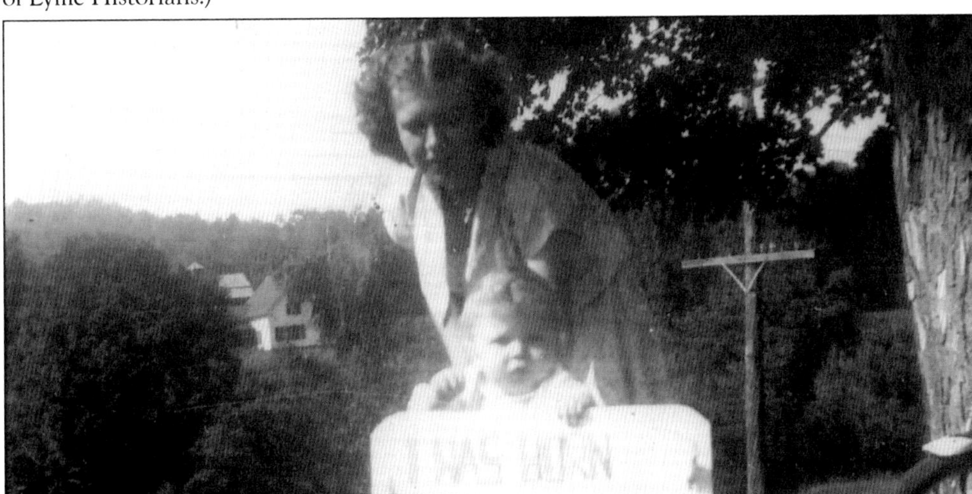

This Lyme youngster and his mother had a better reason than most to be fans of Lyme's old home day, celebrating both the holiday and his birthday together. Baseball, buffets, band concerts, and square dancing were all part of the celebration in the year of this youngster's birth. (Courtesy of Lyme Historians.)

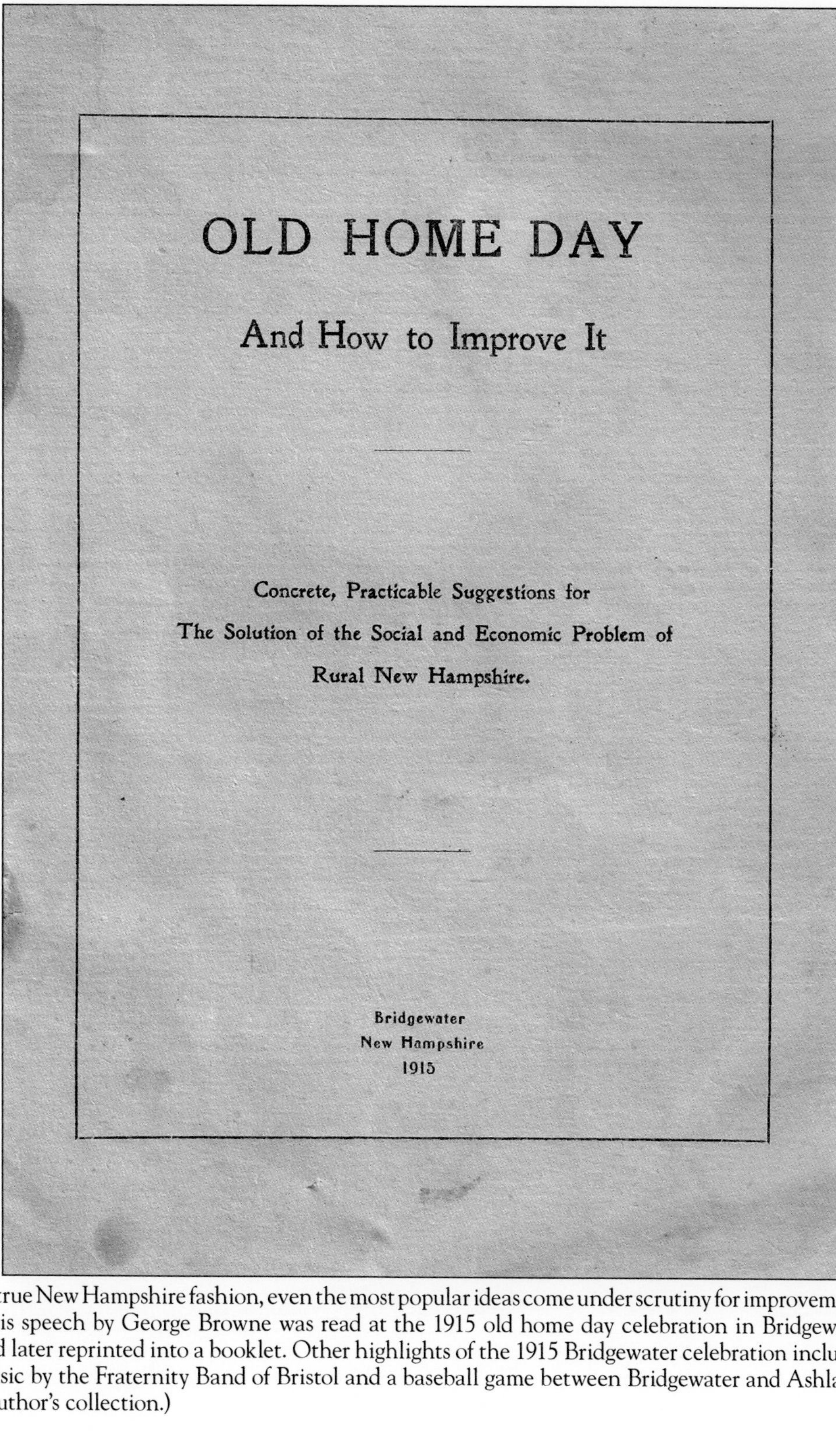

OLD HOME DAY

And How to Improve It

Concrete, Practicable Suggestions for
The Solution of the Social and Economic Problem of
Rural New Hampshire.

Bridgewater
New Hampshire
1915

In true New Hampshire fashion, even the most popular ideas come under scrutiny for improvement. This speech by George Browne was read at the 1915 old home day celebration in Bridgewater and later reprinted into a booklet. Other highlights of the 1915 Bridgewater celebration included music by the Fraternity Band of Bristol and a baseball game between Bridgewater and Ashland. (Author's collection.)

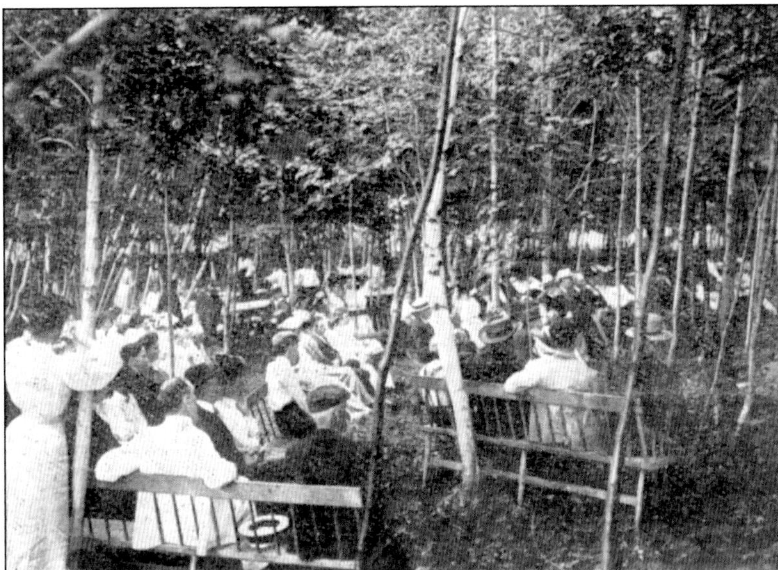

Bridgewater is one of the New Hampshire communities that has celebrated continuously since the initial old home proclamation in 1899. Like other early celebrations in the state, Bridgewater residents gathered for speeches and musical entertainment, one of which was probably the attraction at this early celebration in the grove. (Author's collection.)

OLD HOME DAY
AT
SMITH MEETING HOUSE
GILMANTON, N. H., THURSDAY, AUGUST 24, 1916.

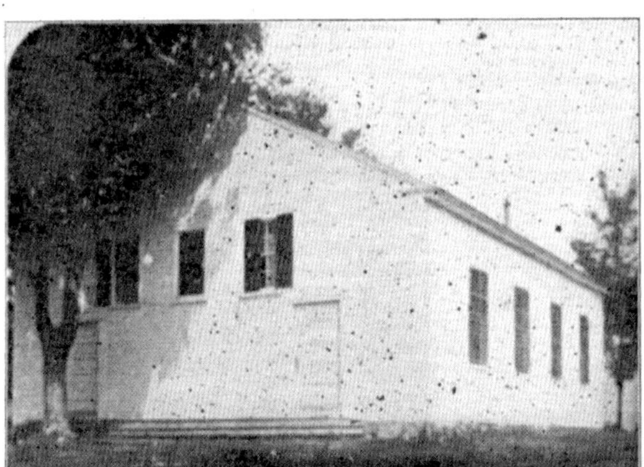

This annual invitation takes the same cordial message from Gilmanton to you---

"COME FOR OLD HOME DAY!"

MRS. BLANCHE AYER,
Sec'y. and Treas.

Address, R. F. D. 4, Pittsfield, N. H.

Gilmanton has celebrated its old home days since 1899. This 1916 invitation picturing the Smith Meeting House shows that the message has remained the same through the years. Come on home or at least send word. (Author's collection.)

Gov. Frank Rollins hoped that the observance of old home day would produce economic benefits for the state as well as camaraderie and pride in community. It produced all of those things along with oceans of poetry from all over the state. This poem, penned by Fred Parker Ham for Gilmanton's 1907 old home day, is just one of hundreds that have been produced since 1899. (Author's collection.)

"BACK ON THE HILL."

After only one short year's absence,
We're back on the hill again;
For we've listened and heard the Old Home Horn
Calling "Don't let me summons in vain."

We found the Old Meeting House opened,
And the key to the doors laid away,
As the purple rays of the Sun's fond gaze
Through the window read "WELCOME TO-DAY."

We renewed the acquaintance, each with each,
In that same old familiar way;
But we thought, though we dared not speak it,
How changed was the other, and gray.

Oh, how life's old tree has been shaken,
Since last we looked into its boughs;
How shattered, how bare are its life leaves there,
How few of them linger now.

We refer to Old Home Day's comforts,
We speak of its meetings of cheer,
While each in his heart depths is thinking
Of those who to-day are not here.

We stroll about through the Groves and the Yard,
And each cold stone's inscription we read,
'Till we pause at the one "SYLVESTER GALE,"
And it seems to call to us "GOD SPEED."

We consider that friend MRS. MOSES,
What she did for the Church, what she said,
'Till she and Sylvester seem living,
And we, the living, seem dead.

We applaud their kind acts 'till it's hard to distinguish
Between their Ghosts and the Guests,
For a mist of tears, the saddest of years,
Steals over our merriest jests.

Composed by FRED PARKER HAM,
and read by him
at the OLD SMITH MEETING HOUSE, Gilmanton, N.H.,
Old Home Day, August 22d, 1907.

Bi-Centennial and Old Home Day

CELEBRATION

AT GILMANTON, N. H.

Will be held at the Smith Meeting House, Thursday, Aug. 25, 1927.

The celebration begins at 12 o'clock at noon.

Speaking at 2 o'clock. Gov. Spaulding has been invited also Col. William B. Greeley, Chief of the U. S. Forestry Service and others.

Do not miss the Senior Girl Scouts Drum and Bugle Corp music with singing around a campfire from 7 to 8. p. m.

A grand display of Fire Works from 8 till 9 .

First-class band music all day.

Catering attendance from 12 o'clock noon to 8 p. m.

MRS. BLANCHE L. AYER, Sec.
Route 4, Pittsfield, N. H.

As with so many other towns, Gilmanton's bicentennial was celebrated with old home day in 1927. Notice the grand display of fireworks offered for the evening. By this time, controlled pyrotechnics had mostly replaced the bonfires of earlier celebrations. Col. William B. Greeley, the nation's third chief of the forest service, spoke at the event. (Author's collection.)

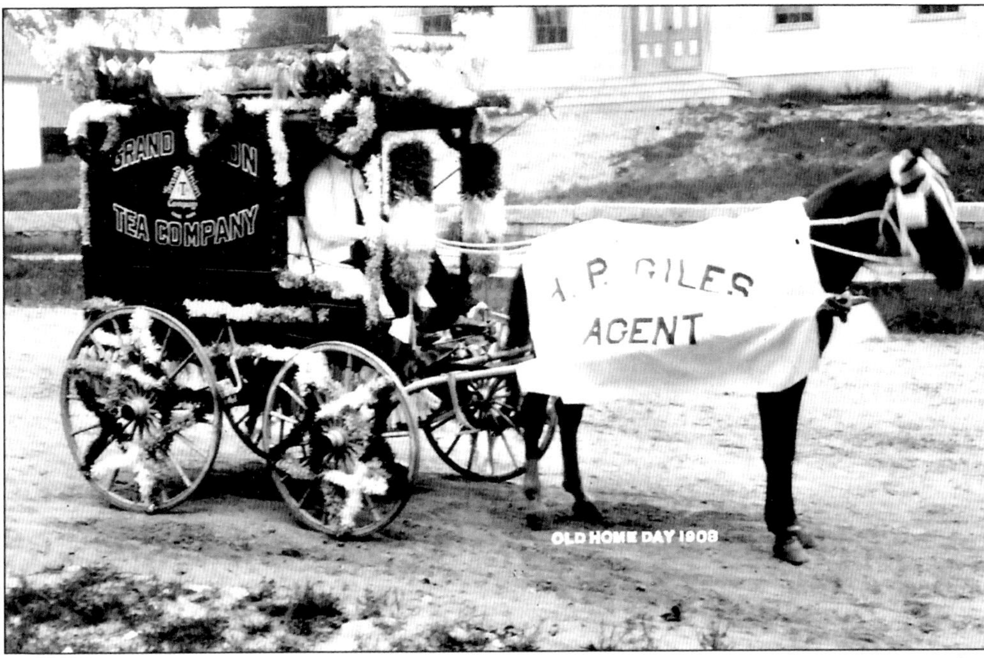

The Grand Union Tea Company, forerunner of the chain of Grand Union Markets, joined in the Pittsfield Old Home Day parade in 1909. Still celebrating New Hampshire's own holiday, citizens of Pittsfield now get together each July for their old home day. (Courtesy of Pittsfield Historical Society.)

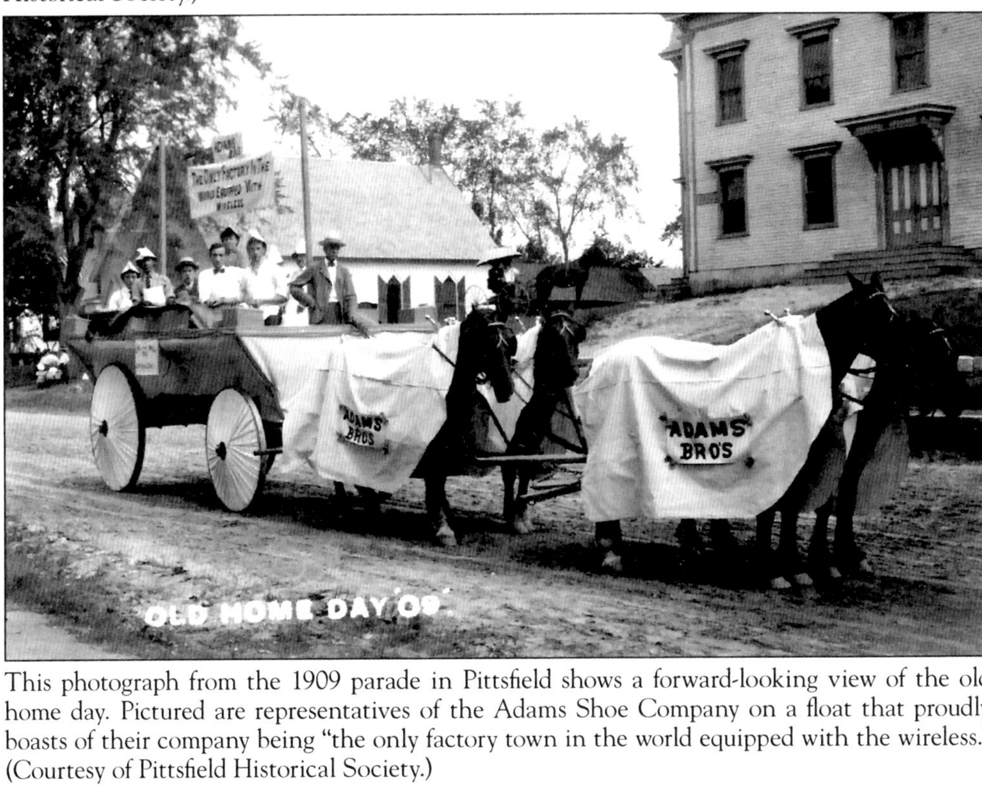

This photograph from the 1909 parade in Pittsfield shows a forward-looking view of the old home day. Pictured are representatives of the Adams Shoe Company on a float that proudly boasts of their company being "the only factory town in the world equipped with the wireless." (Courtesy of Pittsfield Historical Society.)

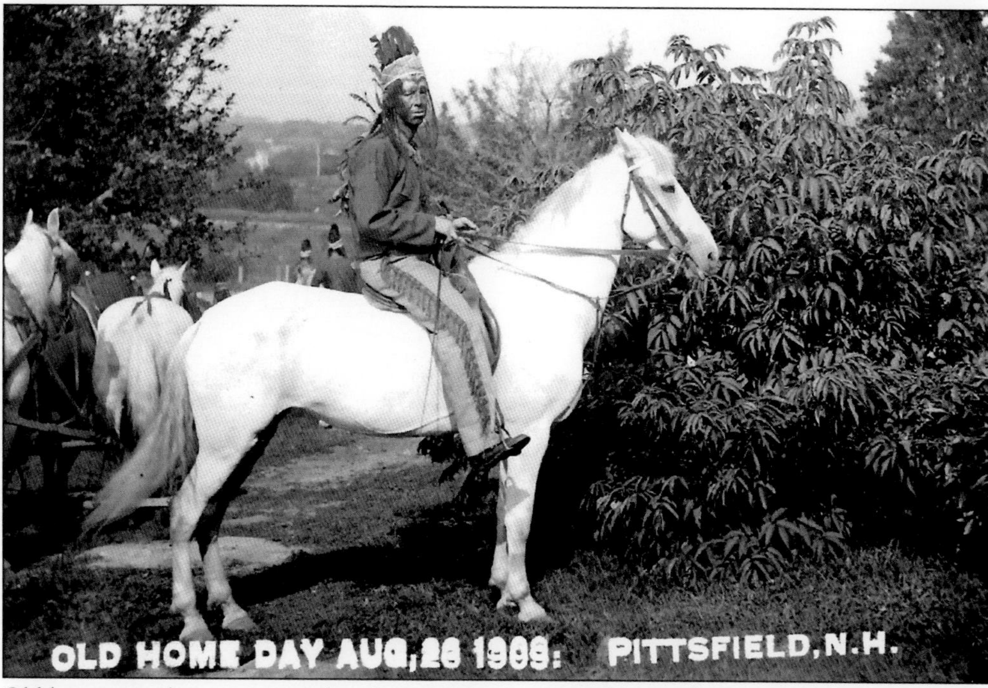

Old home parades are as varied as the participants. In 2008, Pittsfield celebrated "South of the Border: A Mexican Fiesta." In this photograph, Native Americans were celebrated during a break from the 1908 parade. (Courtesy of Pittsfield Historical Society.)

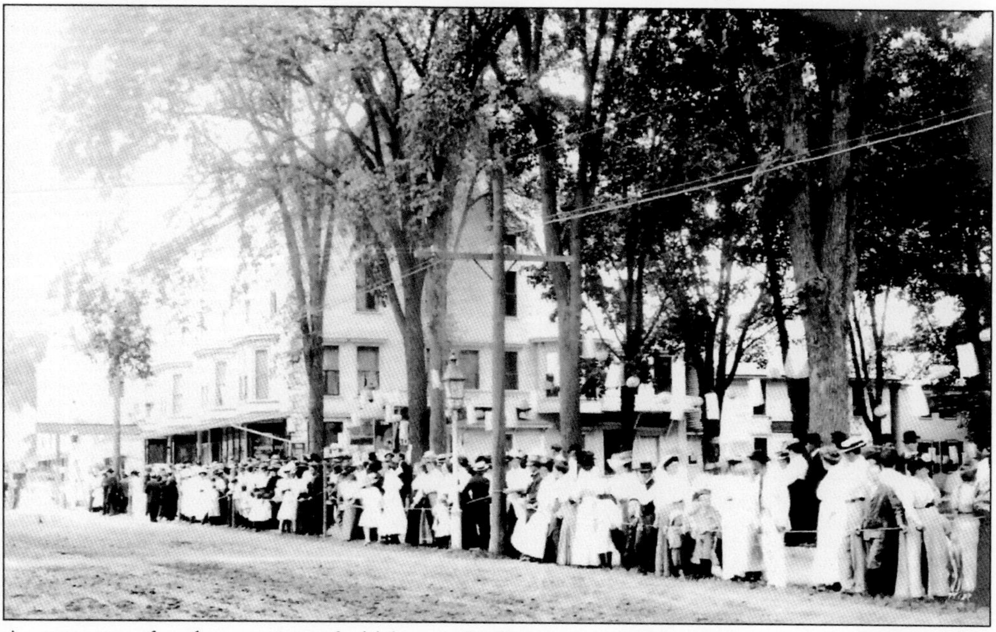

Anticipation for the coming of old home day became a yearly summer ritual in many New Hampshire towns, and nothing was more anticipated than the big parade. Throughout the history of the celebration, the grand parade has been the culmination and highlight of the festivities. Here the Main Street of Pittsfield is lined with onlookers waiting for the marchers in 1909. (Courtesy of Pittsfield Historical Society.)

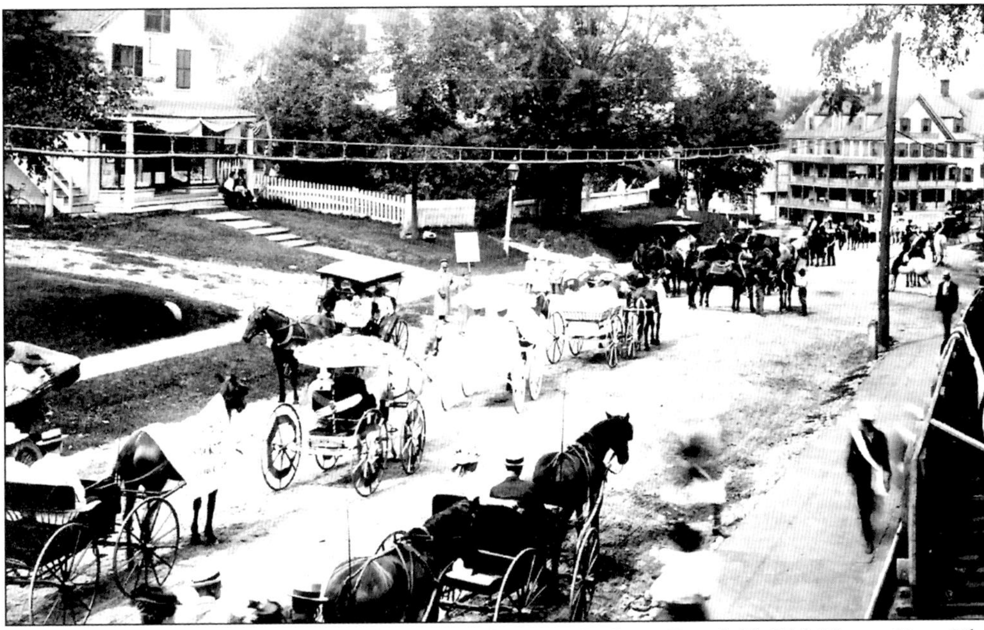

A time of change is reflected in this 1908 photograph from Pittsfield Old Home Day. The promenade of carriages drawn by horses represent what was soon to become the past, while the overhead telegraph wires presage a future of mass communication. Forty years later, Pittsfield observances consisted of a program held on a Monday evening at the Catamount Grange. (Courtesy of Pittsfield Historical Society.)

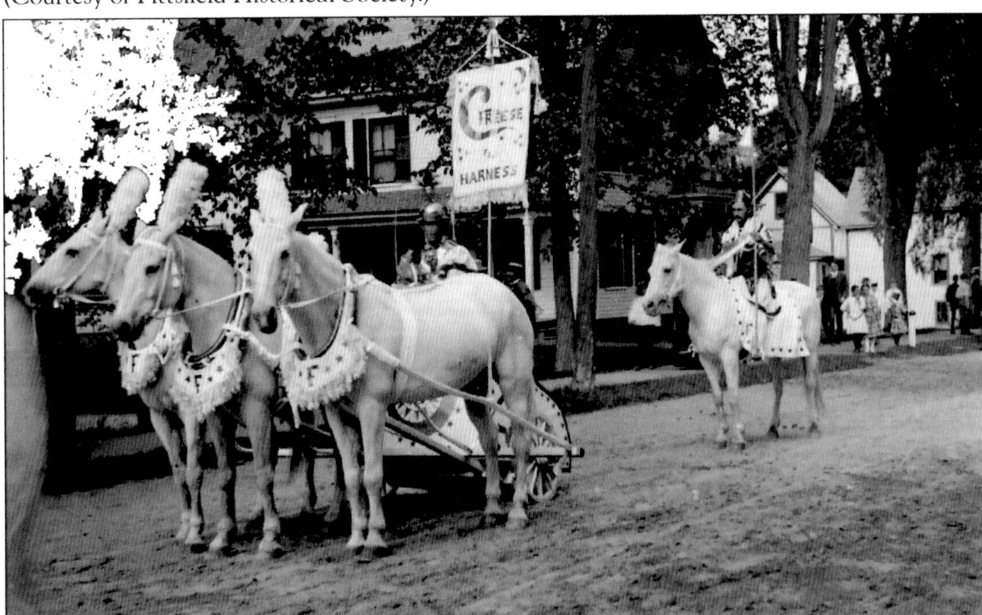

Roman chariots and gladiators were the theme for this Freese Harness Company float in Pittsfield's 1909 parade. While the harness business was on its way out in 1909, Courtland Freese was busy building up Globe Manufacturing, which is still based in Pittsfield today and is one of the leading manufacturers of protective clothing for firefighters. (Courtesy of Pittsfield Historical Society.)

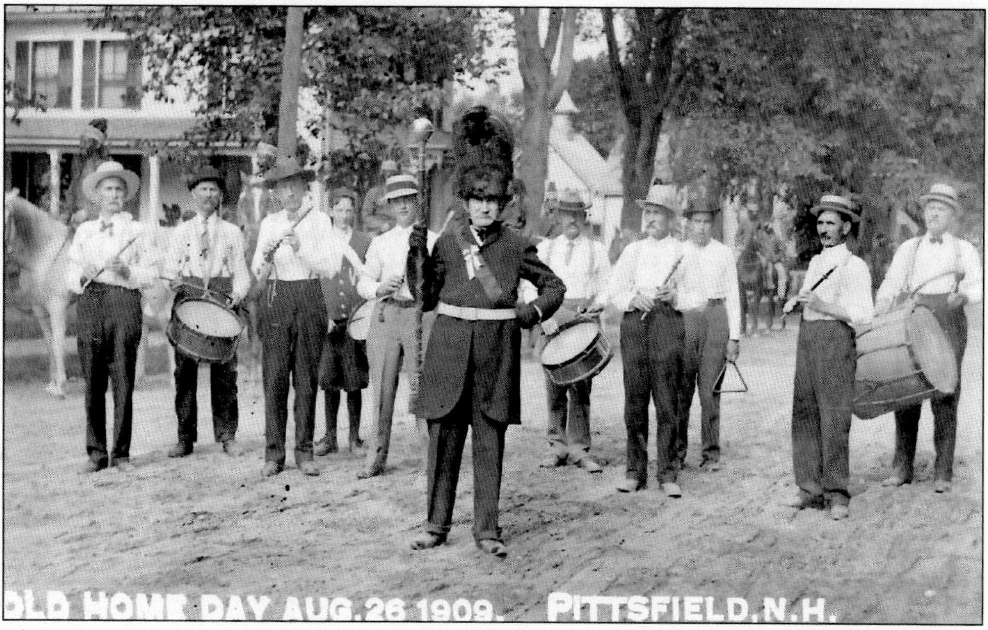

This group from the 1909 Pittsfield Old Home Day is representative of the local musical groups and talents that have always been a part of the holiday. In 1921, Pittsfield held one of its largest events ever during old home week as it celebrated the town's 150th anniversary. Music that year was supplied by both the Suncook Union Coronet Band and the American Band of Pittsfield. (Courtesy of Pittsfield Historical Society.)

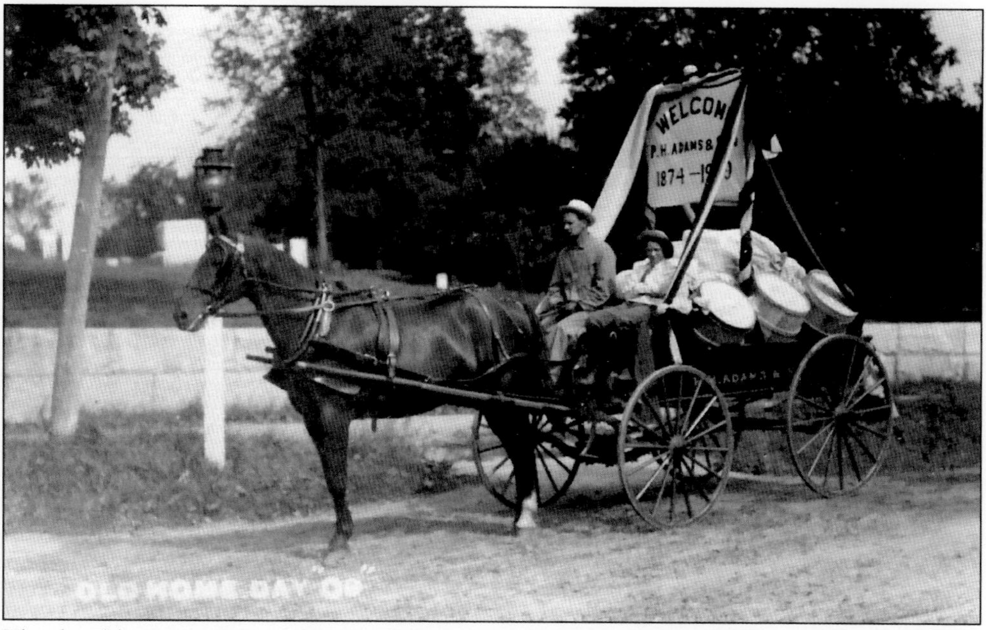

This local business, P. H. Adams and Son, put the simple message, "Welcome," on its float in the 1909 Pittsfield Old Home Day parade. That message is still important at celebrations today. Like towns throughout the state, Pittsfield residents used old home days as a special welcome for returning World War I soldiers 10 years later. The formal welcome home that year honored 66 veterans of the war. (Courtesy of Pittsfield Historical Society.)

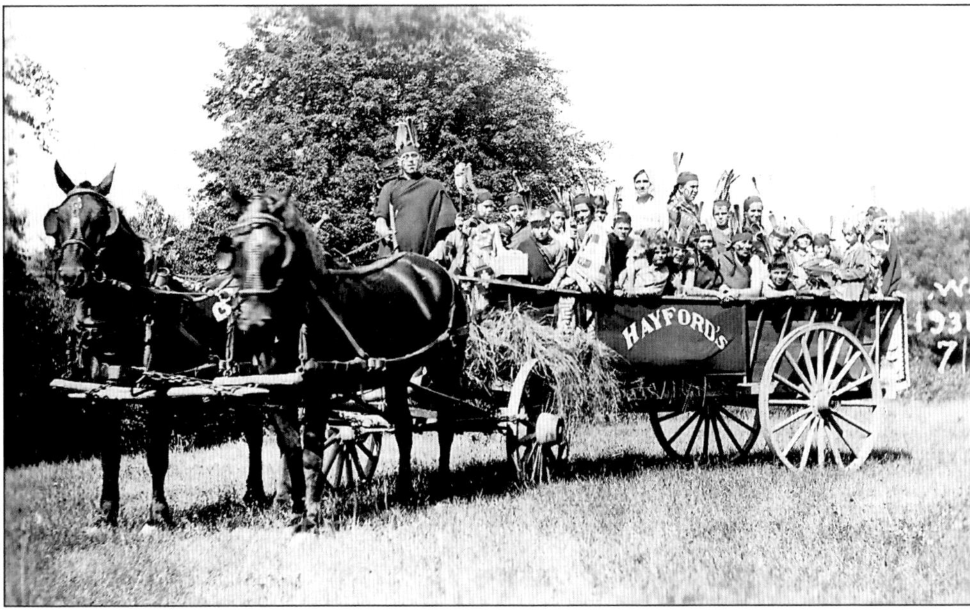

This Hayford's float was just one of 25 that took part in the parade that highlighted the 1931 Tamworth Old Home Day observances. On hand to help residents celebrate and give speeches were Gov. John G. Winant and Francis Grover Cleveland, son of former president Grover Cleveland. (Author's collection.)

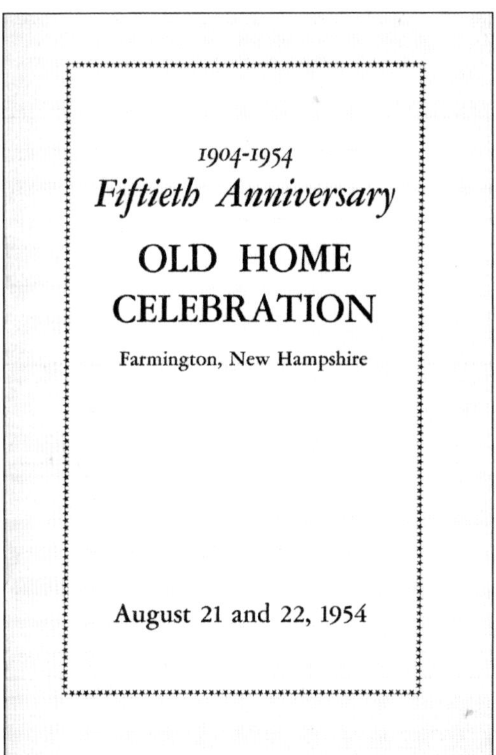

1904-1954
Fiftieth Anniversary
OLD HOME CELEBRATION
Farmington, New Hampshire

August 21 and 22, 1954

Through its many old home celebrations, commemorated here at the 50-year mark, Farmington residents took part in all of the traditional methods of observance. Perhaps one of the town's biggest old home days was the 1919 welcome home for World War I soldiers. Included that year were a grand parade, free band concert and dance, and a baseball match-up between a team from Dover and the Atlantic Corporation of Portsmouth. (Courtesy of the Granite State Collection, Sam Allen.)

Six

MERRIMACK VALLEY

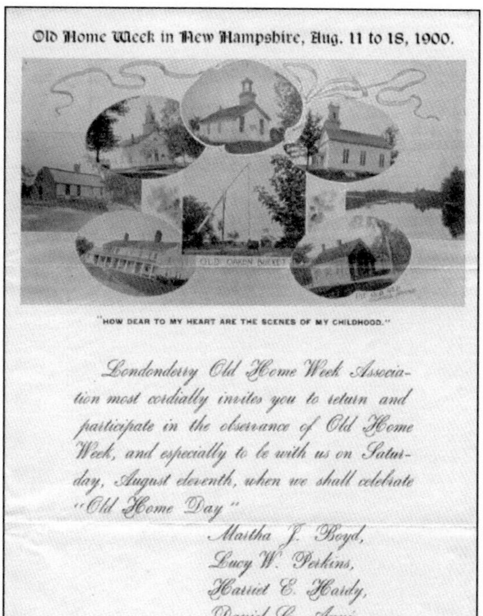
Old Home Week in New Hampshire, Aug. 11 to 18, 1900.

"HOW DEAR TO MY HEART ARE THE SCENES OF MY CHILDHOOD."

Londonderry Old Home Week Association most cordially invites you to return and participate in the observance of Old Home Week, and especially to be with us on Saturday, August eleventh, when we shall celebrate "Old Home Day."

Martha J. Boyd,
Lucy W. Perkins,
Harriet E. Hardy,
Daniel G. Annis,
Rev. G. A. McLucas,
Invitation Committee.

Londonderry has celebrated old home day since its inception in 1899. Just a small community when the observances began, it is now one of the largest towns in the state holding old home festivities. This 1900 invitation calls on several images of home and family to get residents into the old home mood. (Courtesy of Londonderry Historical Society.)

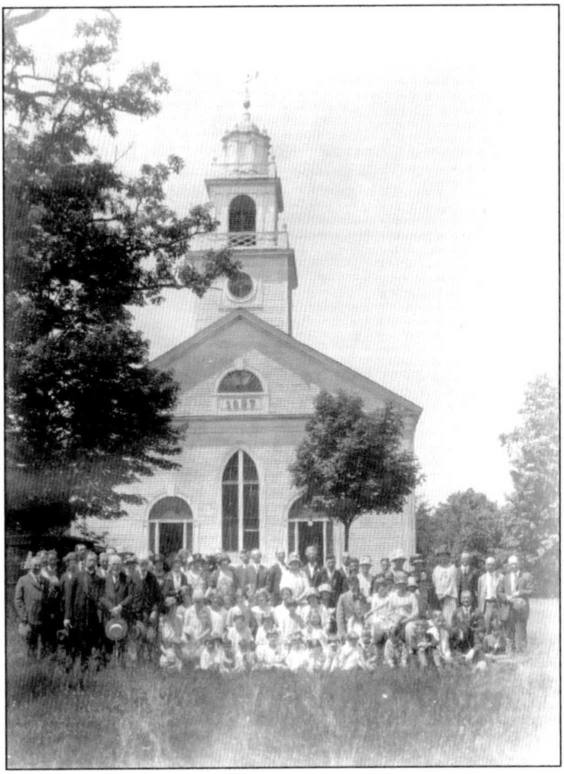

It is hard to get large parts of a community together for photographs today. This group photograph was taken during old home week around 1920 in front of Londonderry's Presbyterian church and represents about 10 percent of the 1,300 town inhabitants at the time. (Courtesy of Londonderry Historical Society.)

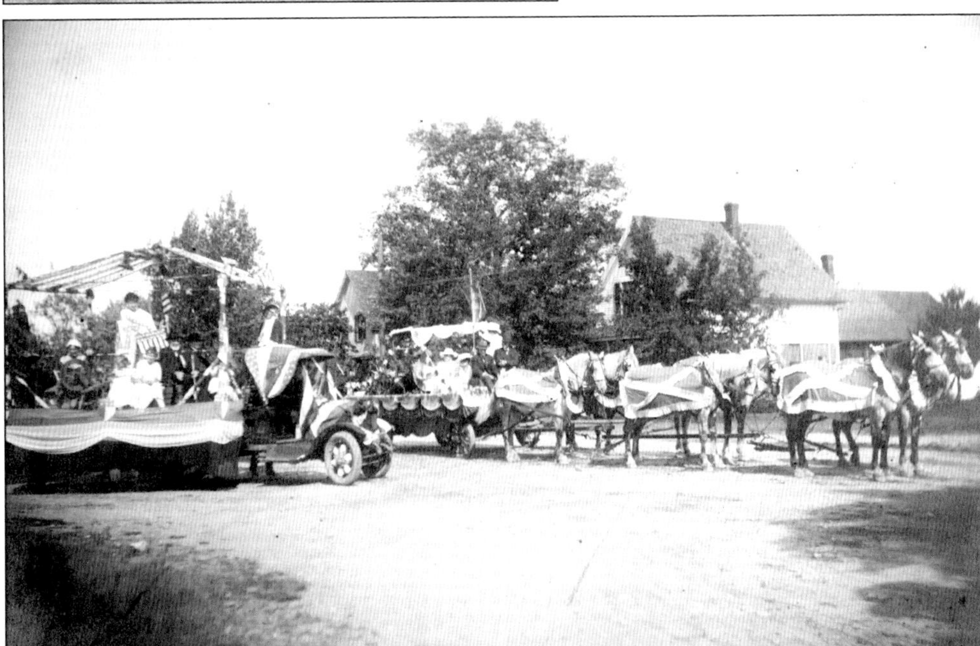

It was the 200th anniversary of the founding of Londonderry as well as the annual Londonderry old home celebration when these cars and floats were decked out in 1919. Parade participants paused for this photograph on the corner of West Broadway (Route 102) and Londonderry Road. (Donated by Ruth and Roy Avery, courtesy of Londonderry Historical Society.)

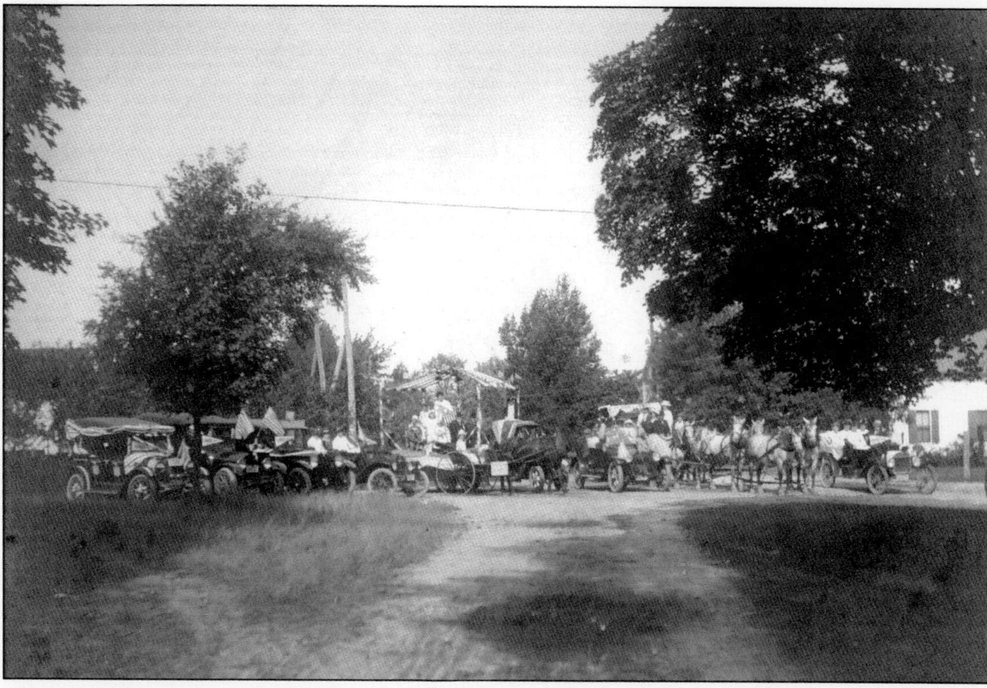

These parade entries are also from Londonderry's 200th anniversary/old home celebration in 1919. Events commenced on Sunday, August 24, as all of the churches in town united for services in the old Presbyterian church in the south of town. The parade contained eight divisions, and each one was headed by a member of the Lester W. Chase post of the American Legion in Derry. (Courtesy of Londonderry Historical Society.)

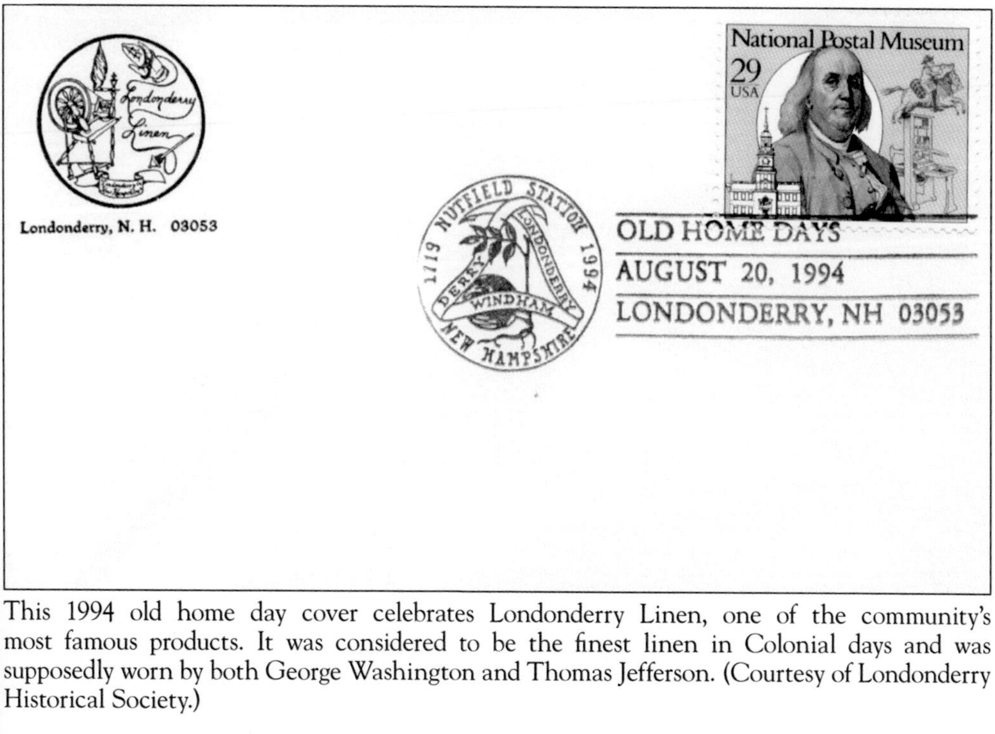

This 1994 old home day cover celebrates Londonderry Linen, one of the community's most famous products. It was considered to be the finest linen in Colonial days and was supposedly worn by both George Washington and Thomas Jefferson. (Courtesy of Londonderry Historical Society.)

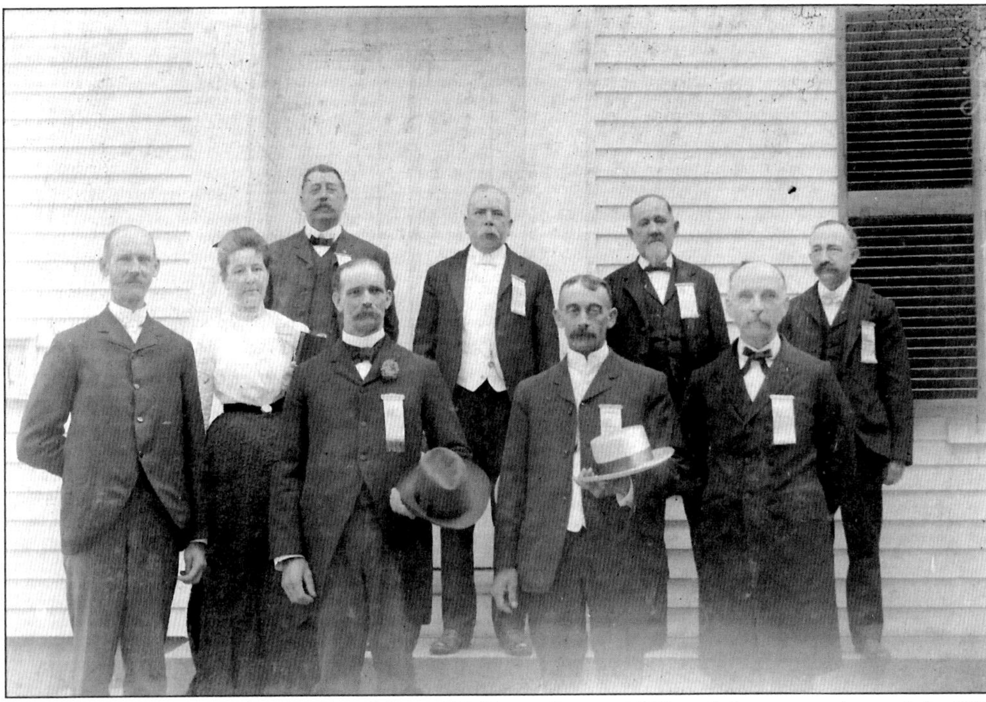

This photograph was taken on Brookline Old Home Day in 1903 and shows members of the Old Home Week Association of Brookline for that year. Events that the association put together in 1903 included a concert by the Ashby Band and a dinner for 25¢ per plate served at Tarbell's Hall. (Courtesy of Brookline Historical Society.)

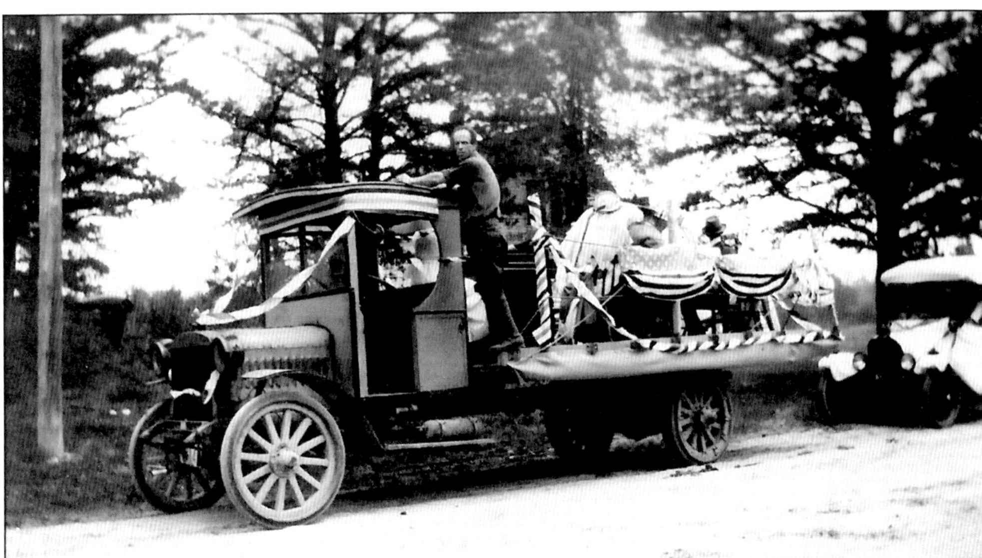

This float from an early Brookline Old Home Day is typical of the work that went into the town's observances of the holiday. In addition to a parade each year, Brookline was always sure to entertain natives and visitors with bonfires and dancing. In 1924, the celebration was held under the auspices of the Frank E. Kilduff post of the American Legion. (Courtesy of Brookline Historical Society.)

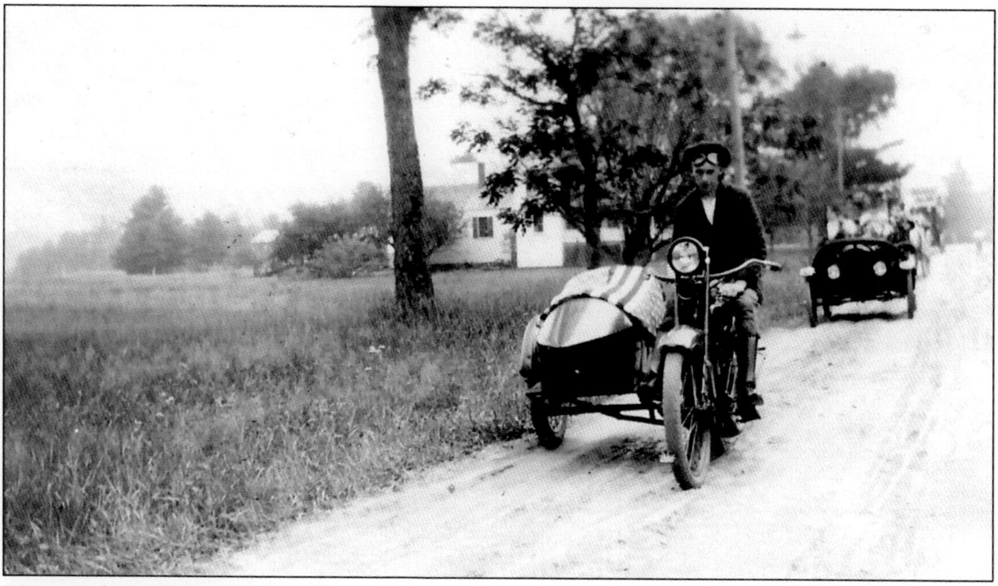

Motorcycle enthusiasts as well as old home fans can appreciate this small entry in the 1921 Brookline Old Home Day parade. In the early 20th century, Brookline celebrated during August, but their full week of observances currently takes place in July. Many of the week's activities take place at the Brookline ballpark. (Courtesy of Brookline Historical Society.)

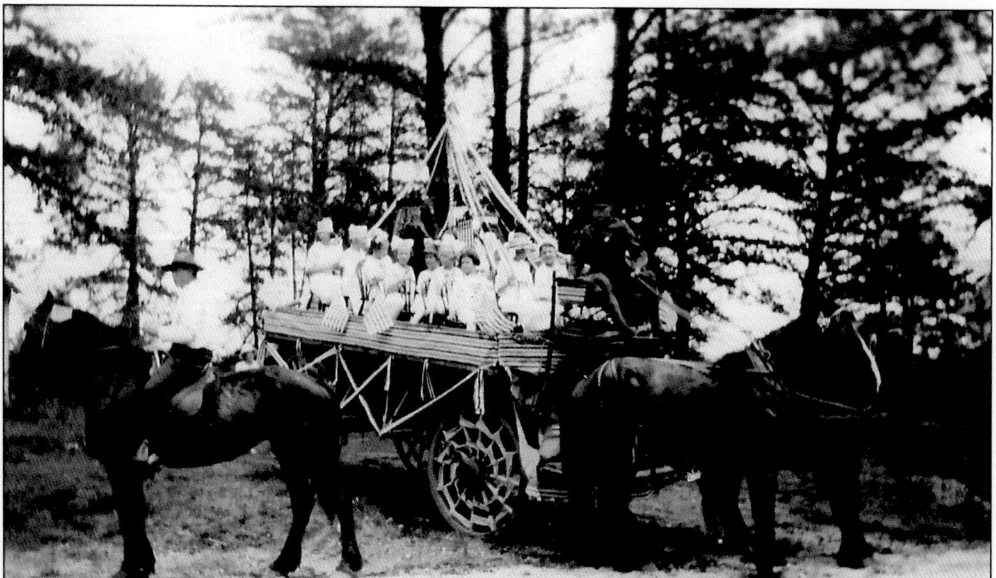

These youngsters aboard an early-1920s parade float celebrate around a Maypole theme for Brookline Old Home Day. Children and families are always at the center of these festivities, but the single set is not forgotten. In 1924, Brookline Old Home Day featured a tug-of-war between married and single men followed by a contest between the married and single ladies. (Courtesy of Brookline Historical Society.)

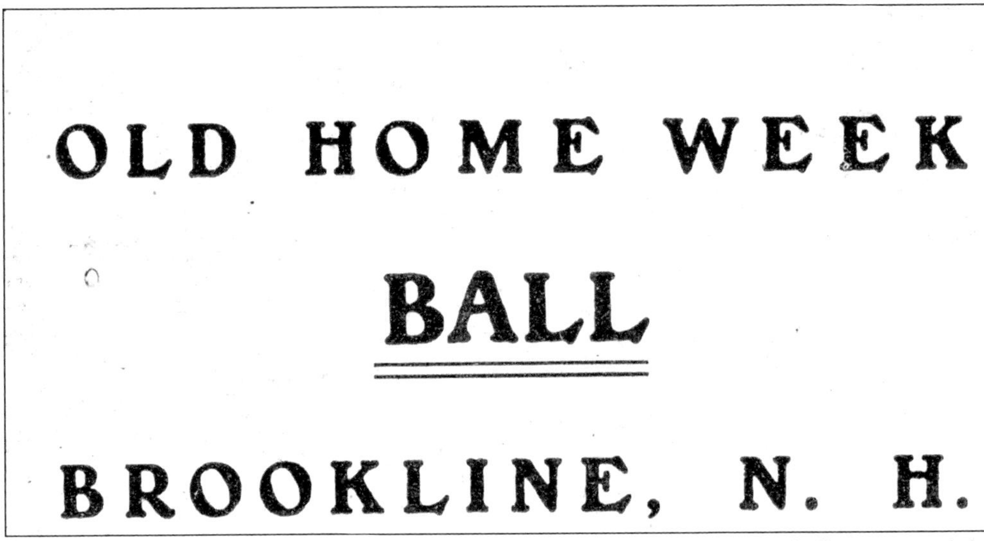

OLD HOME WEEK

BALL

BROOKLINE, N. H.

In the early days of Brookline celebrations, the Brookline Old Home Day ball was one of the highlights of the entire week of events, and a ticket like this one was a coveted item. In 1909, there was dancing from 9:00 p.m. until 2:00 a.m. to the sounds of the Columbia Orchestra of Lawrence, Massachusetts. Floor director was Eldorus C. Fessenden. (Courtesy of Brookline Historical Society.)

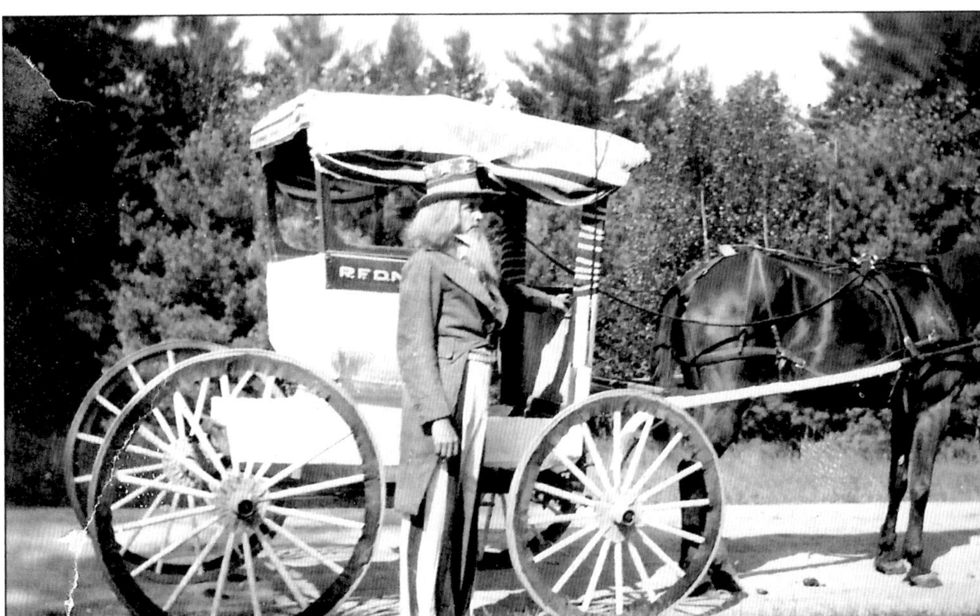

Rural free delivery mail and Uncle Sam are two icons of America represented in this 1921 entry for the Brookline Old Home Day festivities. Uncle Sam's boyhood home was in nearby Mason, but all of New Hampshire had him on display when it was time to celebrate old home days. (Courtesy of Brookline Historical Society.)

The historic Daniels Academy building was featured on the front of the 1924 program for Brookline Old Home Week. Activities that took place in the building during 1924 observances included an apron fair, entertainment by the Ladies Aid Society, and a concert by the Townsend Band. (Courtesy of Brookline Historical Society.)

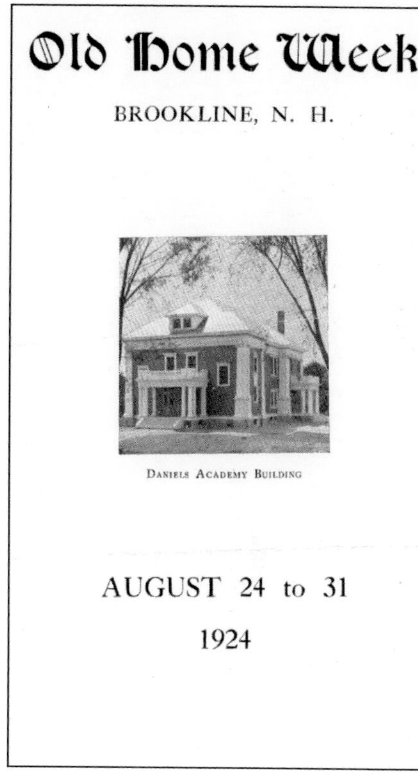

Old Home Week

BROOKLINE, N. H.

DANIELS ACADEMY BUILDING

AUGUST 24 to 31

1924

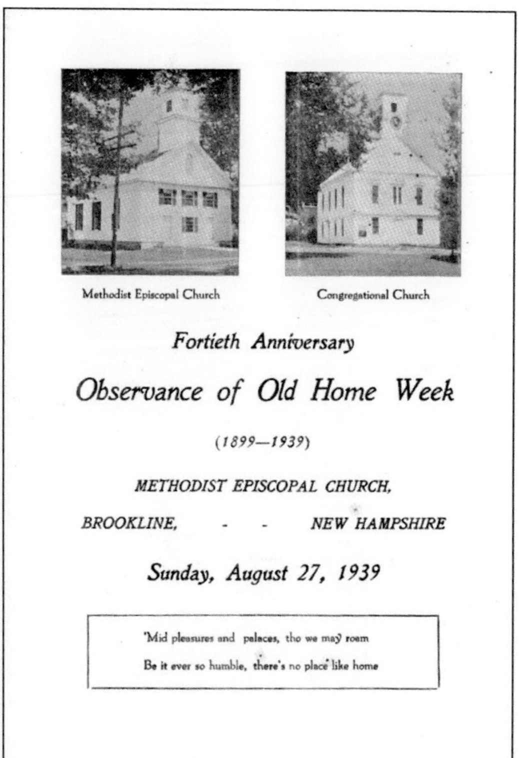

Methodist Episcopal Church

Congregational Church

Fortieth Anniversary

Observance of Old Home Week

(1899—1939)

METHODIST EPISCOPAL CHURCH,

BROOKLINE, - - NEW HAMPSHIRE

Sunday, August 27, 1939

'Mid pleasures and palaces, tho we may roam
Be it ever so humble, there's no place like home

The Methodist Episcopal church and the Congregational church joined their services in the spirit of Brookline Old Home Week in 1939. The ceremonies at the Methodist Episcopal church opened with an organ playing "Home Sweet Home" and closed to the strains of "God Be With You Till We Meet Again." (Courtesy of Brookline Historical Society.)

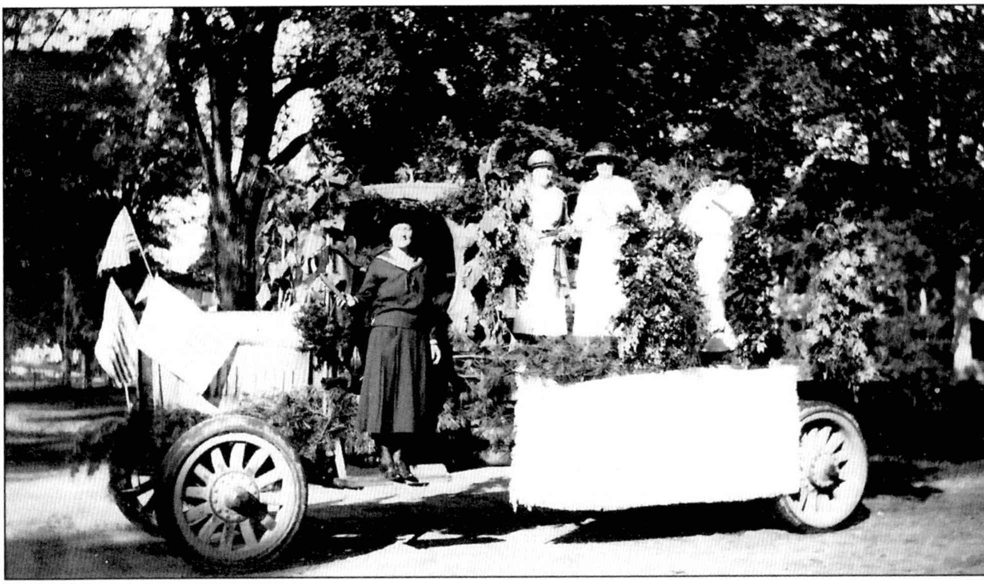

These Brookline ladies posed proudly with their float from the 1921 Brookline Old Home Day celebration. The time spent in preparation for any town's celebrations has always been a factor in the camaraderie created. In Brookline, as in other communities, ladies were always instrumental in the preparations through the main committee, Ladies Aid Society, Grange, or other organizations. (Courtesy of Brookline Historical Society.)

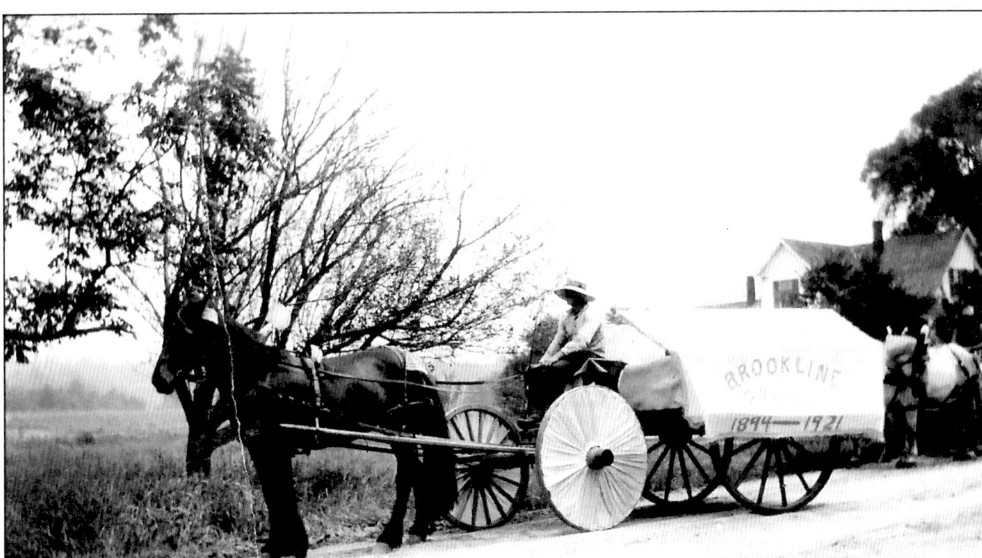

New Hampshire Old Home Week began as a way to reinvigorate rural parts of the state, and the Grange was always an active participant. Shown here is the 1921 float of Brookline Grange No. 211, founded in 1894. Today Grange No. 211 is the combined Brookline/Wilton Grange. (Courtesy of Brookline Historical Society.)

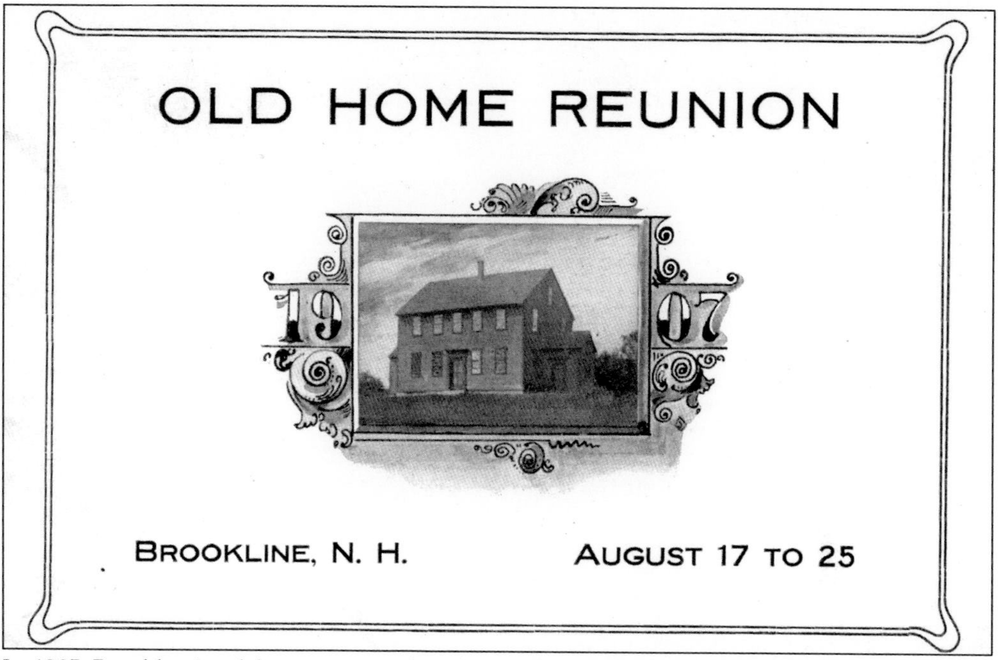

In 1907, Brookline's celebration was referred to as the "old home reunion," and on a town-wide scale, that is just what most communities had. Brookline marked the beginning of what was its sixth-annual old home week with bonfires on neighboring hills and the ringing of church bells. (Courtesy of Brookline Historical Society.)

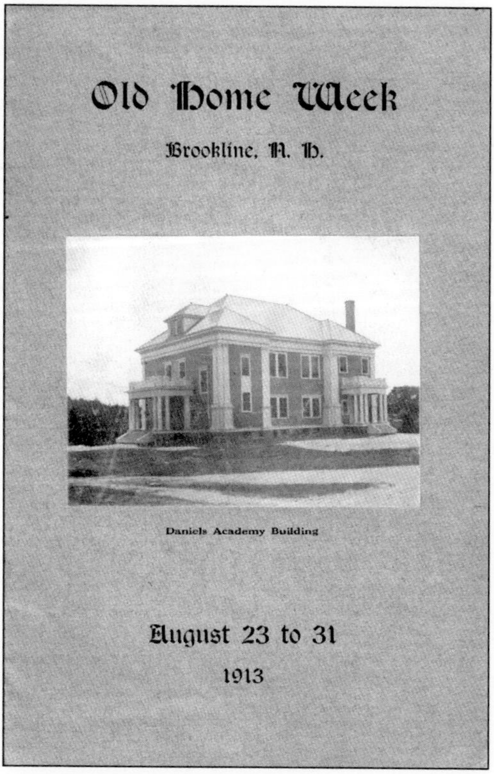

In 1913, Brookline had many neighbors taking part in the festivities. There were concerts by the Townsend Brass Band and Flanagan's Singing Orchestra of Marlboro. On Friday afternoon, a baseball game was held between the Brookline Athletic Association and the visiting Milford Camera Club. (Courtesy of Brookline Historical Society.)

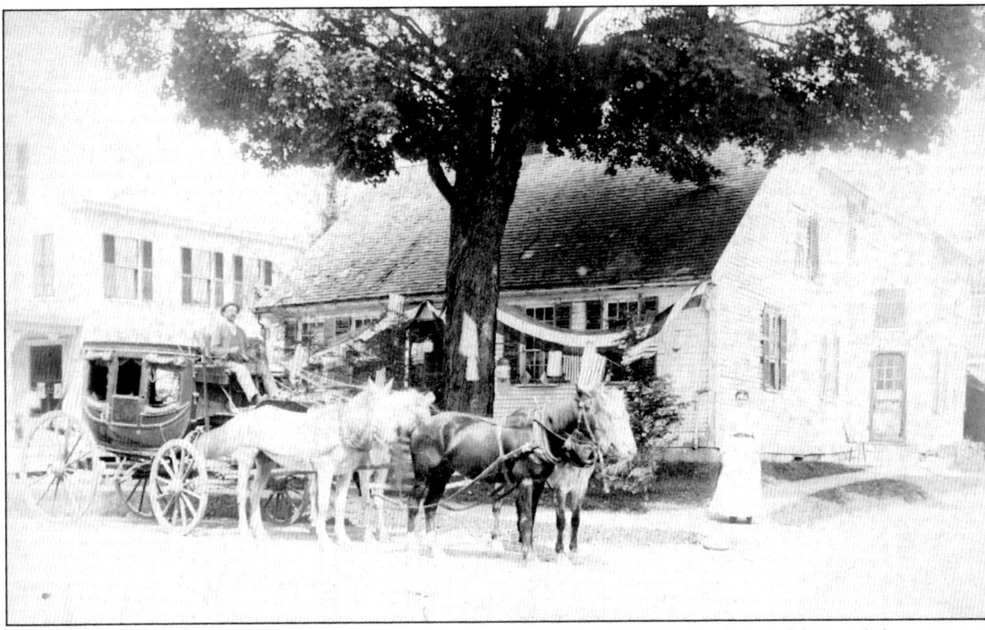

Beginning with its first old home day in 1899, Mont Vernon always hosted big celebrations in the early years. This picture of an early Mont Vernon Old Home Day shows how houses and coaches were decorated. In 1900, Gov. Frank Rollins was on hand for the festivities. The musical highlight was an afternoon performance by the Tobasco Banjo, Mandolin, and Guitar Club of Lowell, Massachusetts. (Courtesy of Mont Vernon Historical Society.)

Philatelists could even get in on the old home spirit, as the state and many towns issued special stationary and stamps in honor of the holiday. Like the idea of old home days, the popularity of coming up with these types of covers spread throughout the region. Today collectors can find the old home day seals from Vermont, Massachusetts, and other states on stamps and envelopes. (Courtesy of Mont Vernon Historical Society.)

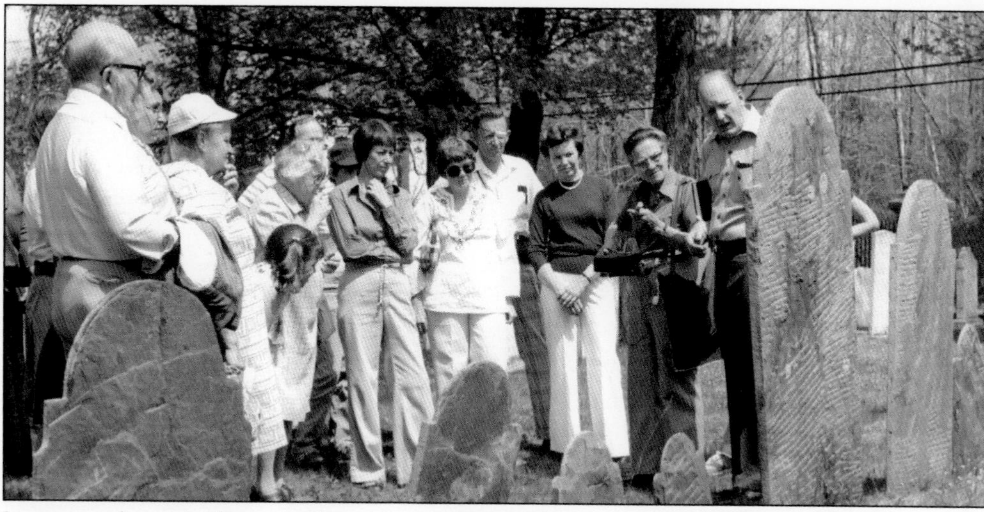

Learning about the history of a town is always a major part of old home days. In this 1978 photograph, Charles E. Buckley on the far right leads a tour and discussion. The tour was named the Greenlawn Cemetery and its Past. (Courtesy of Mont Vernon Historical Society.)

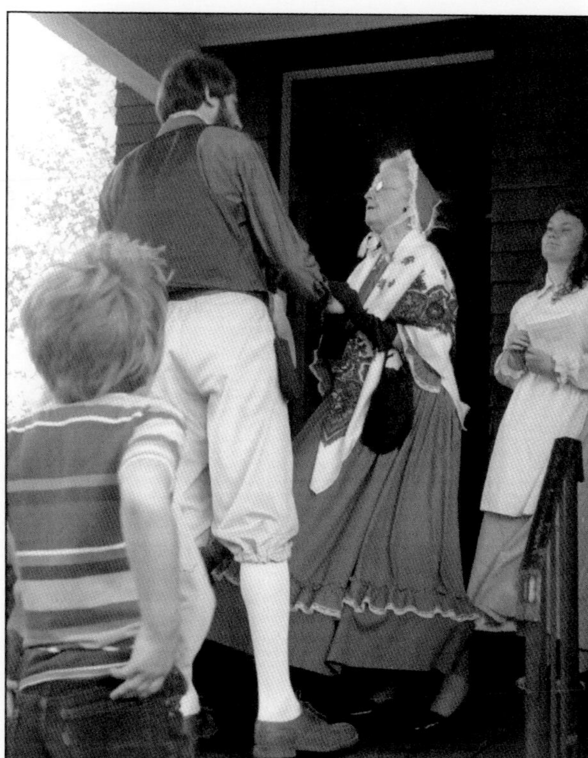

Old home days and the 175th anniversary of the town were the reasons for Mont Vernon residents to don the costumes of their ancestors in 1978. Conversing in the center of this picture are Gary McCullough, with his back to the camera, and Maude Smith. The young lady behind the couple is Jodi Wood. (Courtesy of Mont Vernon Historical Society.)

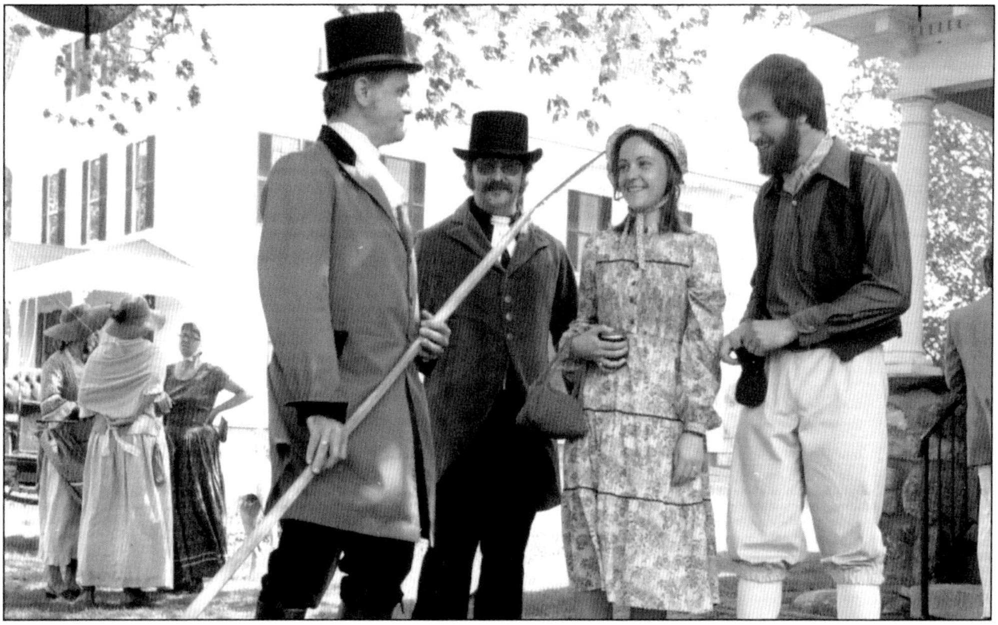

In 1978, the entire town of Mont Vernon was involved for the town's 175th birthday. From left to right, the reenactors pictured are Malcolm Winsor, Pastor Richard Tulip, Jeanne McCullough, and Gary McCullough. When Gov. Frank Rollins arrived in town in 1900 on his tour of towns celebrating the holiday, he was greeted by "forty-four young ladies in white, a platoon of caddie boys, and the First Regiment Band." (Courtesy of Mont Vernon Historical Society.)

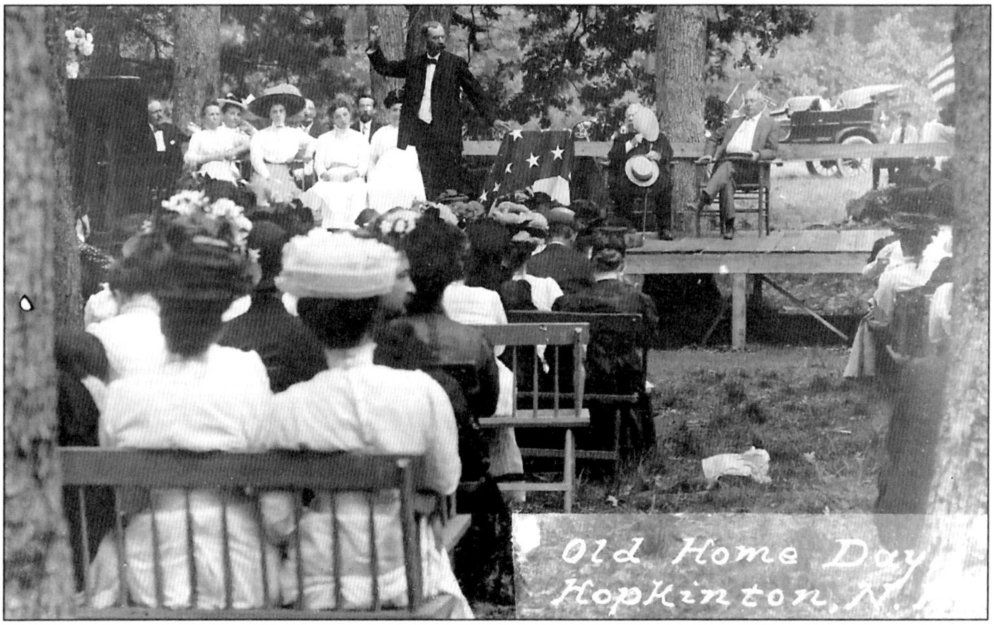

Hopkinton celebrated sporadically early in the century. This postcard of the 1910 Hopkinton Old Home Day shows that orators were popular just like everywhere else. Hopkinton also celebrated along with the town's 150th anniversary in 1915. In 1919, it joined towns throughout the state and used its old home days as a vehicle for welcoming home soldiers. That year, speakers included Gen. Clarence Edwards and Capt. Milton Bebee. (Author's collection.)

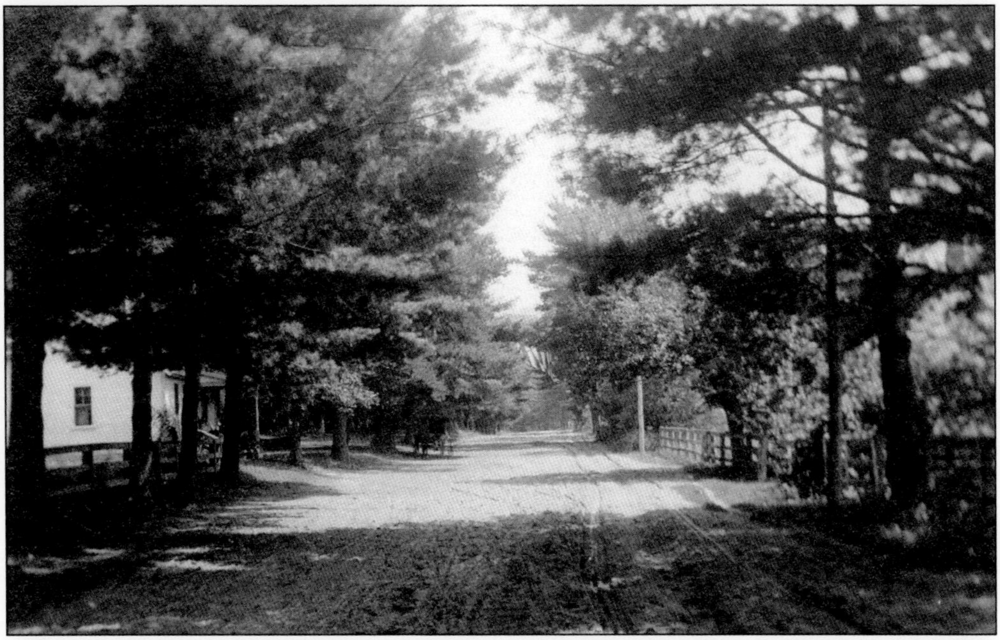

This souvenir from an early Epsom Old Home Day may not seem too festive at first, but tree-lined and dirt-covered main thoroughfares were the norm around 1900. During early old home days, Epsom residents and visitors gathered for picnics and concerts in Tennant's Grove near the old Short Falls railway station. (Courtesy of the Granite State Collection, Sam Allen.)

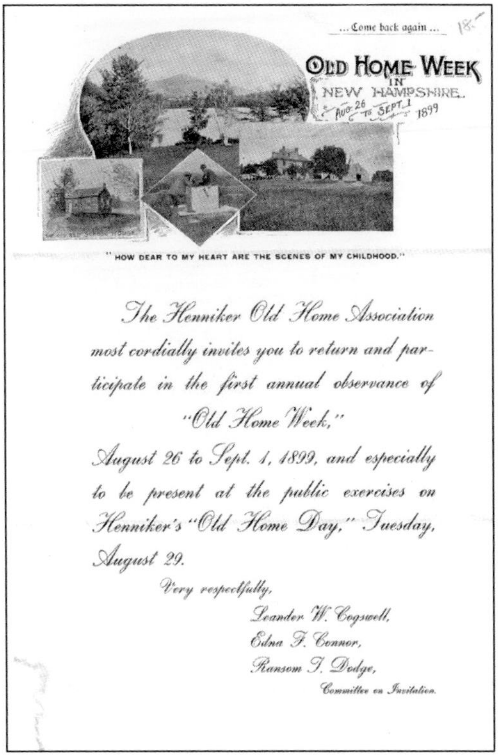

... Come back again ... 18

OLD HOME WEEK IN NEW HAMPSHIRE. AUG 26 TO SEPT 1 1899

"HOW DEAR TO MY HEART ARE THE SCENES OF MY CHILDHOOD."

The Henniker Old Home Association most cordially invites you to return and participate in the first annual observance of "Old Home Week," August 26 to Sept. 1, 1899, and especially to be present at the public exercises on Henniker's "Old Home Day," Tuesday, August 29.

Very respectfully,

Leander W. Cogswell,
Edna F. Connor,
Ransom F. Dodge,
Committee on Invitation.

"How dear to my heart are the scenes of my childhood," was a common theme for all of the towns that first responded to the governor's call. This copy of Henniker's invitation to the very first old home day in 1899 reflects those sentiments. Henniker was also the birthplace of poetess Edna Dean Proctor who penned many poems on the subject of old home days. (Author's collection.)

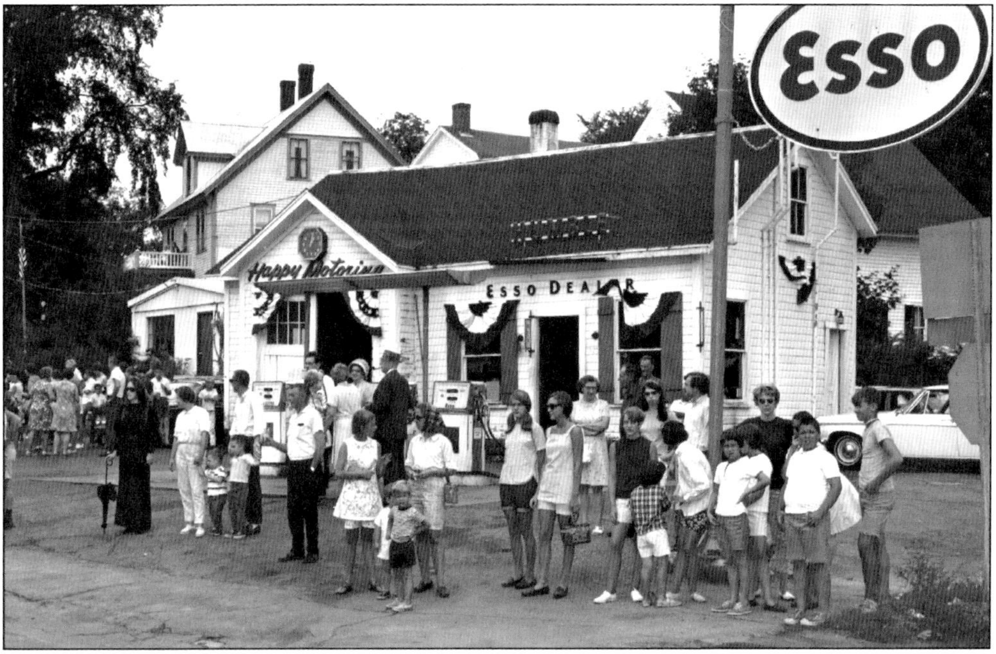

The year 1968 was a turbulent time in most of the world, but in Henniker, the crowds turned out enthusiastically for the old home day parade. Here a crowd waits for the start of the annual parade in the only Henniker on earth. In 1946, Henniker Old Home Days honored World War II soldiers with three full days that included a formal welcome home at the Cogswell Memorial Auditorium. (Courtesy of Henniker Historical Society.)

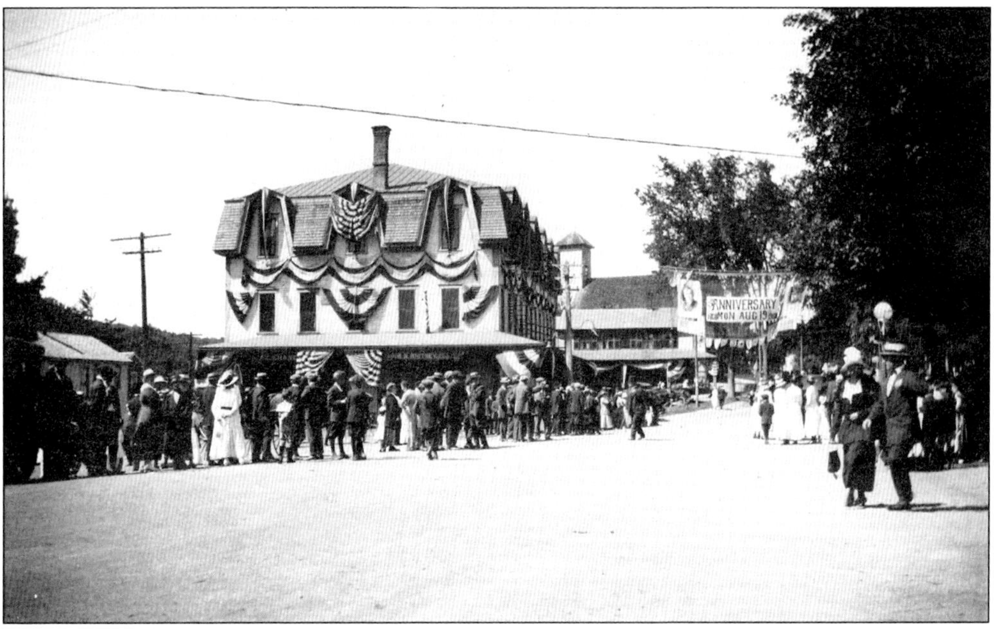

Fans lined the streets to watch the parade and celebrate Henniker Old Home Days and the 150th anniversary of the town's incorporation in 1768. With homecoming on their minds, these 1918 onlookers could not know that the best homecoming of all was just three months away with the November end of World War I. (Courtesy of Henniker Historical Society.)

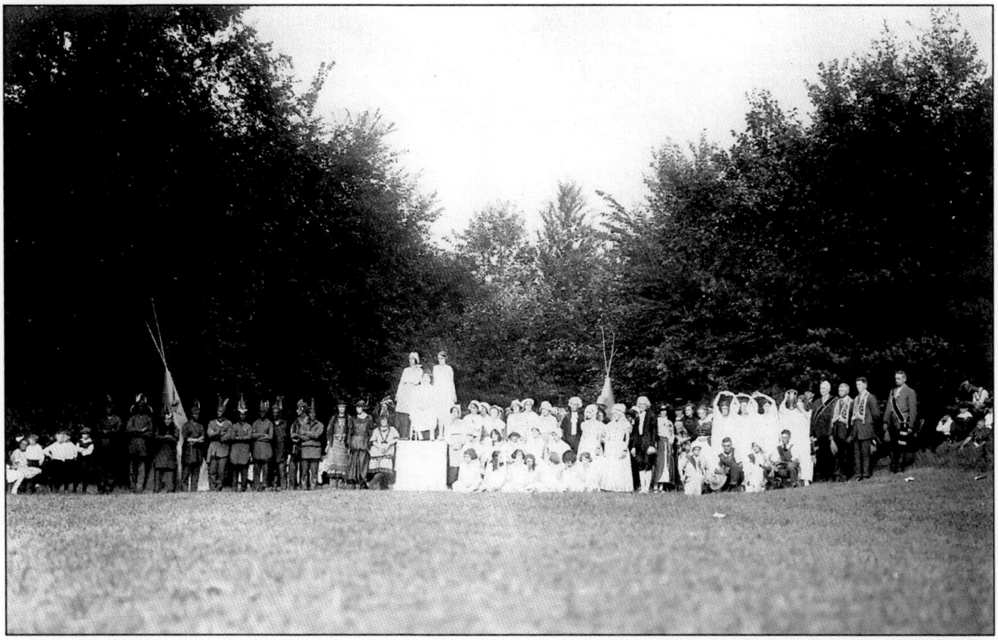

Town pageants were one of the most popular activities at early old home celebrations. Props, costumes, and a lot of preparation went into these town wide projects that centered on the community's history. All of those were evident in this picture of the finale of the 1922 Hooksett Old Home Days pageant. (Author's collection.)

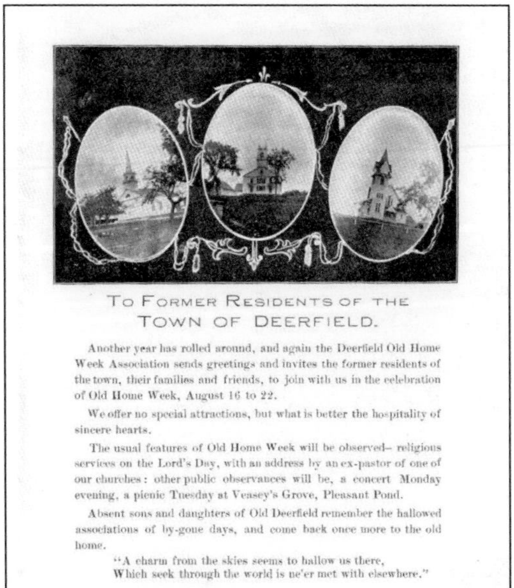

TO FORMER RESIDENTS OF THE TOWN OF DEERFIELD.

Another year has rolled around, and again the Deerfield Old Home Week Association sends greetings and invites the former residents of the town, their families and friends, to join with us in the celebration of Old Home Week, August 16 to 22.

We offer no special attractions, but what is better the hospitality of sincere hearts.

The usual features of Old Home Week will be observed– religious services on the Lord's Day, with an address by an ex-pastor of one of our churches: other public observances will be, a concert Monday evening, a picnic Tuesday at Veasey's Grove, Pleasant Pond.

Absent sons and daughters of Old Deerfield remember the hallowed associations of by-gone days, and come back once more to the old home.

"A charm from the skies seems to hallow us there,
Which seek through the world is ne'er met with elsewhere."

Very cordially,
C. R. BROWN, President.
J. HENRY PRESCOTT, Vice President.
E. S. CHASE, Treasurer.

G. W. BROWN,
BYRON SWETT,
WOODBURY J. HARVEY. } Executive Committee.
GEORGE F. BRADFORD, Secretary.

DEERFIELD, N. H., AUGUST 1, 1902.

This 1902 Deerfield invitation is aimed directly at former residents of the town in an attempt to bring them home for a visit. As with most of the early celebrations, religious ceremonies, music, and community picnics were a large part of the allure. In 1902, Veasey's Park was the site of the Deerfield Old Home Day picnic. (Courtesy of Deerfield Historical Society.)

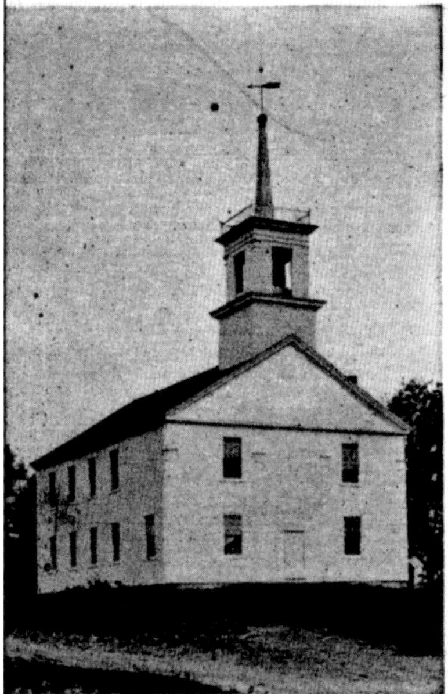

"Should Auld Acquaintance be forgot"

YOU are cordially invited to be present at our

Old Home Day Celebration

Loudon Town Hall

Tuesday, August 18, 1914.

Come and bring your friends.

Per Order,

Invitation Committee.

Spending Tuesday at the town hall was the order of the day for Loudon Old Home Day in 1914, the year the town first observed the holiday. Loudon Old Home Day is still going strong, but now the date is always the second Saturday in August with events taking place at the recreation fields in Loudon Village. (Courtesy of the Granite State Collection, Sam Allen.)

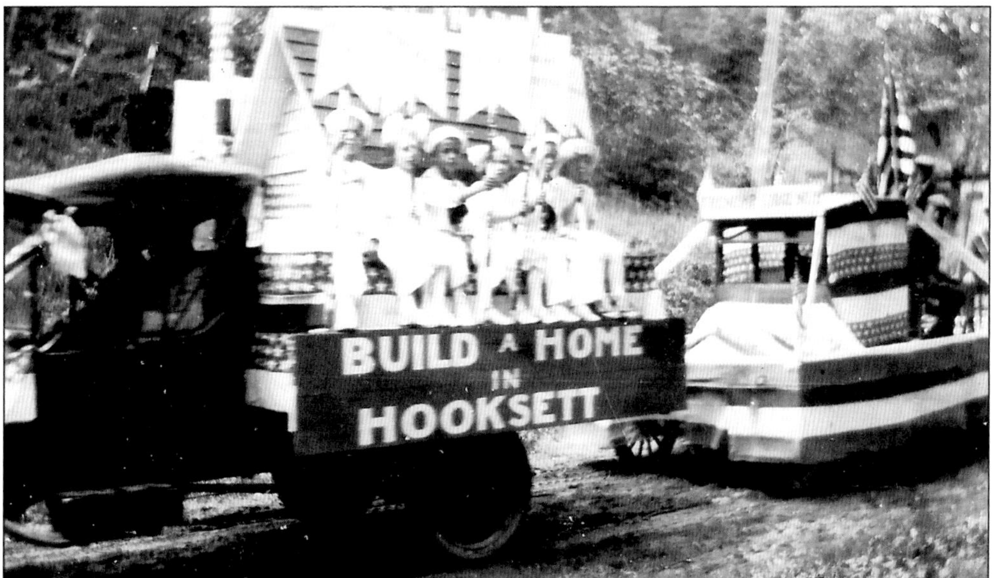

This float, welcoming not just returning natives but also newcomers, was entered by the local board of trade in the 1922 Hooksett Old Home Day parade. That year marked Hooksett's second old home celebration and the 100th anniversary of the town. (Author's collection.)

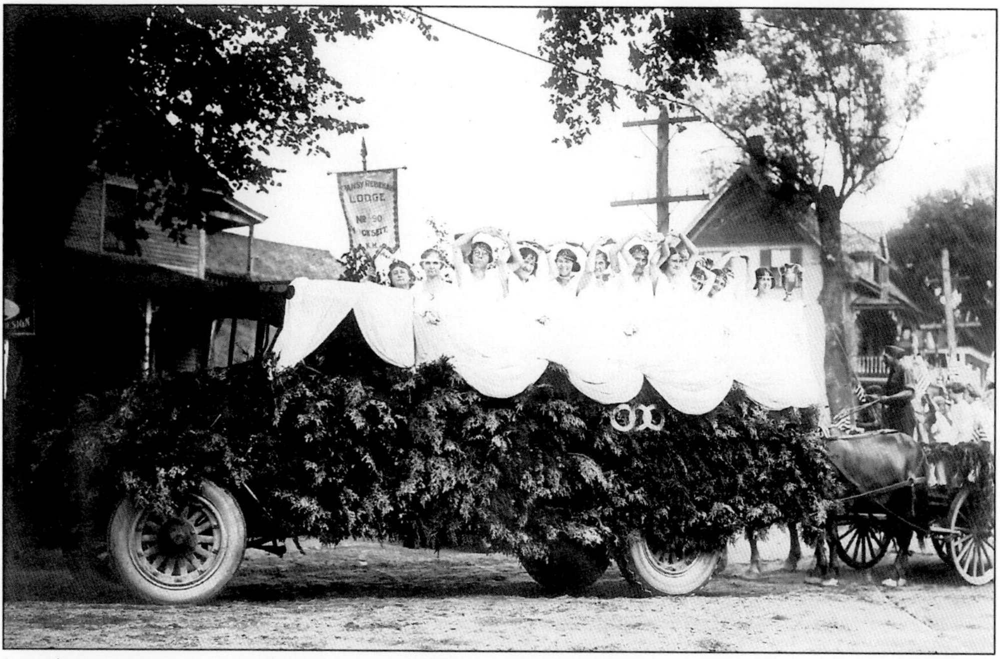

Local organizations are always out in full force when it comes to the old home day parade. In 1922, a crowded float represented the Hooksett Pansy Rebekah lodge. The parade was led by Rainey's Band. Rainey's later had the whole town dancing at a concert and dance held at the public hall. (Author's collection.)

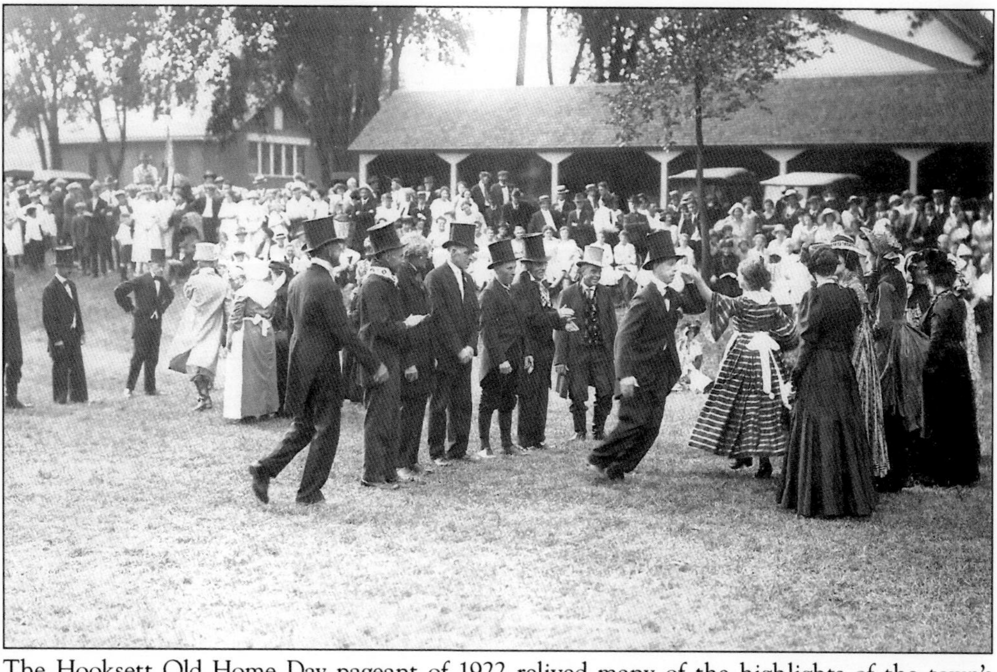

The Hooksett Old Home Day pageant of 1922 relived many of the highlights of the town's past. As part of the commemoration of a visit by Pres. Andrew Jackson in the summer of 1833, dancing of the day was featured. A state historical marker in Bow commemorates the president's visit to the state. (Author's collection.)

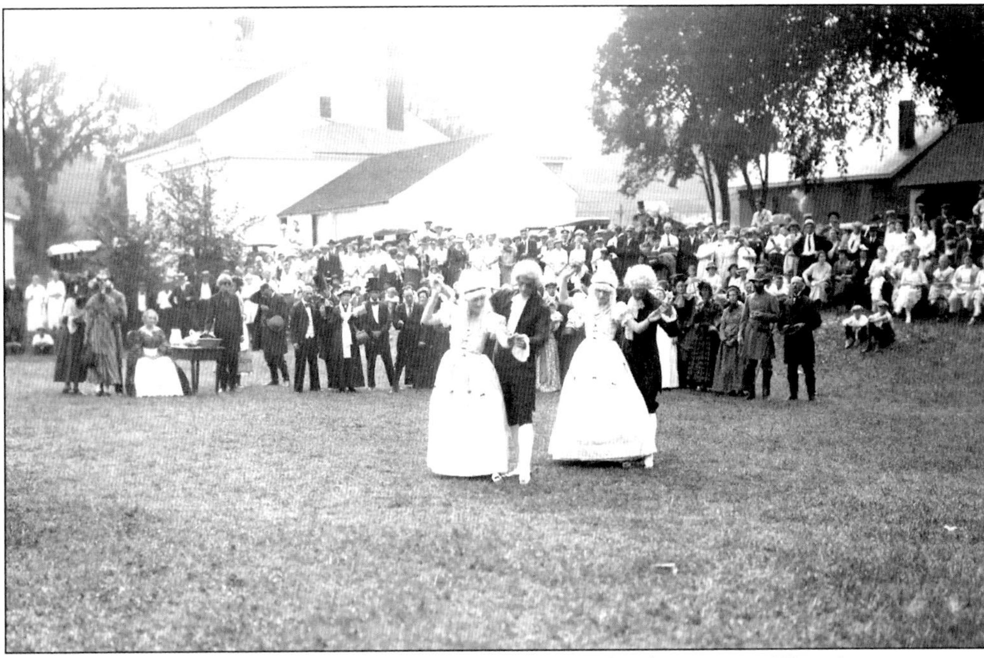

A more genteel form of dance took stage in this portion of Jackson's visit. The play was written by a Miss Dickerman of Concord and was staged by Pearl Johnson of Hooksett. The obviously important and busy role of dance instructor was filled by Margaret Allan of Manchester. (Author's collection.)

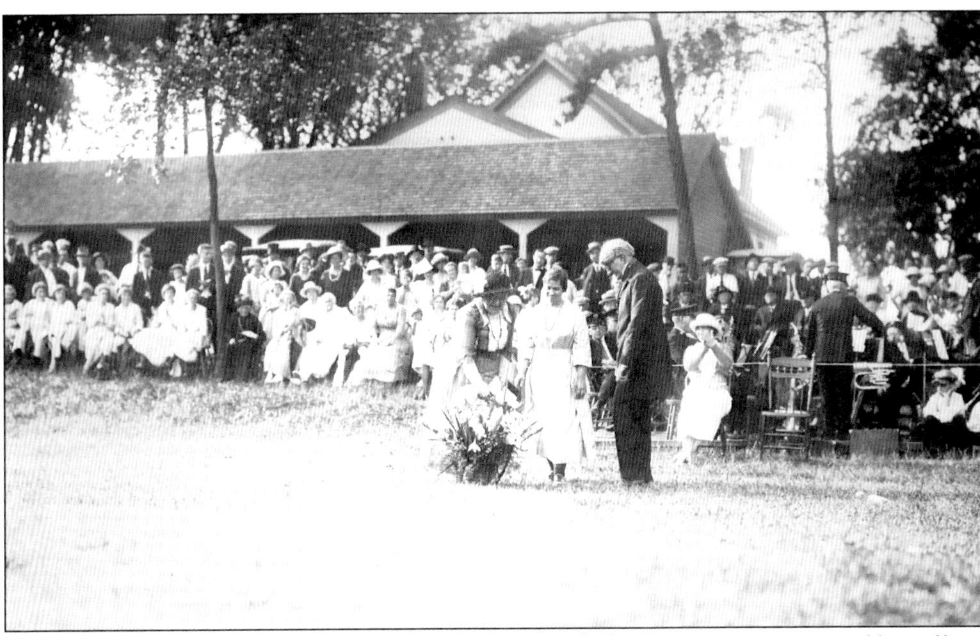

A grateful cast and audience presented Dickerman with flowers in appreciation of her efforts. Organization of the 1922 gala celebration in Hooksett was led by committee president Samuel Head, secretary-treasurer Clifton Sanborn, and executive members John Kimball, Ida M. Gage, and Hild Fozzell. (Author's collection.)

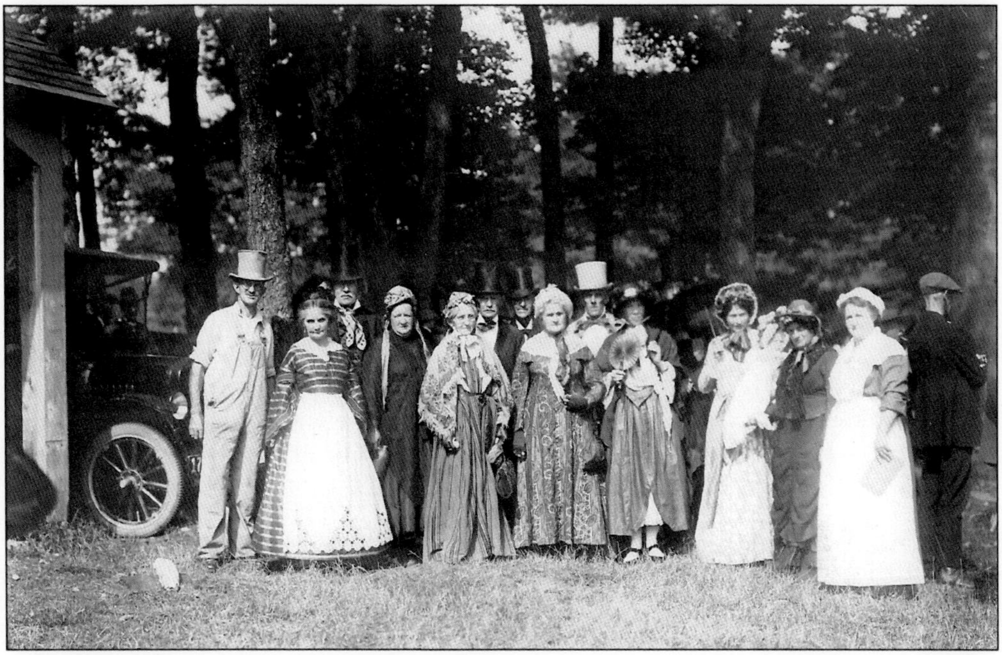

It was Hooksett's old home day in 1922, and this group picture, titled "Ye Old Folk," fit in quite nicely as people took a break from their acting chores. Former pastor J. H. Bliss of Penacook returned for the old home week/centennial festivities and delivered the Sunday sermon at the Congregational church. (Author's collection.)

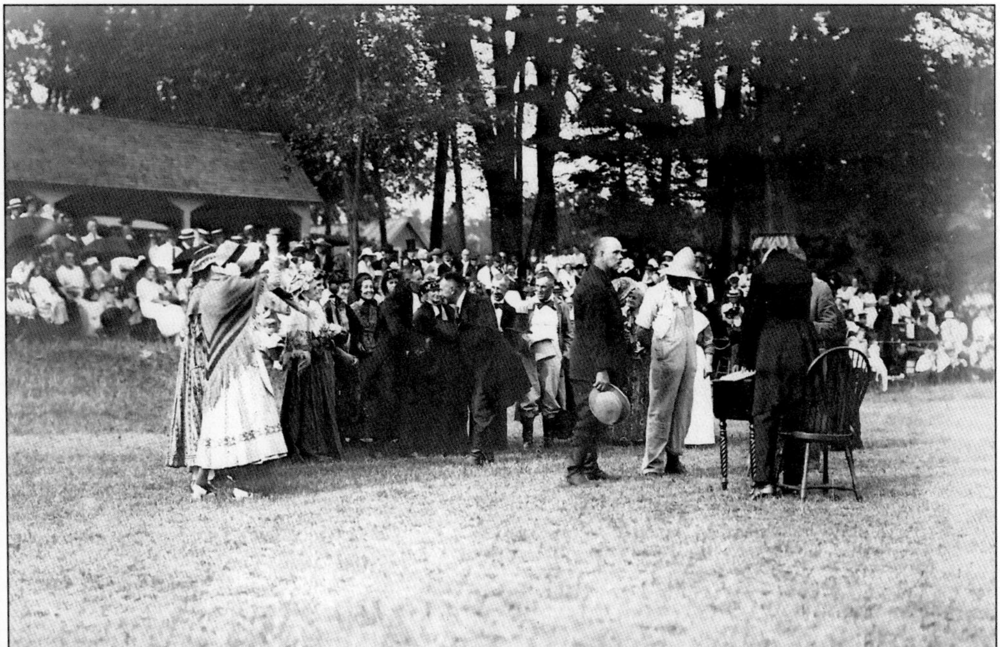

Nothing played a larger role in the political life of New Hampshire than the annual town meeting. This portion of the 1922 Hooksett pageant, *Jackson's Visit*, acknowledged that importance with this reenactment of a typical town meeting scene. (Author's collection.)

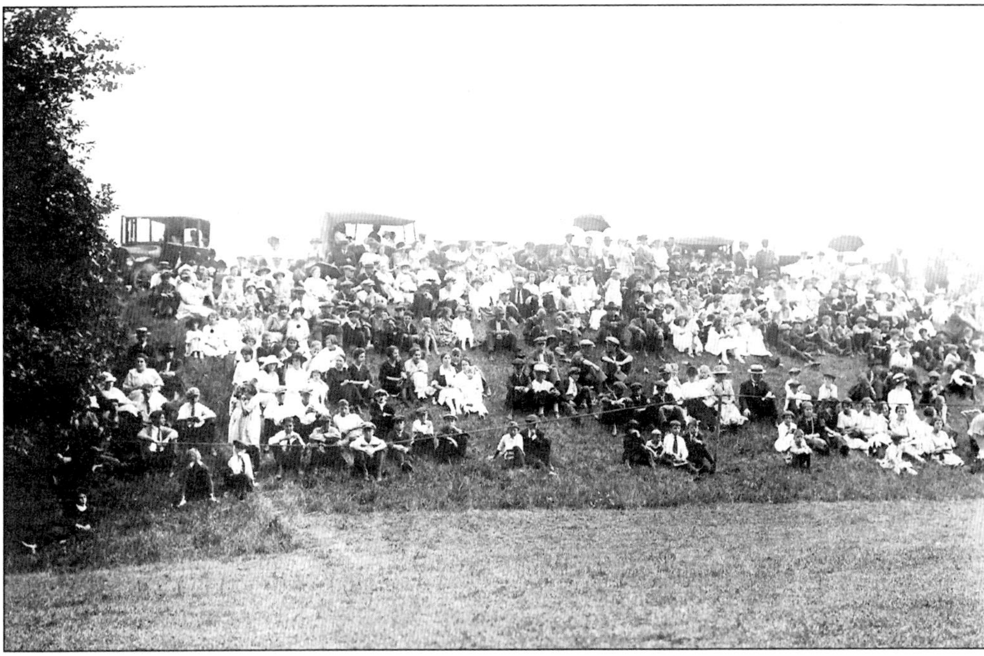

Over 1,200 spectators were estimated to have been on hand for Hooksett's pageant commemorating the visit of Pres. Andrew Jackson to the town. As was the case in many small towns, the only place big enough to house these pageants was the outside. Part of the big crowd is seen here enjoying their natural viewing site for the play. (Author's collection.)

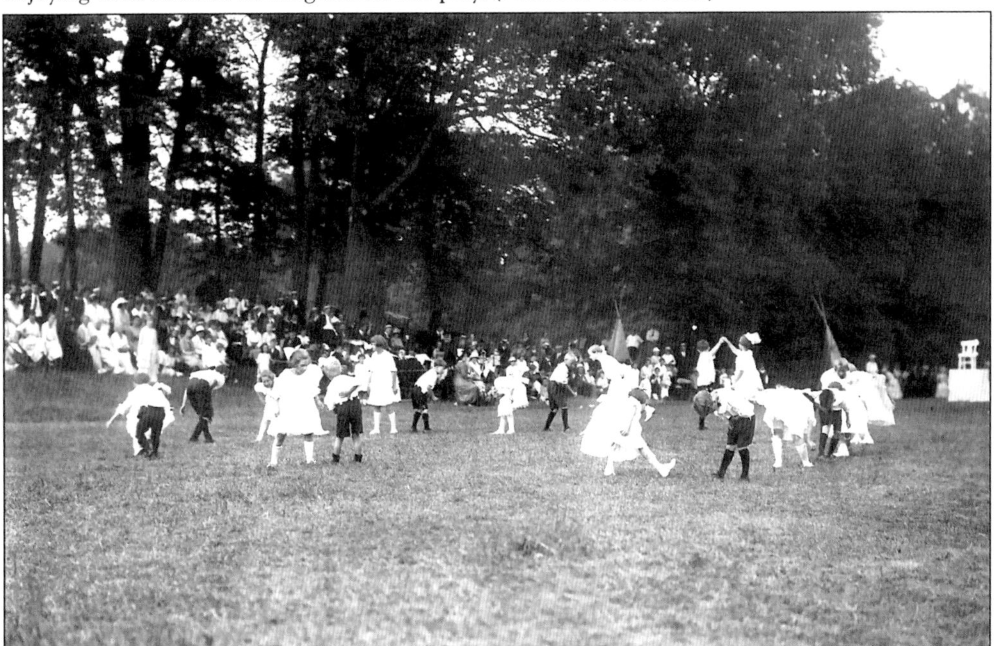

Old home week is about a town's past but always involves and entertains the future citizens. Here local children got in on the party with some dancing of their own during Hooksett's 1922 festivities. Later in the day, Gov. Albert O. Brown was on hand to speak to the crowd. (Author's collection.)

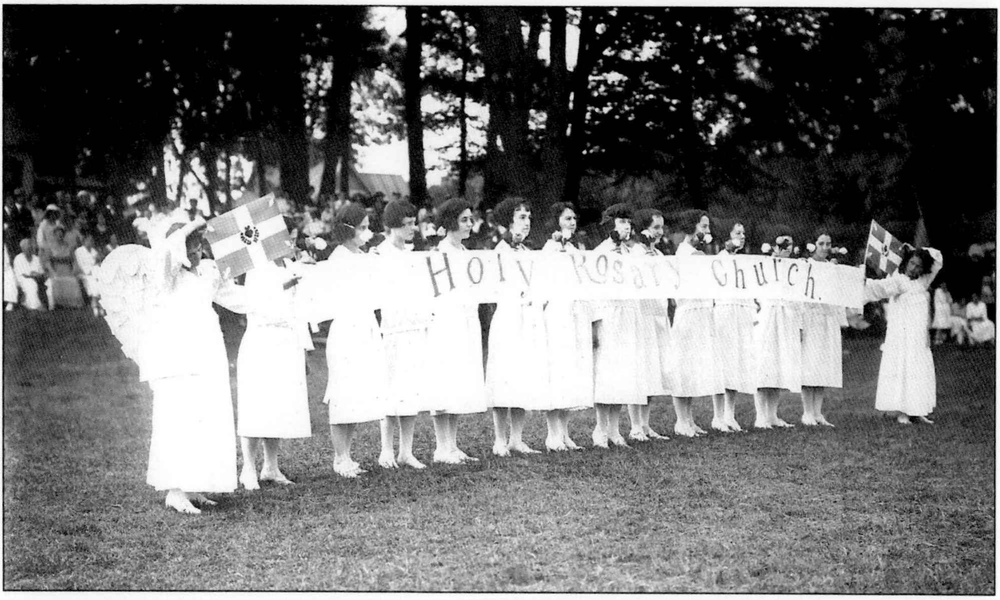

As part of the 1922 Hooksett Old Home Day, this group from the Holy Rosary Church took part in the pageant with this banner. Although 1922 saw Hooksett celebrating in August, the town moved its event a few years earlier. In 1919, it moved ceremonies to Labor Day to welcome home soldiers from World War I. (Author's collection.)

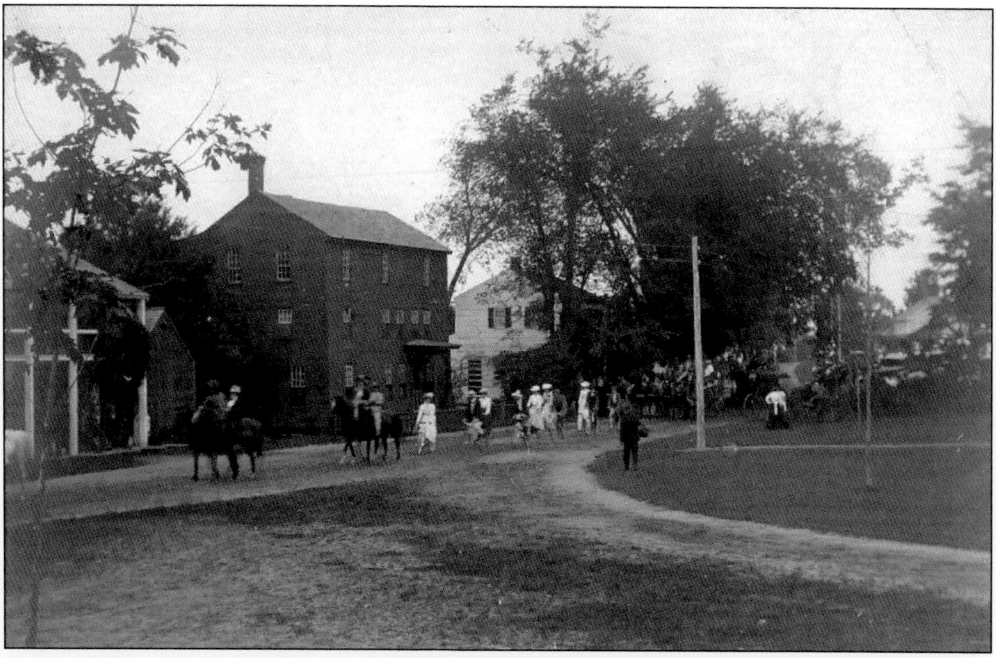

This was the scene at parade time for Weare's first old home day on August 29, 1900, in Weare Center. The parade included over 60 bicycle riders, and the entire day's events were presided over by Medora Edmunds Currier. A special train made a trip from Manchester to bring seven carloads of participants to Weare for the occasion. (Courtesy of Weare Historical Society.)

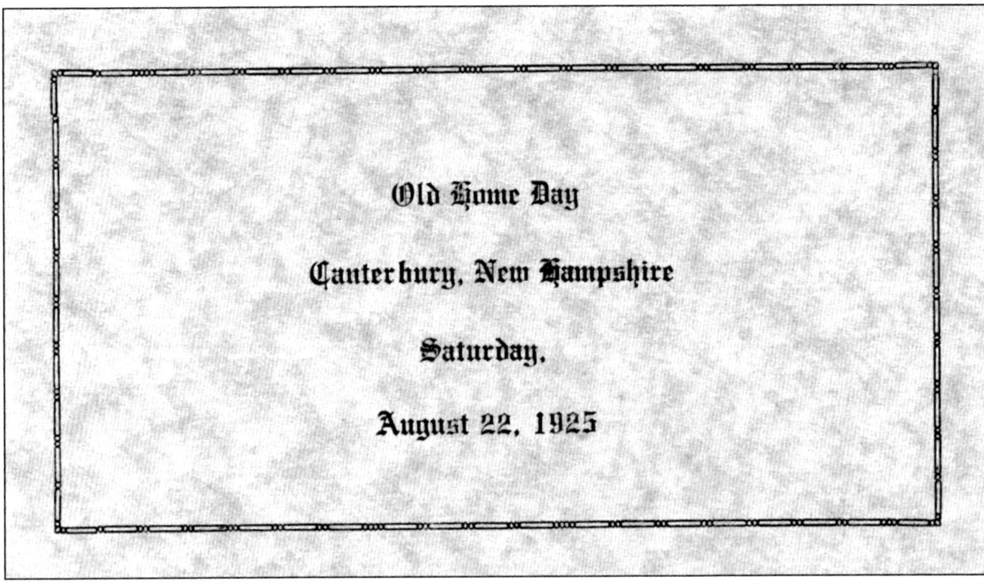
Old Home Day

Canterbury, New Hampshire

Saturday,

August 22, 1925

Canterbury's 1925 celebration was a one-day affair, but it was a full day that included a baseball game pitting the town's married men against the single men. After the game concluded in a tie score, basket lunches were the order of the day with free hot coffee served by the Ladies Aid Society. (Courtesy of the Granite State Collection, Sam Allen.)

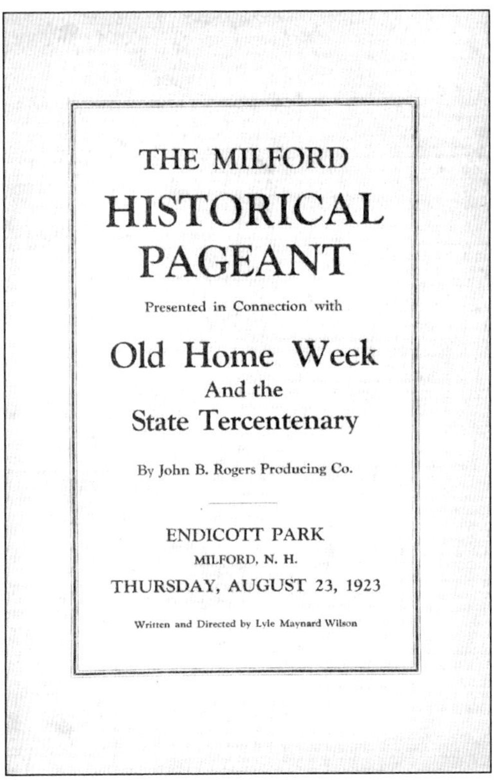
THE MILFORD

HISTORICAL PAGEANT

Presented in Connection with

Old Home Week

And the

State Tercentenary

By John B. Rogers Producing Co.

ENDICOTT PARK

MILFORD, N. H.

THURSDAY, AUGUST 23, 1923

Written and Directed by Lyle Maynard Wilson

Although it does not have a long history of old home day participation, Milford did get on board in 1923 with a historical pageant that involved the talents of over 300 townspeople. Another highlight of the day was a baseball game between a group of veterans and the East Milfords. (Courtesy of the Granite State Collection, Sam Allen.)

Bonfires were an early component of old home day observances, and Nashua's must have been one of the most impressive in 1902. Thousands watched from Godfrey Heights in the south end of the city as officials lit 1,200 railroad ties, 25 cords of wood, 120 barrels of shavings, 5 cords of slabs, 300 empty barrels, 100 barrels of tar, and 50 street railway poles. (Courtesy of the Granite State Collection, Sam Allen.)

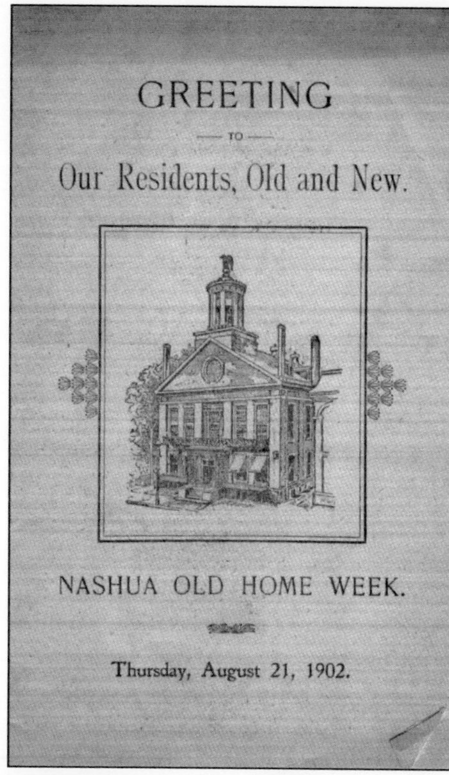
GREETING

TO

Our Residents, Old and New.

NASHUA OLD HOME WEEK.

Thursday, August 21, 1902.

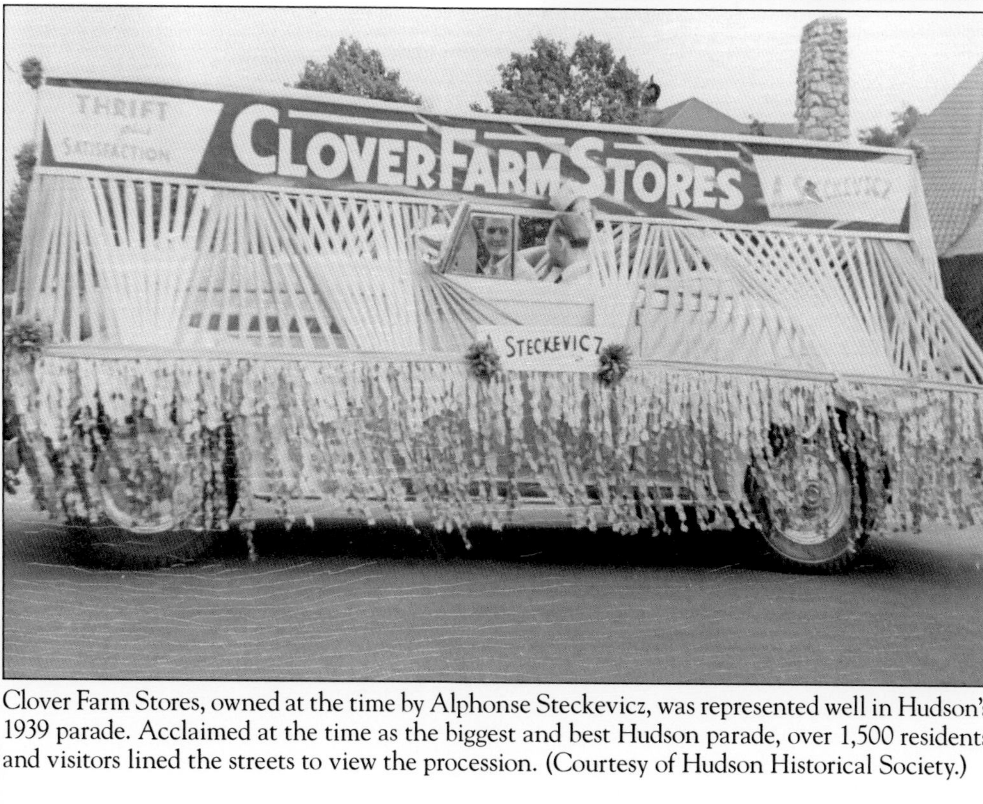

Clover Farm Stores, owned at the time by Alphonse Steckevicz, was represented well in Hudson's 1939 parade. Acclaimed at the time as the biggest and best Hudson parade, over 1,500 residents and visitors lined the streets to view the procession. (Courtesy of Hudson Historical Society.)

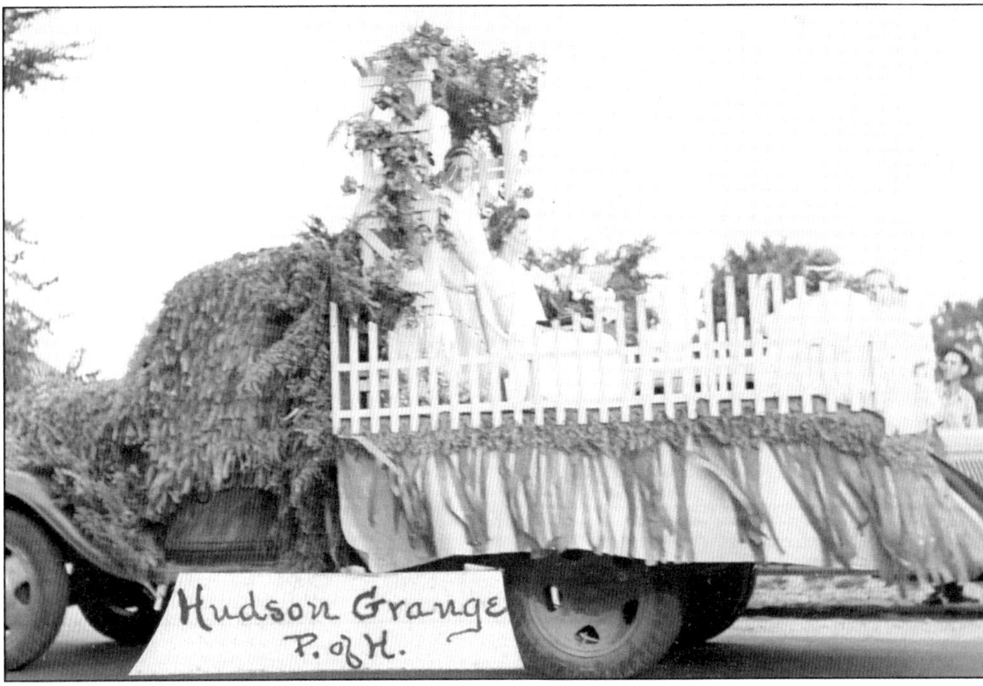

The Hudson Grange, always an active participant in old home week celebrations, was front and center again in 1939. In addition to entering this parade float, the Wattannick Grange also presented an old home program earlier in the week. (Courtesy of Hudson Historical Society.)

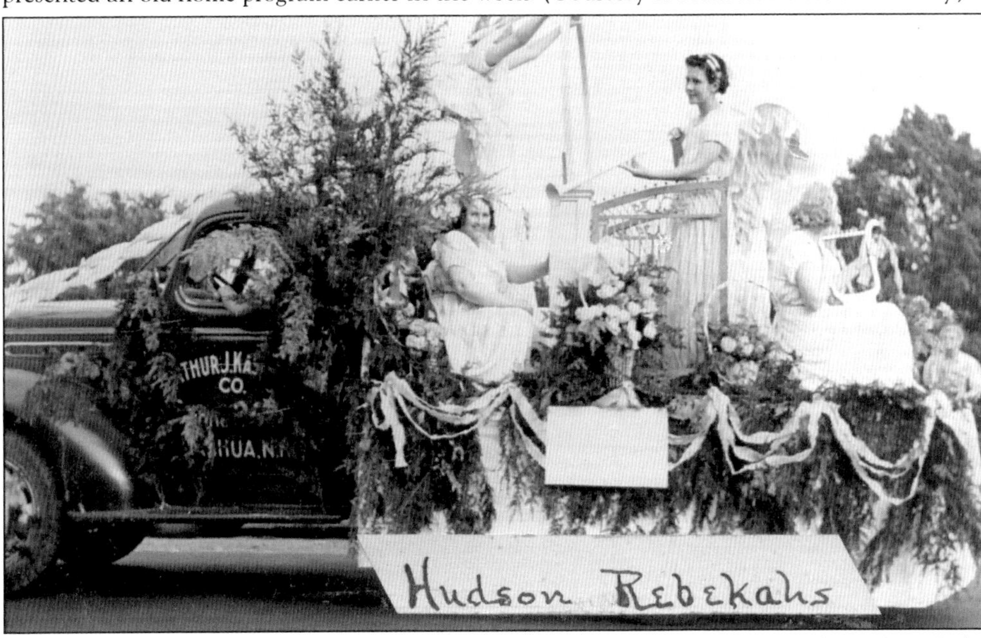

As in many New Hampshire towns, the Rebekahs, the ladies auxiliary of the Independent Order of Odd Fellows, was one of the more active groups in town and almost always participated in the parade. Following the parade, Arthur S. Andrews, a Hudson native and president of the Hudson Old Home Week Association, presided over a short program of speeches and music. (Courtesy of Hudson Historical Society.)

Over the first 50 years of old home celebrations in New Hampshire, many towns regularly reported to the state organization about their activities for a given year. Shown here is a list of reporting towns for the year 1900. (Courtesy of Hudson Historical Society.)

STATE OF NEW HAMPSHIRE.

OLD HOME WEEK ASSOCIATION.

CONCORD, July 14, 1900.

The following local Old Home Week associations and dates of meetings for 1900 have been reported to this office.

TOWN.	PRESIDENT.	DATE.
Alstead,	E. M. Smith,	
Andover,	Henry A. Weymouth, M. D.,	August 14.
Antrim,	W. C. Hills,	
Boscawen,		
Bristol,	Ira A. Chase,	
Claremont,	Dr. O. B. Way,	
Chesterfield,		
Concord,	Hon. J. B. Walker,	August 17.
Deerfield,		August 15.
Dunbarton,	Col. William H. Stinson,	August 15. 1st
Eaton,	Dr. C. M. Stanley,	August 15.
Epsom,	Warren Tripp,	August 15.
Francestown,	E. W. Farnum,	
Freedom,	S. W. Fowler,	August 16.
Gilford,	Thomas E. Hunt,	
Gilsum,	Israel A. Loveland, M. D.,	August 14.
Grantham,	Imla S. Brown,	August 15.
Hancock,	Charles H. Dutton,	August 23.
Hanover,	John M. Fuller,	August 16.
Henniker,	Hon. George C. Preston,	August 14.
Hollis,	Hon. Franklin Worcester,	August 15.
Hudson,	Kimball Webster,	
Kensington,	Charles E. Tuck,	August 15.
Lebanon,	Charles E. Cooper,	
Lempster,	Andrew J. Mitchell,	
Litchfield,	Rev. John P. Newell,	
Londonderry,	Wesley Adams,	August 11.
Marlborough,	Merrill Mason,	August 14.
Marlow,	Elgin A. Jones,	August 16.
Merrimack,	Walter Kittredge,	August 17.
Milan,	D. M. Cairns.	August 16.
Mont Vernon,	Hon George A. Marden,	August 15.
New Hampton,	Richard Pattee,	August 14.
Newton,	Enoch H. Nichols,	
Nottingham,	James H. Kelsey, 2d,	
Pembroke,	George E. Fowler,	August 14.
Peterborough,	Ezra M. Smith,	August 18.
Piermont,	George H. Reneau,	August 16.
Rochester,	Horatio L. Cate,	
Rollinsford,	Joseph D. Roberts,	August 11.
Salem,	Charles T. Woodbury,	August 14.
Sandwich,	Charles B. Hoyt,	August 15.
Somersworth,	Hon. A. J. Seavey,	
South Hampton,	Jacob Eaton,	August 15.
Springfield,	Hon. Charles McDaniel,	August 13.
Stark,	C. A. Cole,	August 15.
Stoddard,	Charles H. Merrill,	
Surry,	M. H. Porter,	
Temple,	Prof. Martin H. Fisk,	
Walpole,	Hon. T. Nelson Hastings,	August 14.
Washington,	Sumner N. Ball,	August 15.
Weare,	Mrs. Medora Currier,	August 14.
Webster,	William W. Burbank,	August 14.
Westmoreland,	Willard Bill, Jr.,	August 16.
Whitefield,	Frank Swett,	August 21.
Winchester,	George W. Pierce,	
Windham,	Horace Berry,	
Wolfeborough,	Hon. Sewall W. Abbott,	
Woodstock,	Elmer E. Woodbury,	August 15.

N. J. BACHELDER, *Secretary.*

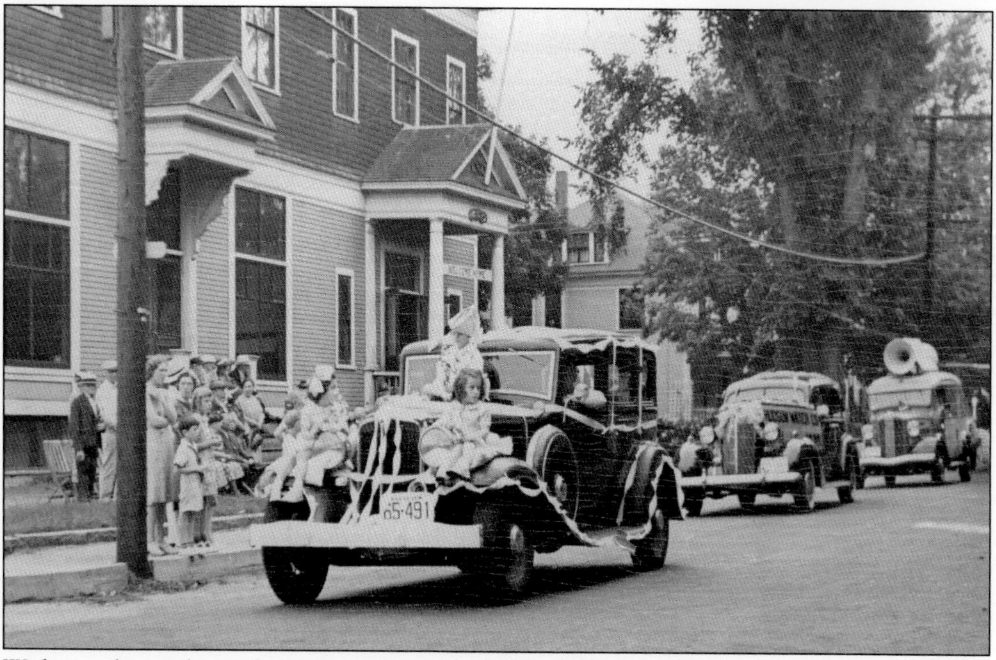

With a welcome home banner on the Odd Fellows hall in the background, three youngsters adorn the float of John Baker. Small-town residents are apt to wear many hats during old home week. In addition to his parade entry, Baker was also in charge of the old home dance held in the evening. (Courtesy of Hudson Historical Society.)

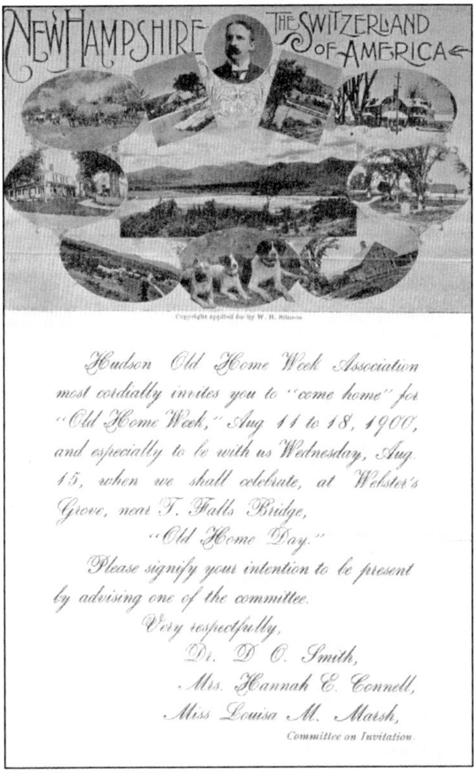

NEW HAMPSHIRE THE SWITZERLAND OF AMERICA

Copyright applied for by W. H. Stinson

Hudson Old Home Week Association most cordially invites you to "come home" for "Old Home Week," Aug 11 to 18, 1900, and especially to be with us Wednesday, Aug. 15, when we shall celebrate, at Webster's Grove, near T. Falls Bridge, "Old Home Day."

Please signify your intention to be present by advising one of the committee.

Very respectfully,

Dr. D. O. Smith,

Mrs. Hannah E. Connell,

Miss Louisa M. Marsh,

Committee on Invitation.

This ornate invitation invited Hudson residents to take part in the state's second old home celebration in 1900. Festivities began at Webster Grove until an afternoon shower drove residents inside the Methodist church. Also held in conjunction with the day's events was the annual reunion of the Cummings family. (Courtesy of Hudson Historical Society.)

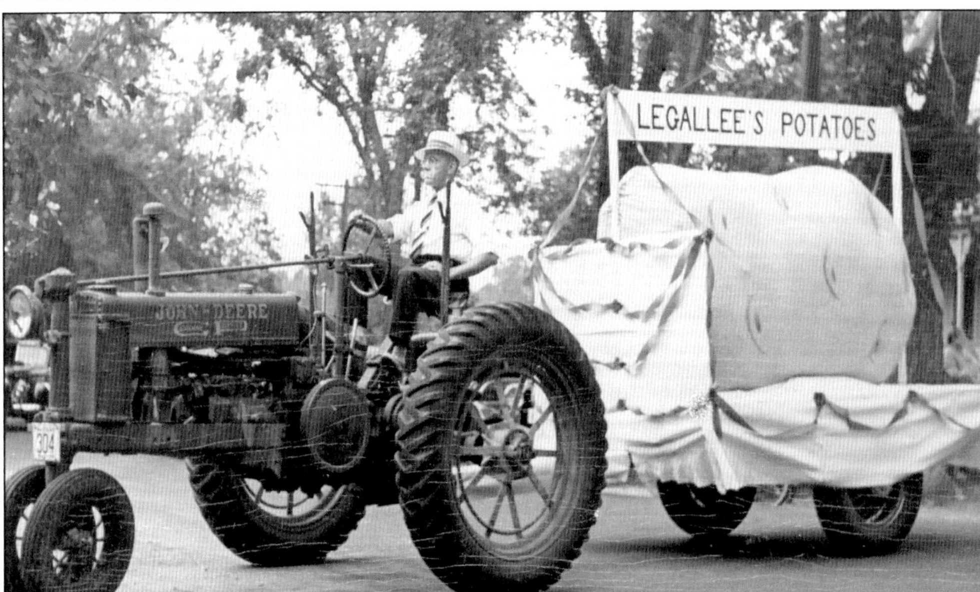

Agriculture played a larger role in Hudson life in 1939, and Legallee's Potatoes was a familiar name to residents. A large part of the program following the old home parade was given over to the recognition of longtime residents and natives of Hudson. Rev. Fred Winn, a descendent of some of Hudson's earliest settlers, presented the event's invocation. Winn traveled from his home in Redwood, California, for the celebration. (Courtesy of Hudson Historical Society.)

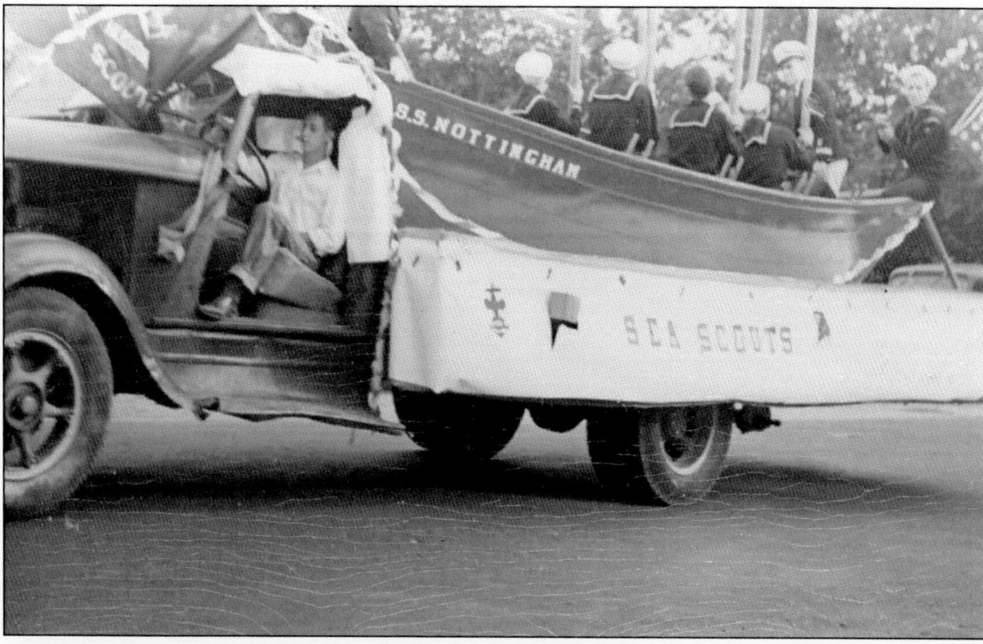

Sea Scouts, members of the international scouting movement, were on hand for the 1939 parade. Today the annual Hudson Old Home Days take place over four days in early August. The festivities are sponsored by the Hudson Historical Society and held on the grounds of the historic Hills House. (Courtesy of Hudson Historical Society.)

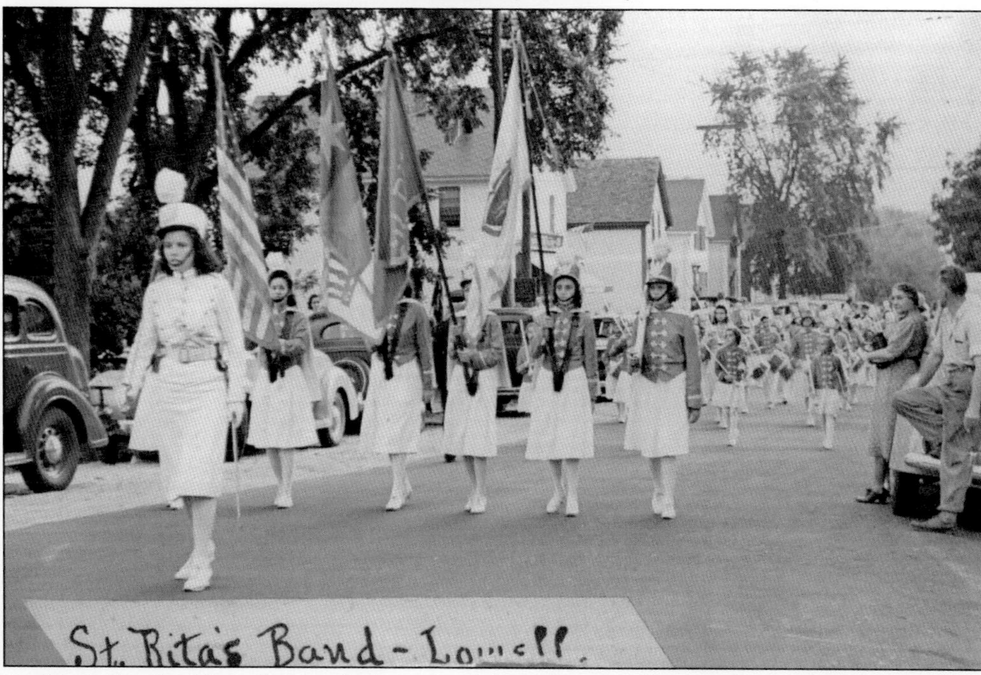

St. Rita's Band of Lowell provided much of the music for the parade in 1939. In 1900, the guest speaker for what was then just a one-day event was Judge Samuel P. Hadley, who also made the trek from Lowell to play a part in the Hudson celebration. (Courtesy of Hudson Historical Society.)

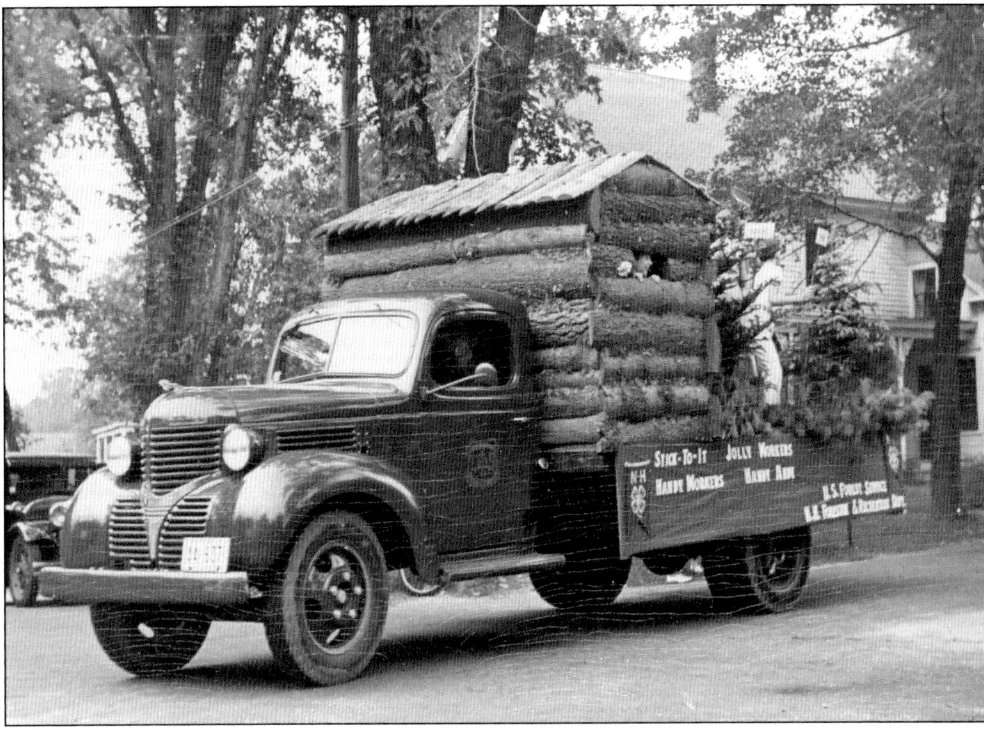

The beginning of the week was stormy for Hudson's 1939 old home day celebration, but by parade day, the sun was shining and the crowds were out. It was estimated that over 1,500 spectators lined the streets on August 24 to watch the floats, including this joint effort of the U.S. Forestry Service and the local 4-H club. (Courtesy of Hudson Historical Society.)

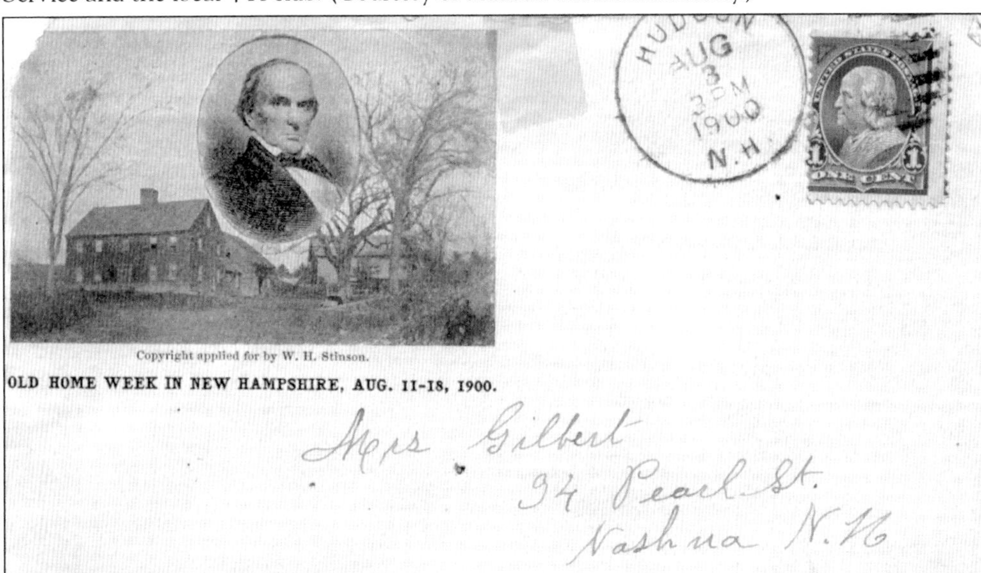

Old home celebrations were aimed at honoring those who stayed in New Hampshire and those who moved away. One favorite New Hampshire son celebrated throughout the state during local festivities was Daniel Webster, who was born and educated in the state. Tributes like this one on old home stationary were common. (Courtesy of Hudson Historical Society.)

Today most towns have gone their own way and celebrate according to each community's wishes. At the beginning of the 20th century, the structure of organization was from the top down, and state officials were quick to let towns know if they were overdue in reporting their plans for the coming year. (Courtesy of Hudson Historical Society.)

State Officers.

President,
Frank W. Rollins.

Secretary,
N. J. Bachelder.

Treasurer,
H. H. Dudley.

Executive Committee,
E. N. Pearson,
H. H. Metcalf,
W. H. Stinson.

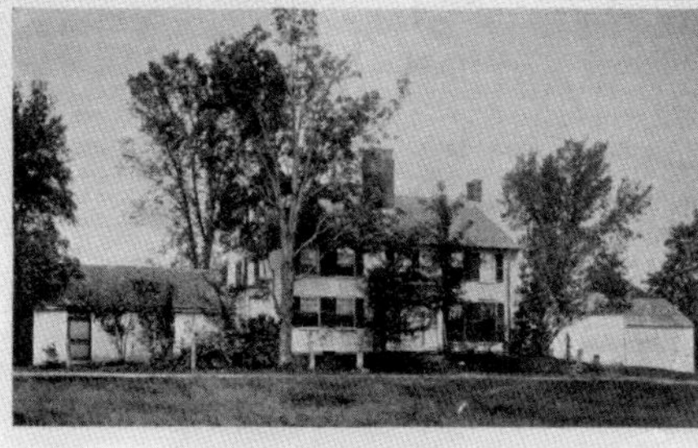

"MY OLD NEW HAMPSHIRE HOME."

OLD HOME WEEK IN New Hampshire.

August 17–24, 1901.

Concord, N. H., June 28, 1901.

Secretary,
Old Home Week Association,
Hudson, N.H.,

Dear Sir:

The state association has not yet received any report as to the likelihood of an Old Home Day observance in your town this year. We are preparing an official list of towns and dates, where and when observances will be held and should very much like to include Hudson. I hope to hear from you favorably in the matter at your convenience.

Yours sincerely,

N. J. Bachelder

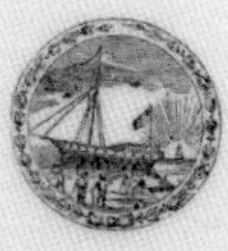

The Hudson Old Home Association

Cordially invites you to participate in the enjoyment of

"Old Home Week," August 16-23, 1902,

And especially solicits your presence Friday, Aug. 22, at Hudson Center, where we hope to meet and greet our friends of

Auld Lang Syne

in a public observance of "Old Home Day"

Please signify your intention to be present by advising one of the Committee.

Very Respectfully,

Dr. D. O. Smith,
Miss Louisa M. Marsh,
Miss Gertrude A. Merrill, } Committee.

This 1902 invitation to Hudson residents promised and delivered a good time for all who answered the call. Among the 1902 highlights were beacon bonfires from atop Barretts Hill, religious services by all three local pastors, and selections of music by the visiting Wilton Orchestra. (Courtesy of Hudson Historical Society.)

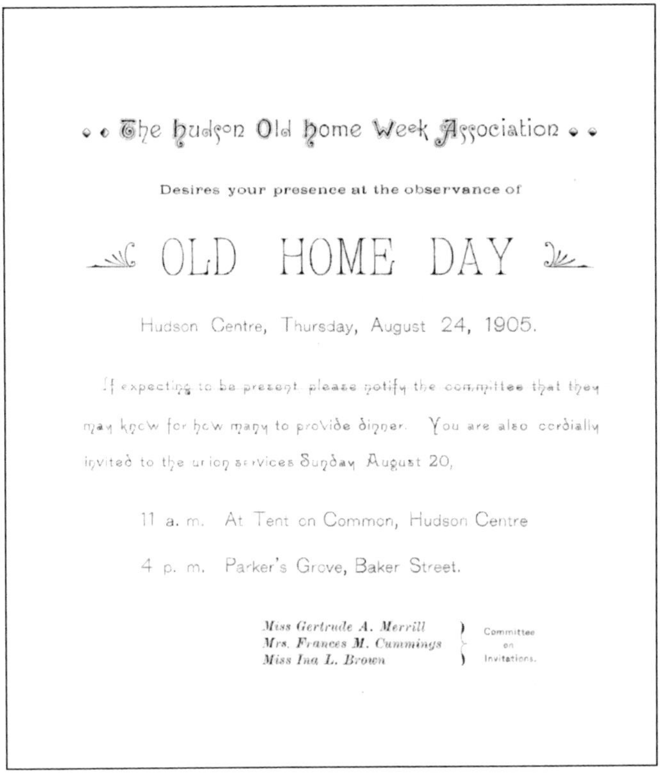

The Hudson Old Home Week Association

Desires your presence at the observance of

OLD HOME DAY

Hudson Centre, Thursday, August 24, 1905.

If expecting to be present please notify the committee that they may know for how many to provide dinner. You are also cordially invited to the union services Sunday August 20,

11 a. m. At Tent on Common, Hudson Centre

4 p. m. Parker's Grove, Baker Street.

Miss Gertrude A. Merrill
Mrs. Frances M. Cummings
Miss Ina L. Brown
Committee on Invitations.

In 1905, Hudson celebrated with events in Parker's Grove and on the town common. Webster's Grove was a popular site of early festivities. Although not mentioned here, another common feature of Hudson's early old home celebrations was its combination with the Cummings family reunion. It was reunions such as this that predated and cleared the way for the statewide old home movement. (Courtesy of Hudson Historical Society.)

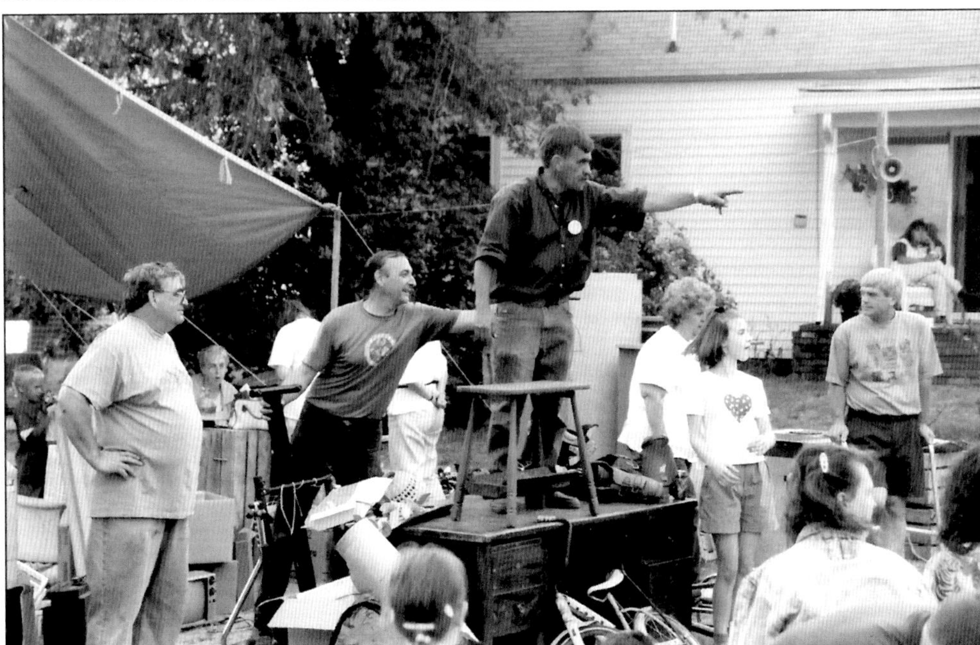

Tradition runs deep in Pelham where old home day has been a local fixture since 1906. Pictured here is former Pelham selectman Victor Spaulding conducting the annual Pelham Old Home Day auction. The event is now known as the Victor Spaulding Memorial Auction. (Courtesy of First Congregational Church of Pelham.)

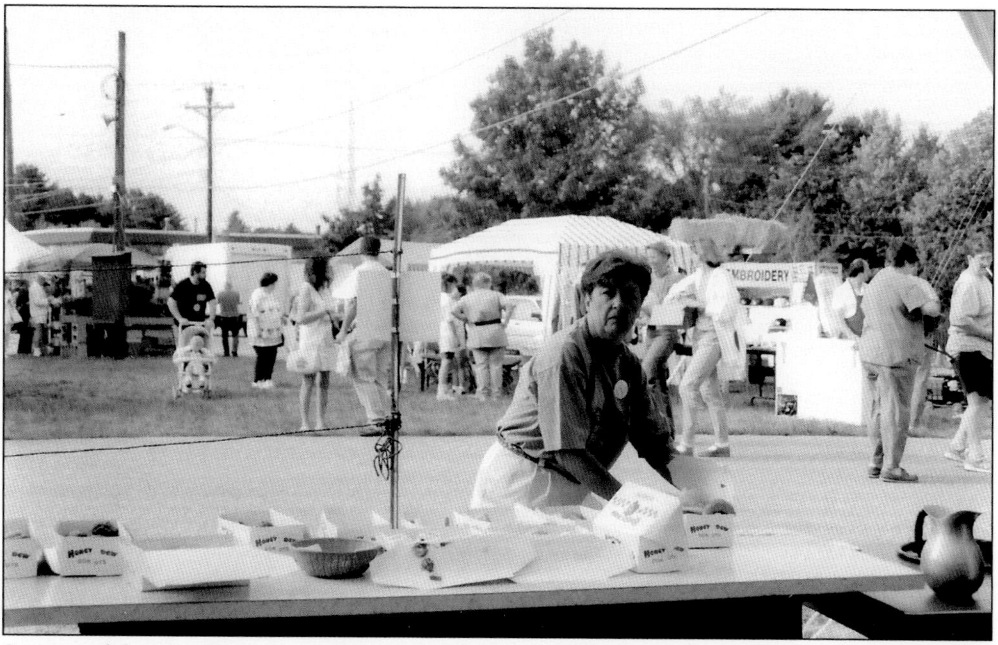

Sponsored by the First Congregational Church of Pelham for over 100 years, vendor food has always been a big part of Pelham Old Home Days. Here Fran Smith prepares coffee and doughnuts to help locals get off to a good start for a day of fun. (Courtesy of First Congregational Church of Pelham.)

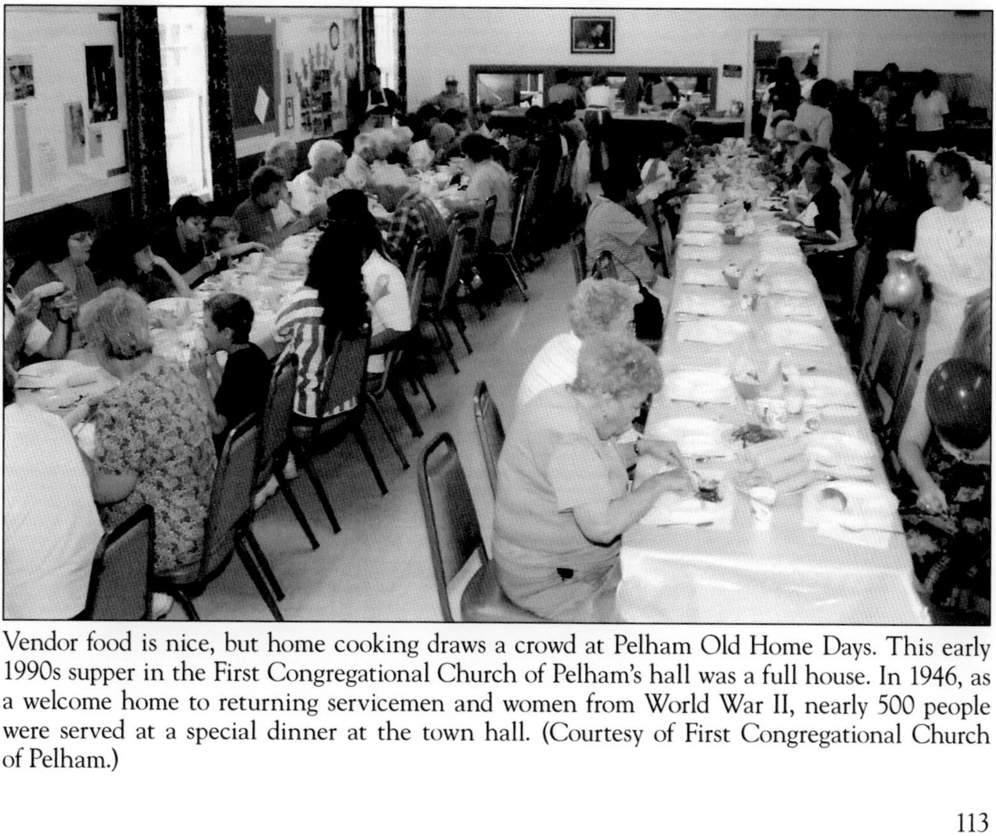

Vendor food is nice, but home cooking draws a crowd at Pelham Old Home Days. This early 1990s supper in the First Congregational Church of Pelham's hall was a full house. In 1946, as a welcome home to returning servicemen and women from World War II, nearly 500 people were served at a special dinner at the town hall. (Courtesy of First Congregational Church of Pelham.)

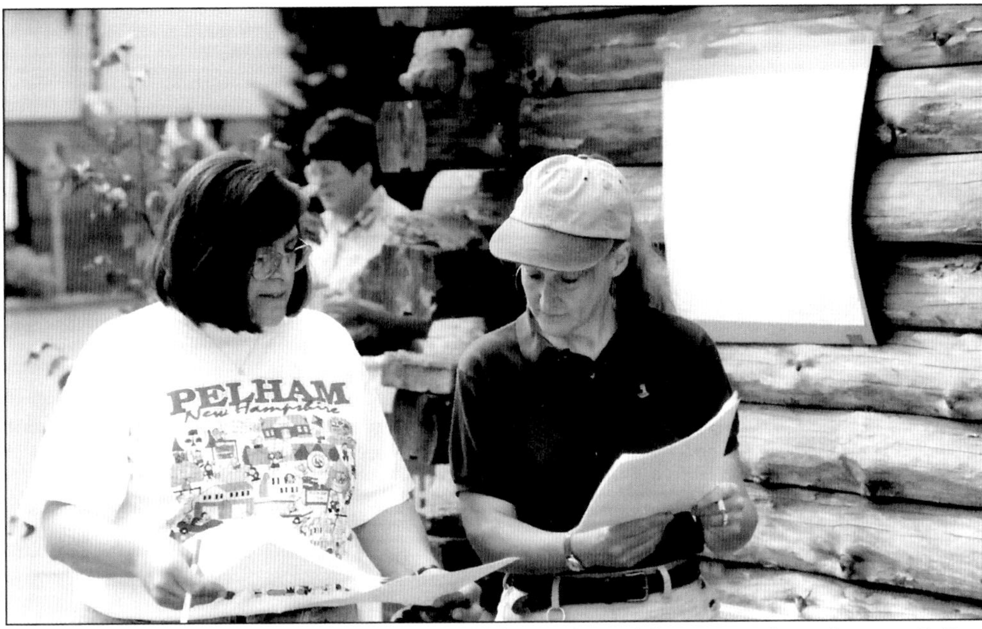

There is plenty of fun for everyone at an old home day celebration such as the one Pelham holds every year on the first weekend after Labor Day. But behind all the fun, there is always a large group of volunteers putting all of the events together. Shown here comparing notes are volunteers Diane Molloy (left) and Jeanne Bedrosian (right). (Courtesy of First Congregational Church of Pelham.)

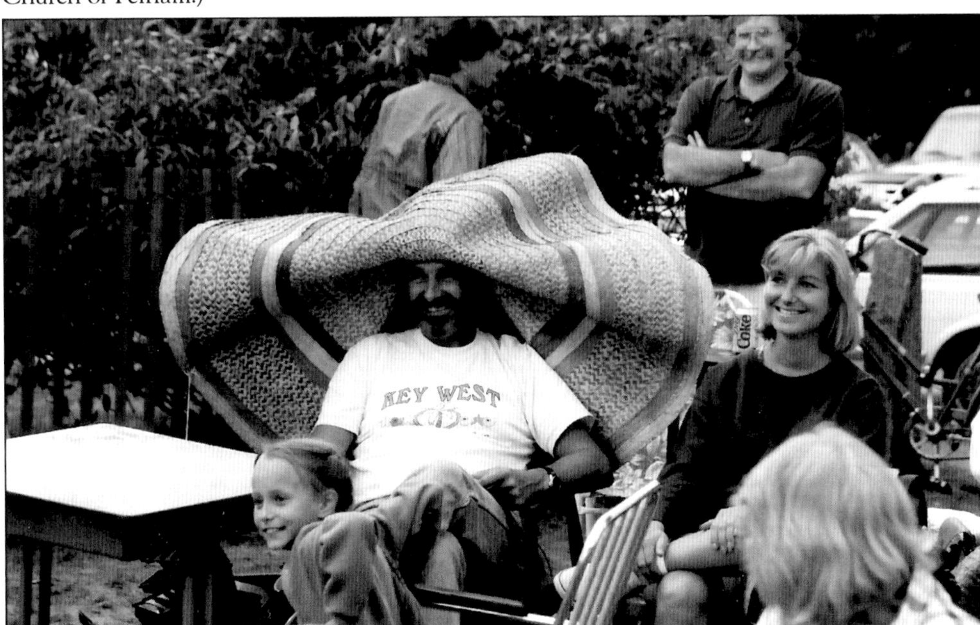

The Victor Spaulding Memorial Auction is always one of the biggest and most popular draws at Pelham Old Home Days. Pictured here is a good example of putting an auction purchase to immediate use in an effort to ward off the September heat. (Courtesy of First Congregational Church of Pelham.)

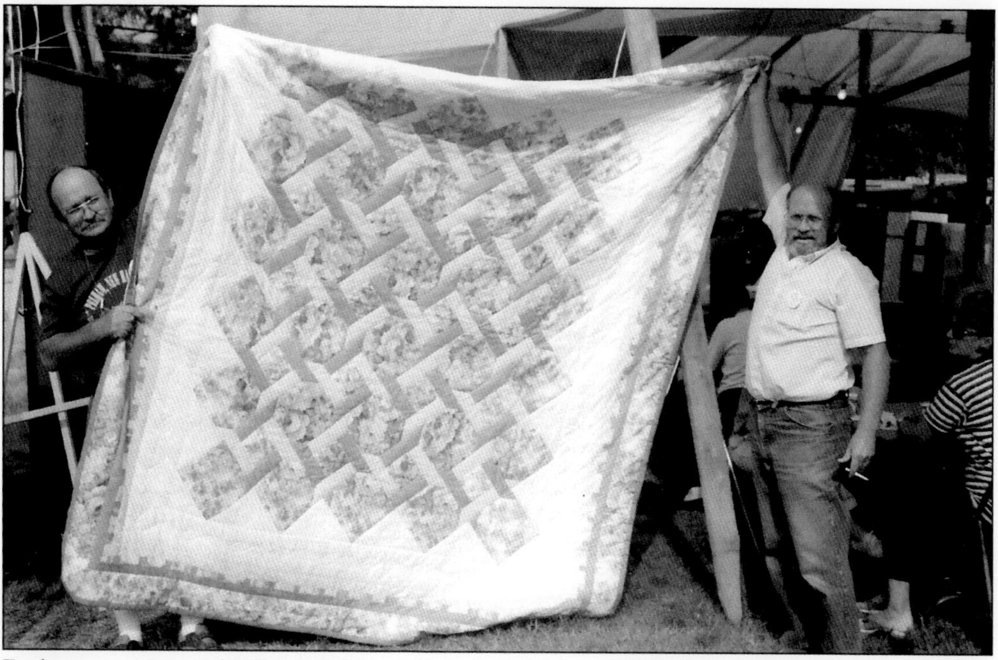

Each year, a group of Pelham ladies makes a quilt to be raffled off as the grand prize in an old home day fund-raiser. Here Wally Cibulski (left) and Ken Fogarty display a year's worth of labor that will soon become the property of a lucky winner. (Courtesy of First Congregational Church of Pelham.)

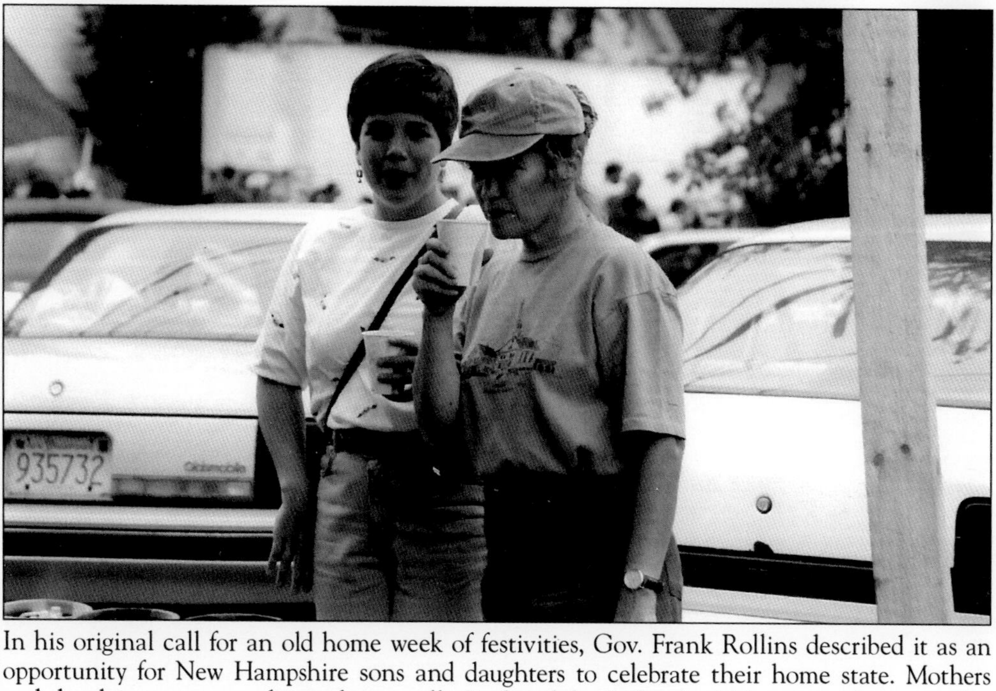

In his original call for an old home week of festivities, Gov. Frank Rollins described it as an opportunity for New Hampshire sons and daughters to celebrate their home state. Mothers and daughters carry on the tradition still. On hand for Pelham's old home week are mother Kathy Coleman (left) and daughter Kristie Coleman. (Courtesy of First Congregational Church of Pelham.)

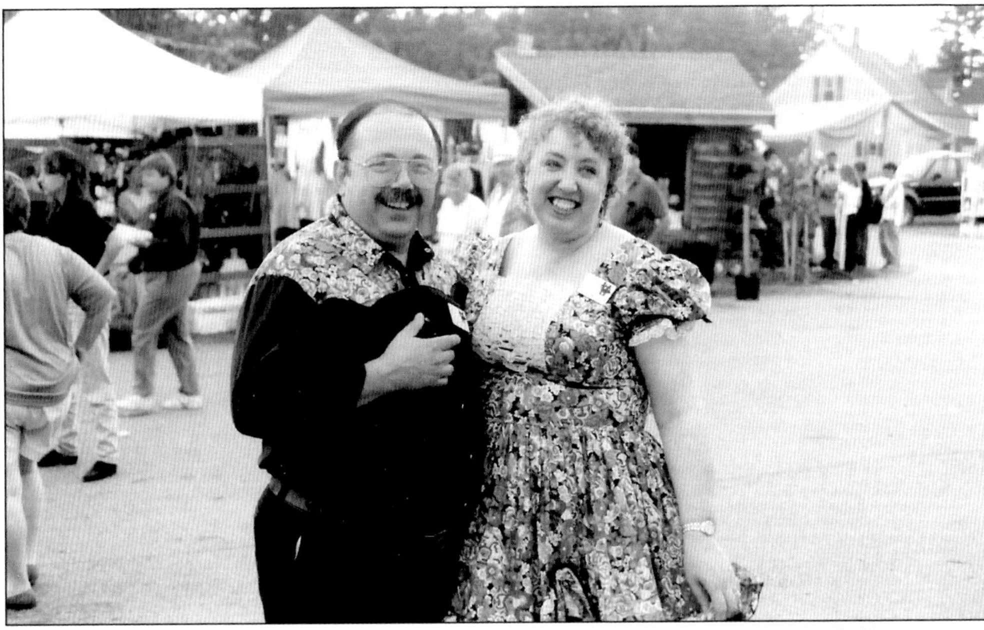

Most old home days celebrate with all sorts of music and entertainment. In Pelham, square dancing is part of the fun. Pictured here are Diego and Kathy Miccichi, members of the square dance group that performed at a recent celebration. Visiting entertainers are always a hit at old home days. In 1946, a show was presented by the Abbott Worsted Band and William (Bill) Elliot, the singing cop from Hampton Beach. (Courtesy of First Congregational Church of Pelham.)

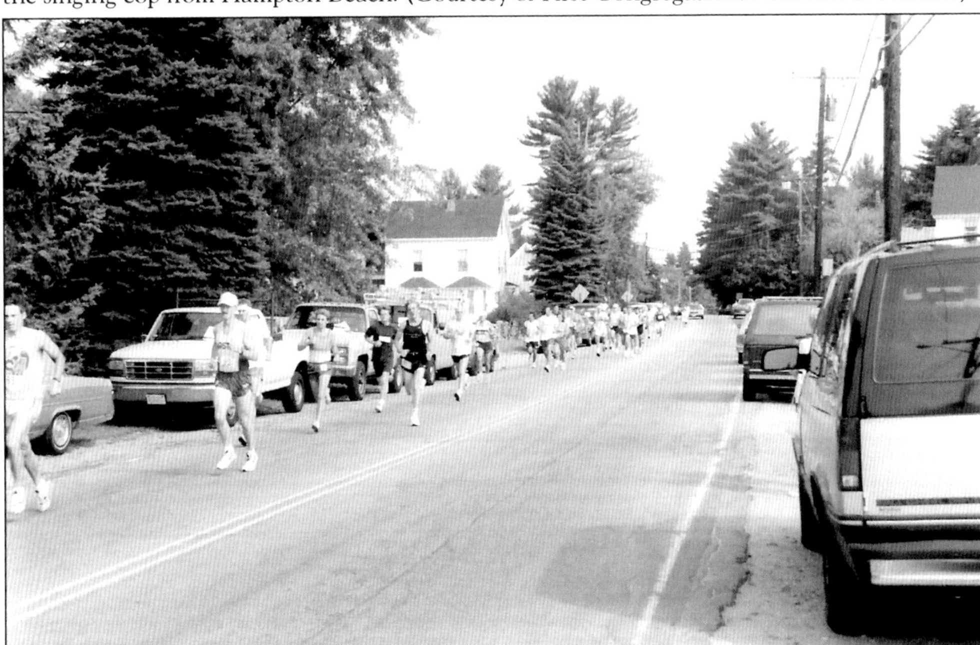

One can spend an entire old home celebration as a spectator and have a wonderful time. However, many local events stress participation. A five-kilometer road race has become a solid tradition in Pelham. Here runners are strung out along Windam Road for a race in the early 1990s. (Courtesy of First Congregational Church of Pelham.)

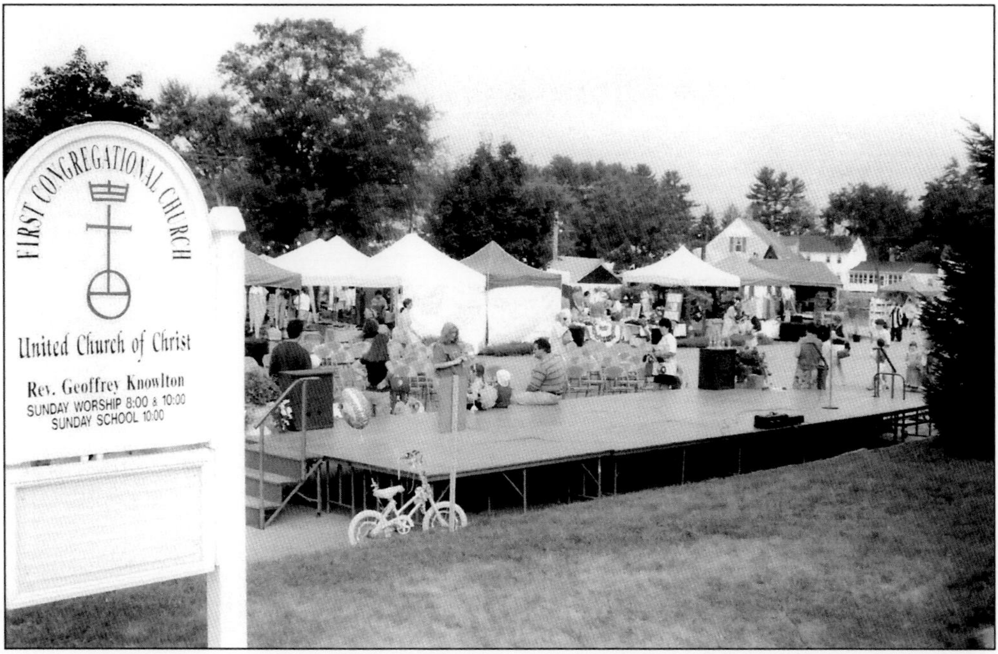

There is always something to do during Pelham's one-day old home celebration. Even when there is no entertainment on stage, plenty of activities are crammed into the day, including a craft fair on the green, a grand parade, a pretty pie contest, hourly raffles, and a chicken supper at the Congregational church. (Courtesy of First Congregational Church of Pelham.)

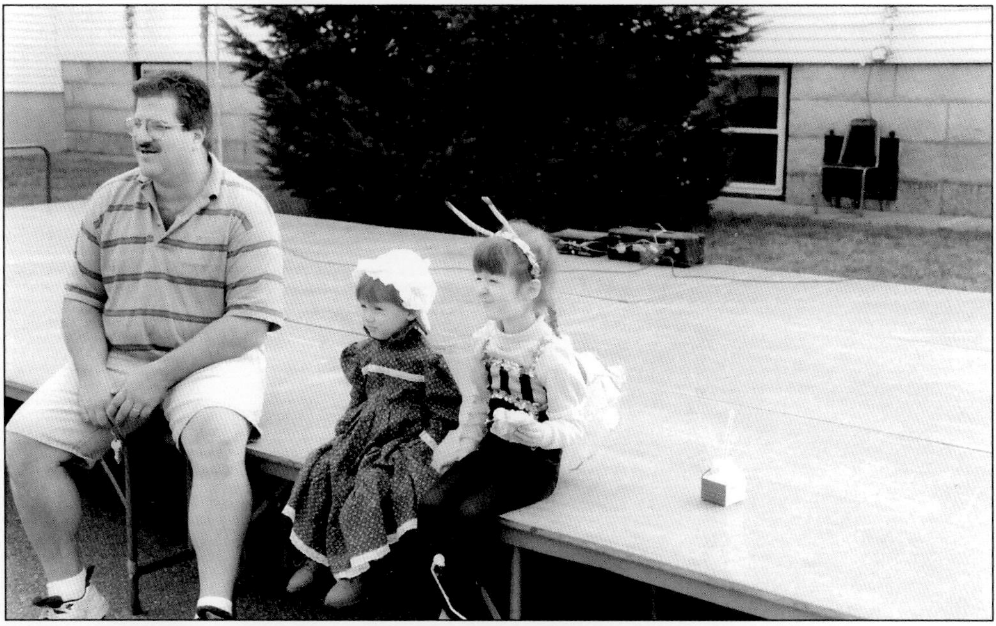

No matter how many great things there are to do at Pelham's old home day, sometimes it is nice to just relax and watch the festivities. These Pelham residents, in costume and out, appear to be doing just that during a break in the action. In 1931, Mrs. Frank Carleton was the general chairperson of a program that included an exhibition of work by 4-H members at the library. (Courtesy of First Congregational Church of Pelham.)

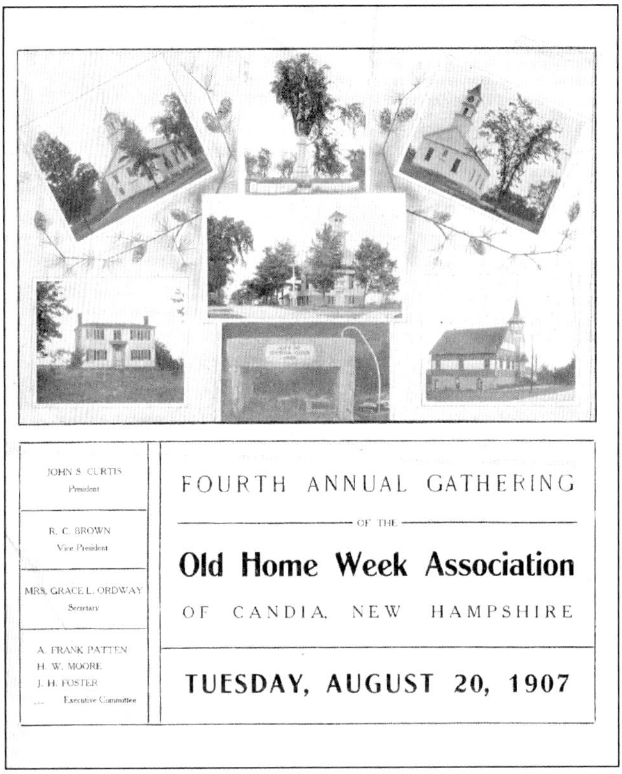

Familiar sites from around town adorned this 1907 invitation to current and former residents of Candia. That year's celebration included a free lawn concert in front of Moores Hall by the Old Home Brass Band immediately followed by a hop given by the six-piece Oakland Orchestra. Gov. Charles Floyd was also on hand and addressed the crowd. (Courtesy of Candia Historical Society.)

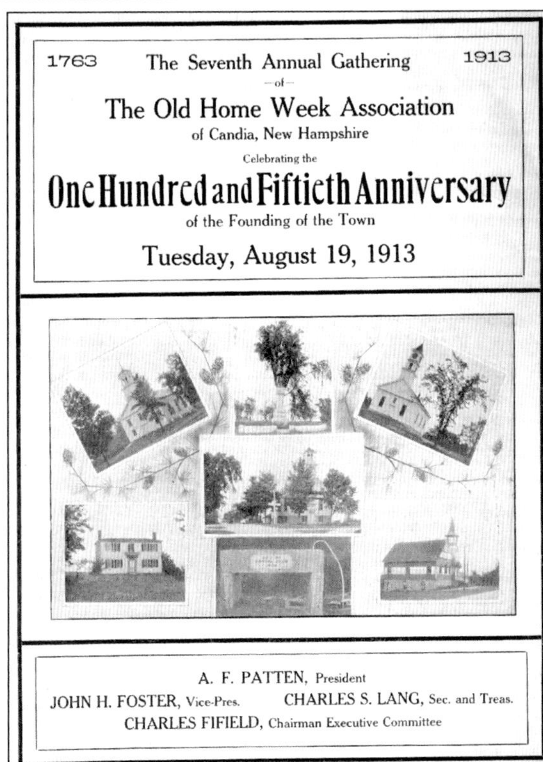

The 150th anniversary of the town and old home week brought people back home to Candia in 1913. Both Gov. Samuel D. Felker and former governor Charles Floyd were on hand for the festivities. A daylong program kicking off the week was highlighted by the Ladies' Orchestra of Manchester, under the direction of Anne Daniels. (Courtesy of Candia Historical Society.)

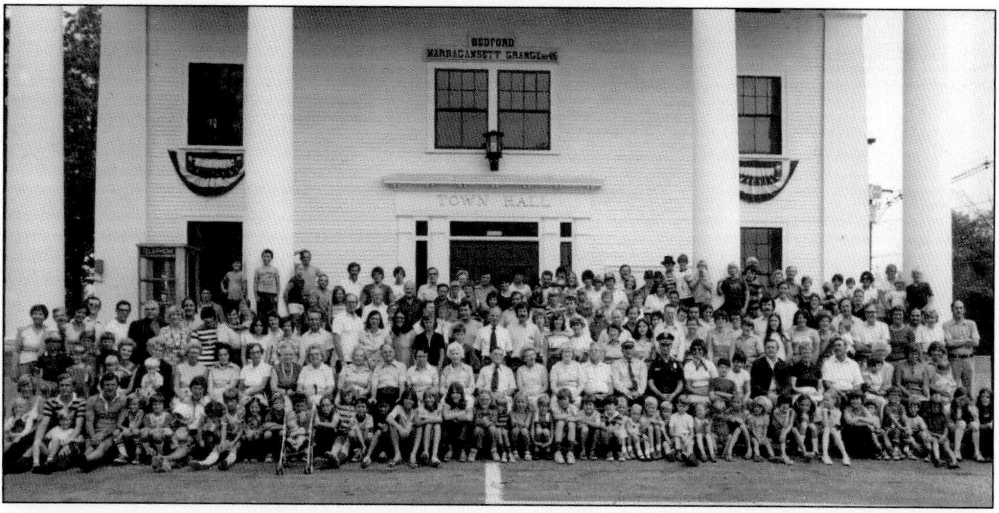

In 1983, a large group of Bedford residents posed in front of the town hall to commemorate old home days. The 1983 celebration came just 60 years after the town's first observance. In 1923, Bedford took part in the old home day festivities for the first time, joining towns throughout the state in marking the 300th anniversary of New Hampshire's settlement. (Courtesy of Bedford Historical Society.)

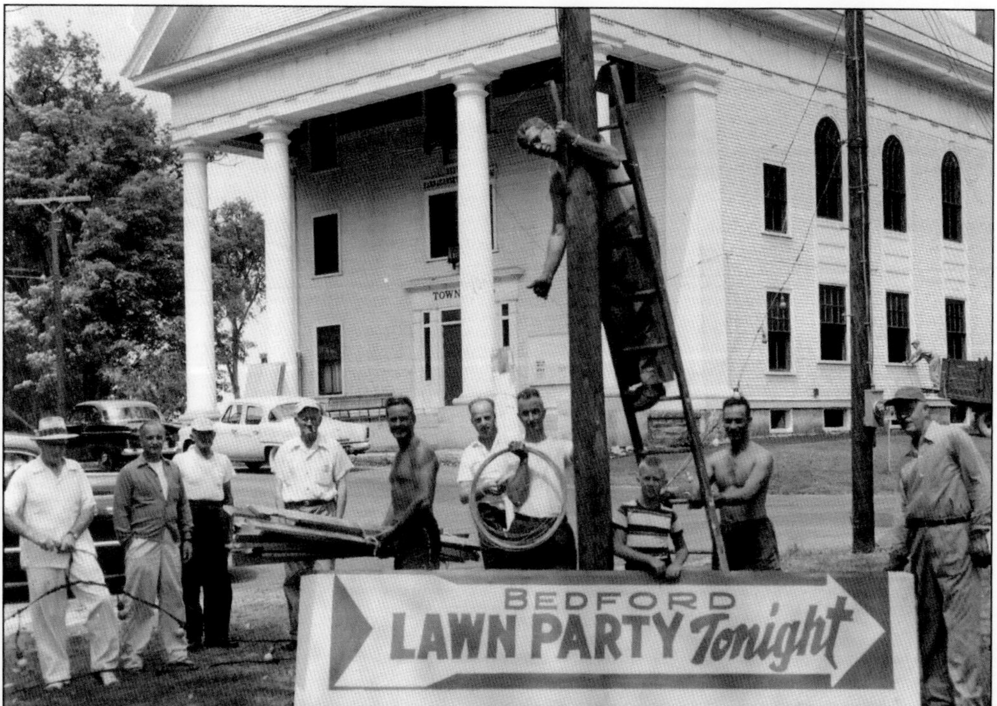

Preparation can provide some of the fun and lots of the camaraderie associated with old home days celebrations. That appears to be the case in this 1954 Bedford Old Home Day picture, as residents young and old prepare for the evening's activities. Not every year included quite so many activities. In 1931, the only observance was an old home night presented at the Bedford Grange. (Courtesy of Bedford Historical Society.)

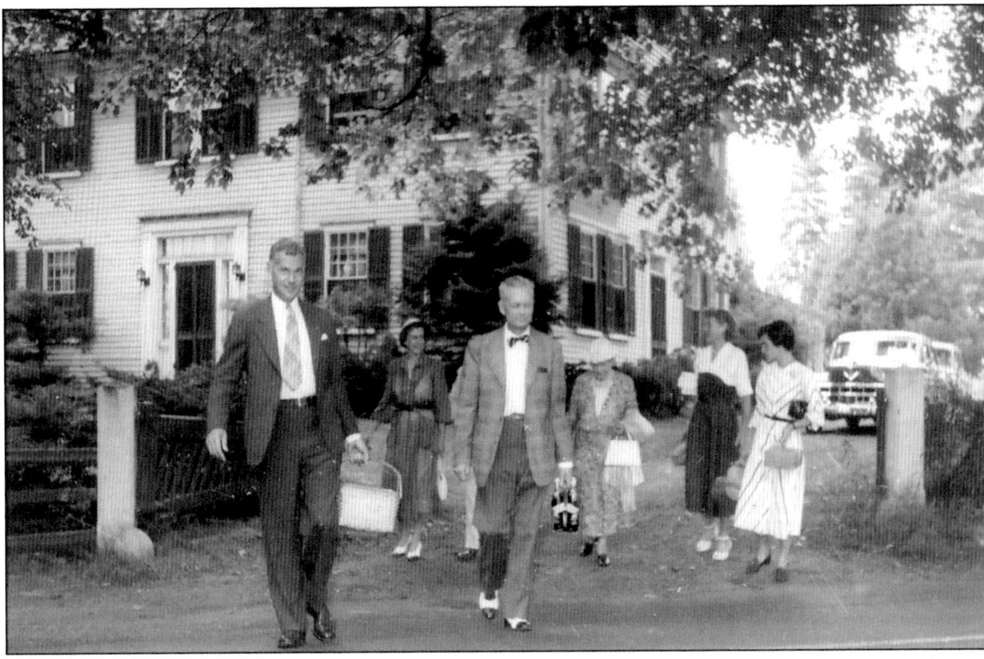

Heading off for a picnic lunch might have been a bit more of a formal affair in 1954 than it is now, but it is still a big part of the holiday. This group from Bedford is heading out for old home day in much the same way it was done in 1899. In 1949, at the 50th anniversary of New Hampshire Old Home Week, entertainment was presented by the Narragansett Grange with refreshments provided by Mrs. Ivan Parkhurst and Mrs. Erwin Parkhurst. (Courtesy of Bedford Historical Society.)

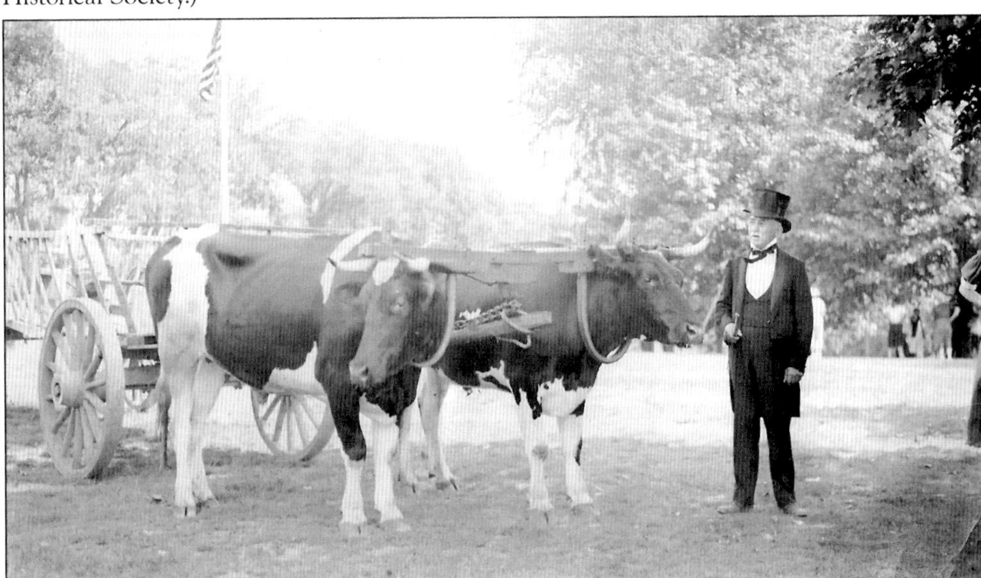

In 1933, oxen and carts were already surpassed as a major mode of transportation, but the idea of Bedford Old Home Day was to hearken back to images of days gone by. Here George Wiggin of Bedford poses in period costume with his oxen for old home festivities. (Courtesy of Bedford Historical Society.)

In 1933, Mrs. Gordon Woodbury was one of many Bedford residents who donned costumes from earlier days. Also taking part in that year's festivities was Charles Shepard, who traveled through town in a horse and buggy acting out the part of the town crier, inviting fellow residents to attend church services. (Courtesy of Bedford Historical Society.)

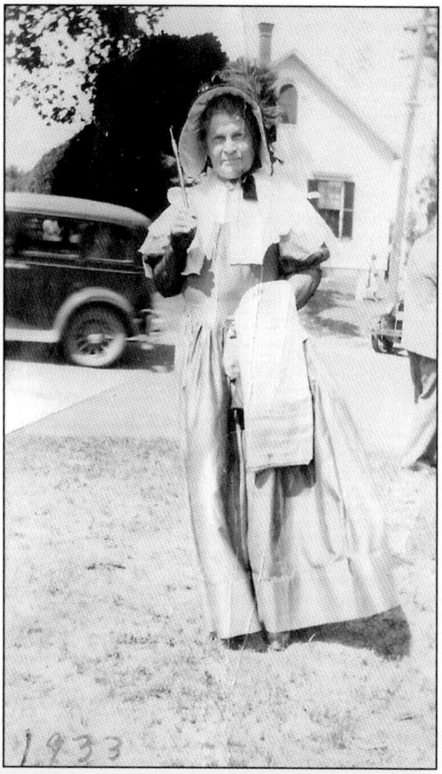

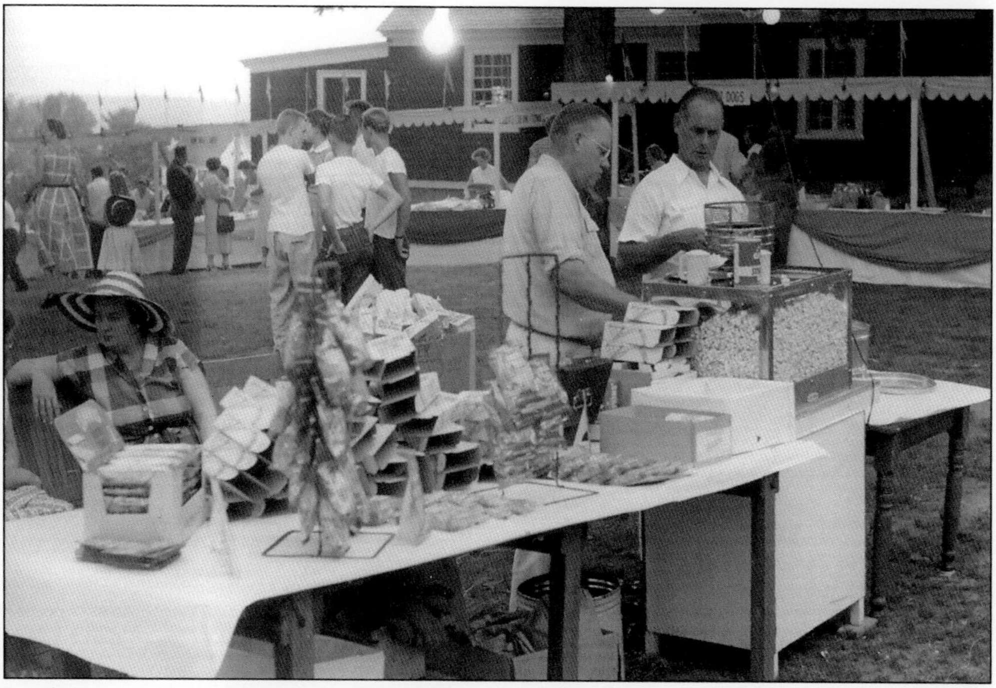

Involving as many organizations as possible is a tried and true method of assuring maximum participation in old home day events. Here members of the Unity Club operate a concession booth for the 1954 Bedford festivities. (Courtesy of Bedford Historical Society.)

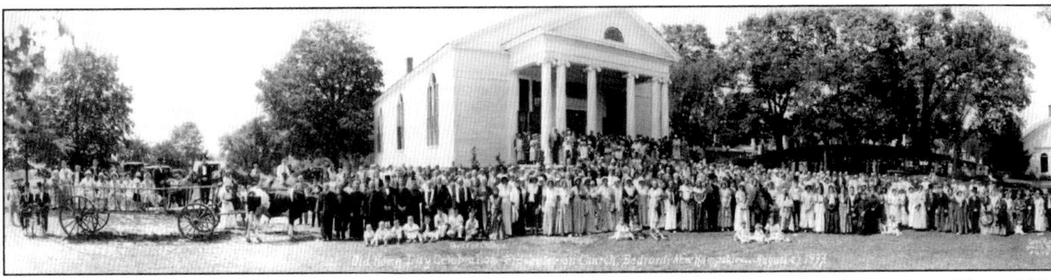

Old home day was truly a town wide affair, as this 1933 Bedford photograph attests. The 1930s saw all-out participation in the pageants and festivities. Also included in 1934 was a biblical pageant that used exotic animals from the Bedford Zoo as well as pigs on loan from Ora Kilton. (Courtesy of Bedford Historical Society.)

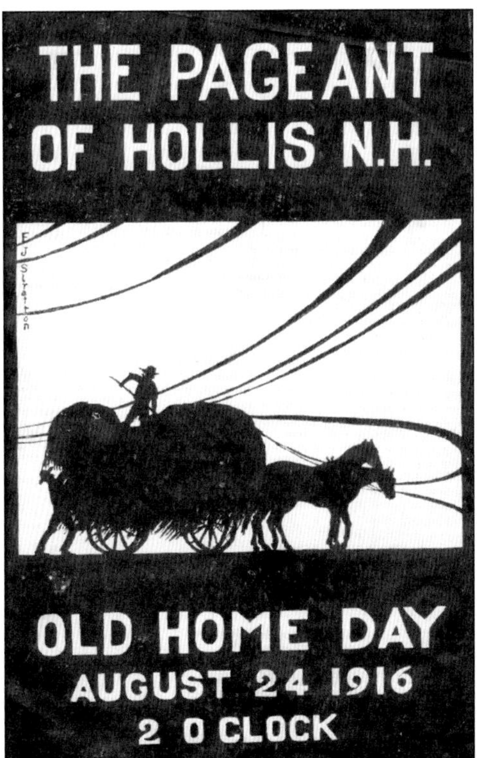

In 1916, Hollis was still very much a farming community, and it was reflected in this cover from the program of that year's big old home pageant. Pageants involving individuals from throughout the town were common, and Hollis was no exception. The 1916 pageant covered the town's history in 10 episodes, from Native Americans through the farms of 1916 Hollis. (Courtesy of Hollis Historical Society.)

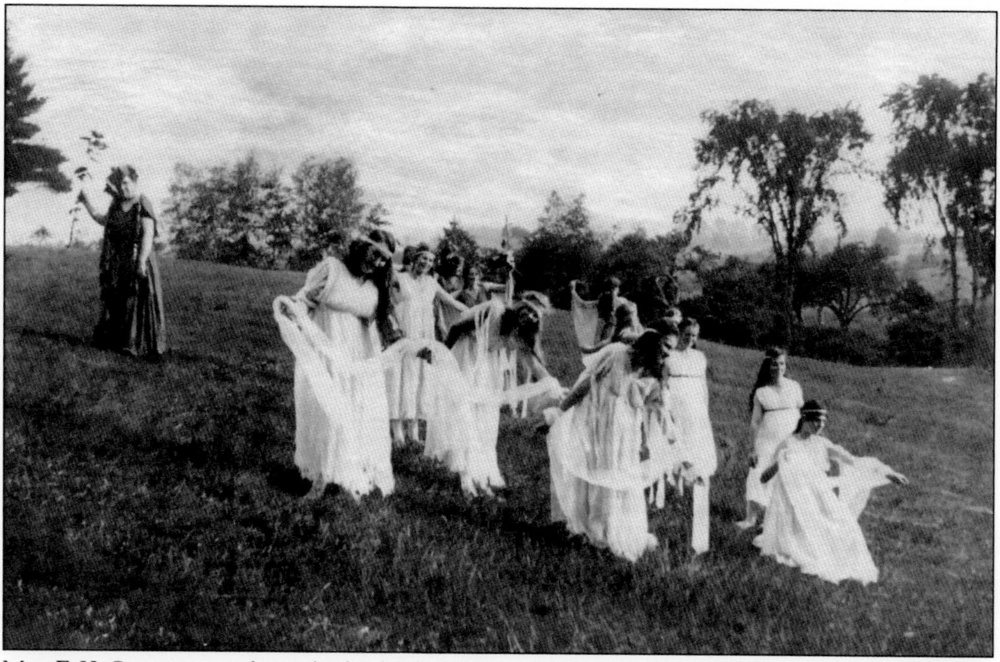

Mrs. F. K. Sweetster took on the lead role of Dame Nature in the opening of the 1916 old home day. Here she is joined by various wood, meadow, and water nymphs in this early depiction of Hollis history. Three years later, Hollis combined its town fair with old home week to welcome home World War I veterans. (Courtesy of Hollis Historical Society.)

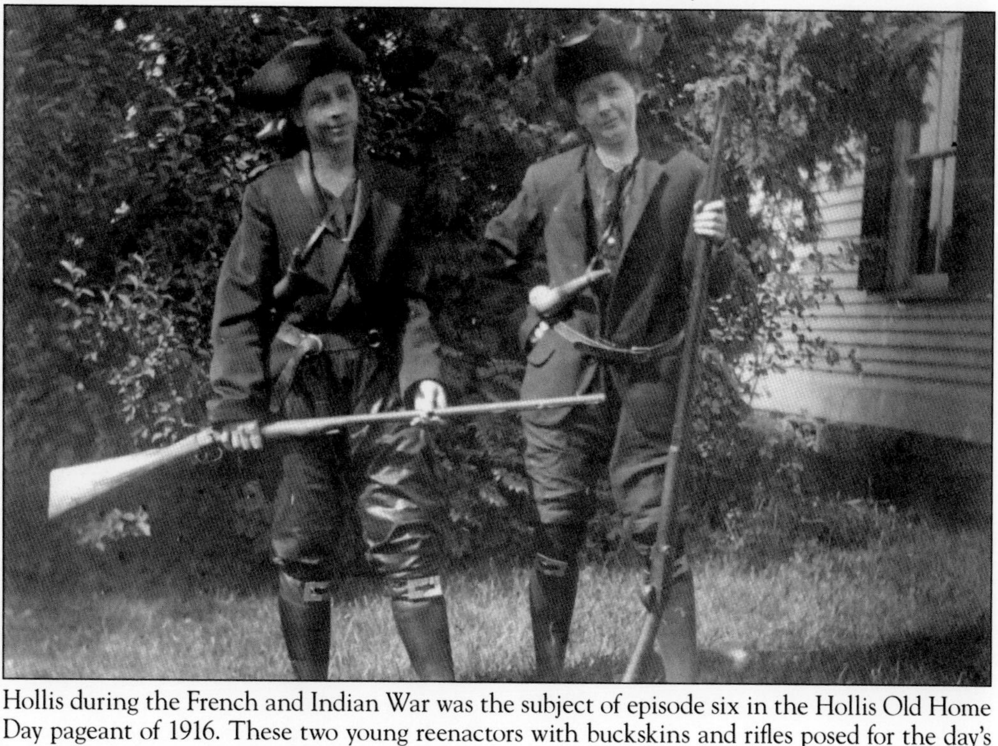

Hollis during the French and Indian War was the subject of episode six in the Hollis Old Home Day pageant of 1916. These two young reenactors with buckskins and rifles posed for the day's event. (Courtesy of Hollis Historical Society.)

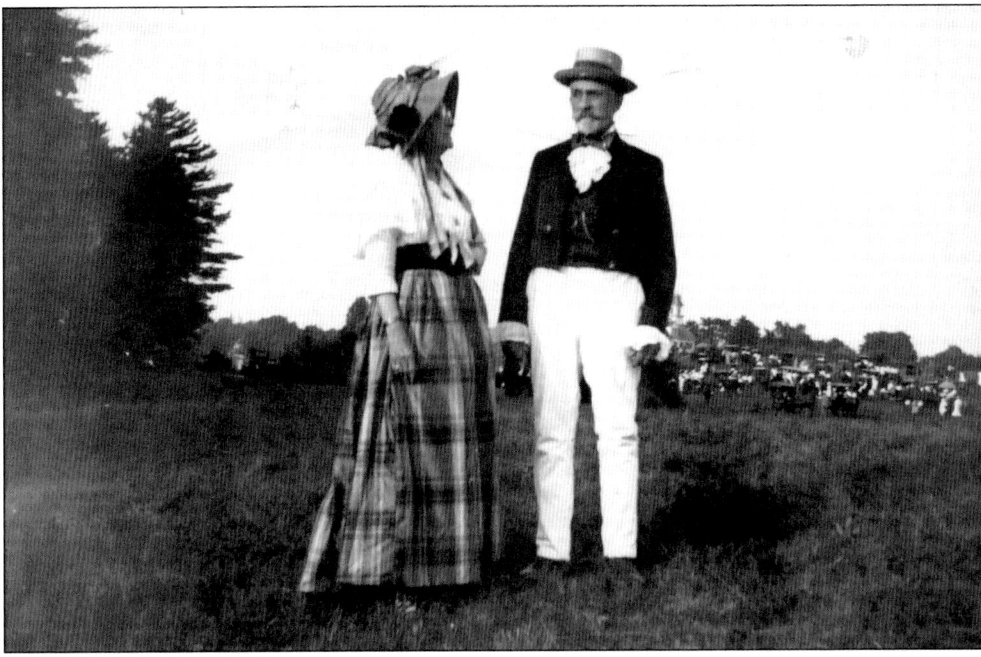

"Good Morning Mistress Powers, this is a glad day for Hollis." The glad day commemorated here was an important one in the life of any New England community. This couple was part of the scene depicting the founding of the first church in Hollis. (Courtesy of Hollis Historical Society.)

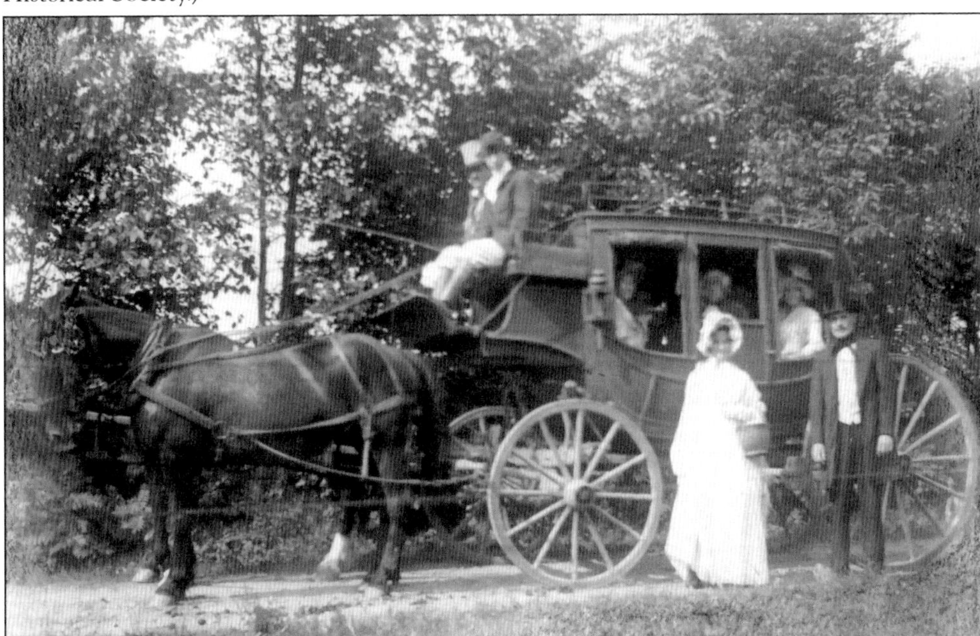

The wedding journey of John and Nancy Haywood in August 1836 was the subject of this old home day scene. After relating the story of his trip by flat-bottom boat up the Merrimack River just in time to catch the Nashua coach to New Ipswich, John and his bride joined in contra dancing with their neighbors. (Courtesy of Hollis Historical Society.)

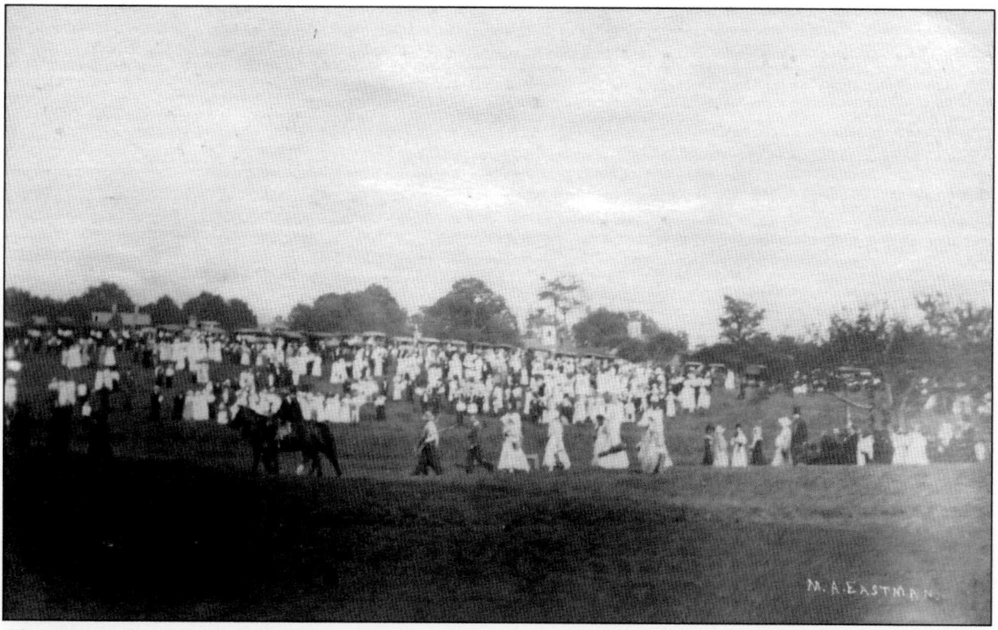

The grand finale of the 1916 pageant gathered all of the participants together. In keeping with the spirit of old home days, the organizers described the pageant of Hollis as "a festival of appreciation given reverently by the native and adopted sons and daughters of this lovely New England village." (Courtesy of Hollis Historical Society.)

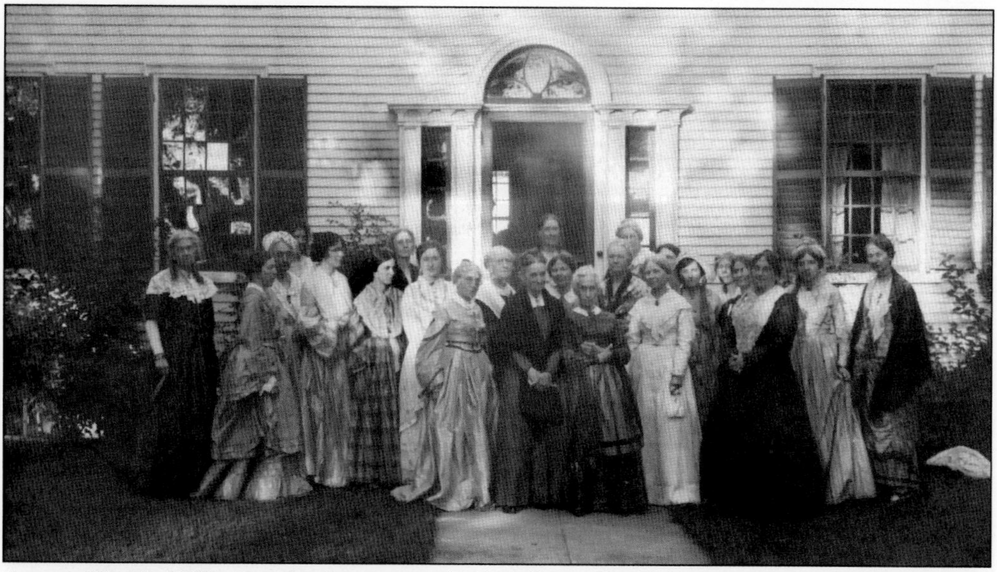

August 20–24, 1930, was the bicentennial of Hollis and old home week. Gathering for the commemoration in front of the home of Abby and Etta Flagg are Nellie Hardy, Jane Stratton, Mary Wassester, Francis Leighton, Irene Wright, Marion Nichols, Helen Bell, Louise Stratton, Emma Coravan, Elizabeth Worcestor, Minnie Colburn, Abby Flagg, Ellen Lovejoy, Patty Hayes, Georgia Proctor, Bertha Colburn, Ruth Goodwin, Lucinda Read, Nellie Lougee, Doris Wheeler, Francis Goodwin, and Flora Hardy. (Courtesy of Hollis Historical Society.)

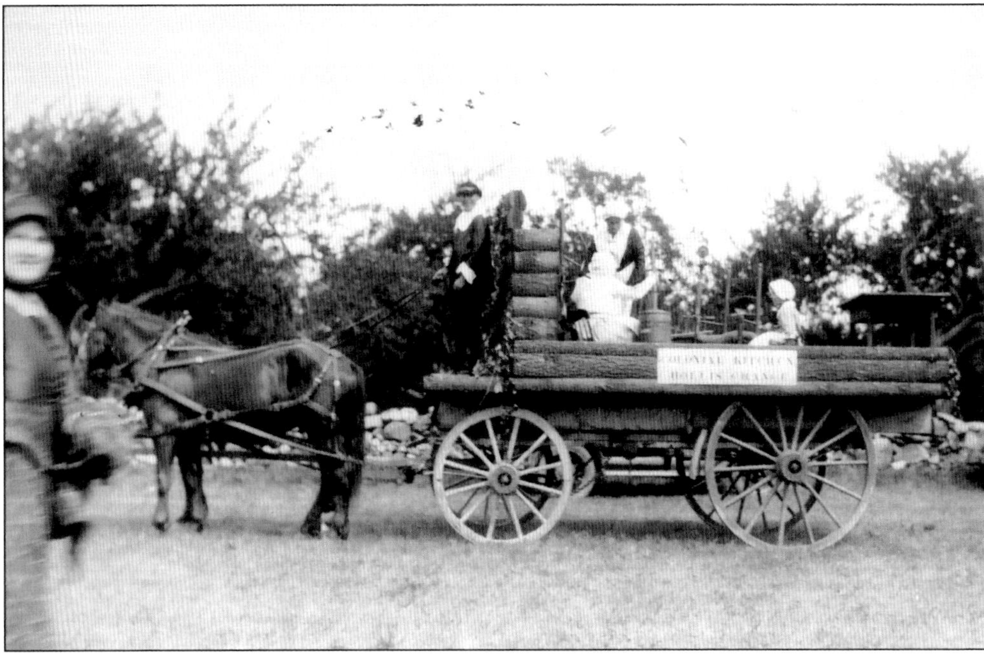

As always, the Hollis Grange was on board for the Hollis Old Home Day parade. This entry was from the 1930 bicentennial/old home celebration. In addition to the parade, there were band concerts on the common—one immediately following the parade and one later in the afternoon. (Courtesy of Hollis Historical Society.)

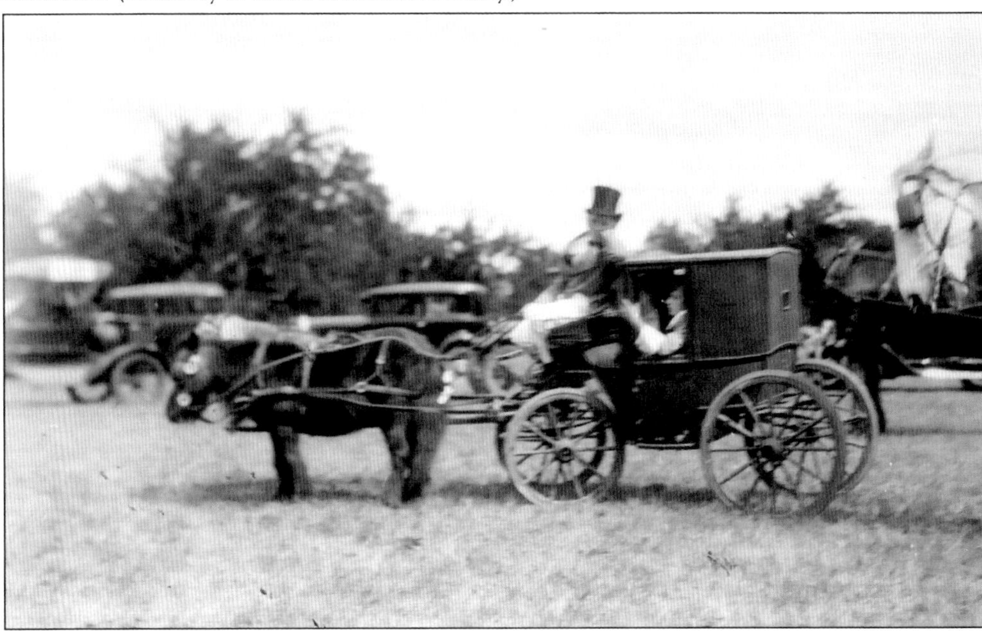

This small coach and horses were part of the historical parade held on Thursday, August 21, 1930, as part of the Hollis bicentennial/old home days. Other events on this second day of festivities included dinner at the lower town hall and Hardy Parish Hall, historical exercises at the church, and the planting of an anniversary tree on the lawn east of the library. (Courtesy of Hollis Historical Society.)

The Daughters of the American Revolution float was just part of the hospitality on display at the 1930 Hollis celebration. As part of the festivities, the houses on Main Street were opened to the public, and there was a display of household articles and heirlooms at all of the residences. In another example of organizing old home day for special events, the 1919 return of soldiers turned out nearly the entire town. (Courtesy of Hollis Historical Society.)

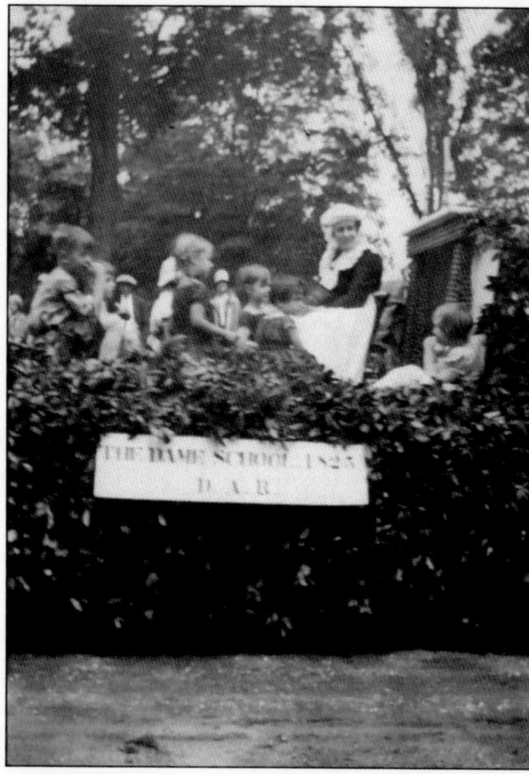

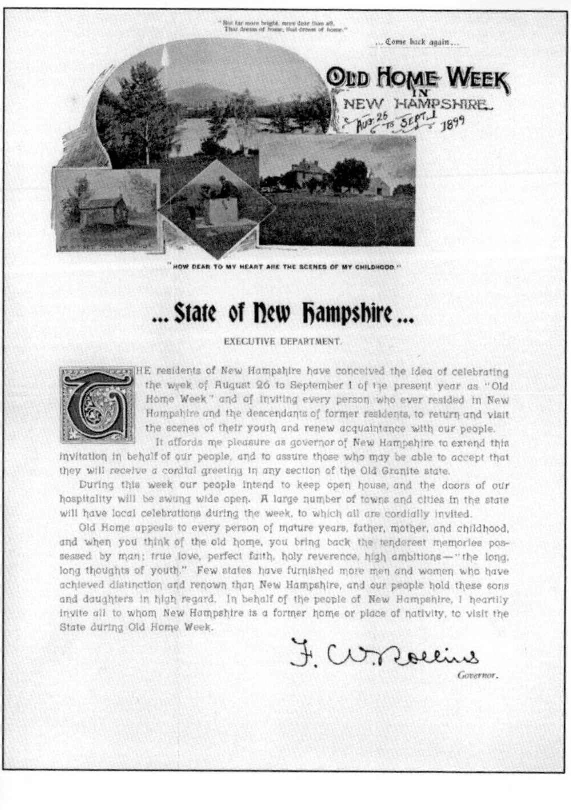

"But far more bright, more dear than all,
That dream of home, that dream of home."

... Come back again ...

OLD HOME WEEK IN NEW HAMPSHIRE. AUG. 26 TO SEPT. 1 1899

"HOW DEAR TO MY HEART ARE THE SCENES OF MY CHILDHOOD."

... State of New Hampshire ...

EXECUTIVE DEPARTMENT.

THE residents of New Hampshire have conceived the idea of celebrating the week of August 26 to September 1 of the present year as "Old Home Week" and of inviting every person who ever resided in New Hampshire and the descendants of former residents, to return and visit the scenes of their youth and renew acquaintance with our people.

It affords me pleasure as governor of New Hampshire to extend this invitation in behalf of our people, and to assure those who may be able to accept that they will receive a cordial greeting in any section of the Old Granite state.

During this week our people intend to keep open house, and the doors of our hospitality will be swung wide open. A large number of towns and cities in the state will have local celebrations during the week, to which all are cordially invited.

Old Home appeals to every person of mature years, father, mother, and childhood, and when you think of the old home, you bring back the tenderest memories possessed by man; true love, perfect faith, holy reverence, high ambitions—"the long, long thoughts of youth." Few states have furnished more men and women who have achieved distinction and renown than New Hampshire, and our people hold these sons and daughters in high regard. In behalf of the people of New Hampshire, I heartily invite all to whom New Hampshire is a former home or place of nativity, to visit the State during Old Home Week.

F. W. Rollins
Governor.

Homecoming and scenes of home are a part of nearly all of the nation's major holidays. In New Hampshire, old home days is a time set aside specifically to welcome people home to the scenes of their youth and to exhibit pride in community. In 1899, this declaration by Gov. Frank Rollins welcomed everyone home. Over 100 years later, the invitation still stands. (Courtesy of Mont Vernon Historical Society.)